SCOTTISH JOURNAL OF THEOLOGY

Current Issues in Theology

Edited by
ALASDAIR HERON
IAIN TORRANCE

SCOTTISH JOURNAL OF THEOLOGY

Current Issues in Theology

Edited by
ALASDAIR HERON
IAIN TORRANCE

This is a series of short books specially commissioned by the editors of *Scottish Journal of Theology*. The aim is to commission books which stand between the static monograph genre and the more immediate statement of a journal article. Following the long tradition of the *Journal*, the editors will commission authors who are questioning existing paradigms or rethinking perspectives. It is hoped that the books will appeal to a wide range of readers.

Believing that living theology needs an audience and thrives on debate, the editors will invite the authors to present the themes of their topics in four public lectures at the University of Aberdeen (*The Scottish Journal of Theology Lectures*), and the books, which will be published subsequently, will be developed from these.

The *Scottish Journal of Theology* is an international refereed quarterly journal of systematic, historical and biblical theology published by T&T Clark Ltd, 59 George Street, Edinburgh EH2 2LQ, Scotland. Subscription details are available on request from the Publishers.

INTERPRETING GOD AND THE POSTMODERN SELF

INTERPRETING GOD AND THE POSTMODERN SELF

On Meaning, Manipulation and Promise

ANTHONY C. THISELTON

T&T CLARK
EDINBURGH

T&T CLARK LTD
59 GEORGE STREET
EDINBURGH EH2 2LQ
SCOTLAND

First published 1995

ISBN 0 567 29302 5

British Library Cataloguing-in-Publication Data
A catalogue record for this book is available from the British Library

Typeset by Waverley Typesetters, Galashiels
Printed and bound in Great Britain by Page Bros, Norwich

Contents

Preface ix

Part I
MEANING, MANIPULATION AND TRUTH

1 God as Self-Affirming Illusion? Manipulation, Truth and
  Language 3
2 Postmodernism, Modernity and the Postmodern Self 11
3 Do All Controlling Models in Religion Serve Manipulative
  Purposes? 19
4 The Rhetoric of Theological Models and Currencies of
  Meaning 27
5 Language, Truth and Life in Theology and Postmodernity 33
6 Non-Manipulative Interpretation and Truth as Relational 41

Part II
INTERPRETING TEXTS AND INTERPRETING THE SELF

7 Respecting the Other: Transcending Prior Categories and
  the Limits of Empirical Method 47
8 Biblical Texts and Pastoral Hermeneutics: History, Science
  and Personhood 53
9 A Temporal Hermeneutic of the Self Through the 'Detour'
  of Texts as 'Other' 59
10 Five Ways in which Textual Reading Interprets the Self 63
11 Self-Deception and Sub-Text: Psychoanalysis, Suspicion
  and Conversation 67
12 Self-Identity within the Temporal Logic of Narrative Plot 73

Part III

POSTMODERN GOD? SEA OF FAITH
OR ABYSS OF BABEL?

13 The Sea of Faith Network: Interpreting God as a Human
Construct   81

14 Successive Stages in Cupitt's Interpretations of God   87

15 'Taking leave of God' as Internalizing, De-objectifying
and Autonomy   93

16 Rehearsing an Over-played Script: 'Facts', World-Views
and Divine Agency   99

17 'God's Second Death' in the Postmodern Self:
An 'Internalized' God Now?   105

18 Pluralism or Propaganda? The Forked Rhetoric of
Postmodern Interpretation   111

Part IV

POSTMODERN SELF AND SOCIETY:
TOWARDS A THEOLOGY OF PROMISE

19 The Collapse of the Hope of the 'Modern' Self:
From Active Agency to Passive Situatedness   121

20 More Social Consequences of Postmodern Selfhood:
Despair, Conflict and Manipulation   127

21 Corporate Power and Corporate Self-Deception   137

22 Present and Future: The Pluriform Grammar of Hope
and the God of Promise   145

23 Further Issues on 'Interpreting God': Christology
and Trinity   153

24 Will-to-Power De-centred, Transformed and Re-centred
in Promise and Love   159

Select Bibliography   165

Index of Names and Subjects   173

Index of Biblical References   179

Preface

NIETZSCHE and Foucault, among others, argue that claims to truth often represent disguised attempts to legitimate uses of power. This study takes these arguments seriously. With the rise of post-modern notions of the self, of language and meaning, and of society, this issue has become perhaps a more far-reaching cause for disbelief about claims to truth on the part of Christian theology than older, more tired appeals to materialist world-views as monolithic responses of secular modernity.

We do not deny that certain forms of religion, even within Christian traditions, have often been reduced to instrumental devices to affirm the human self, or, worse, to seek to legitimate power over others. But can all Christian claims be interpreted in this way? Such a sweeping diagnosis, I argue, would fail to come to terms with substantial counter-arguments and counter-examples.

Postmodernism also tells part of the story about the human self, but not the whole story. It takes account of imposed role-performances within society with a greater degree of realism than the partly illusory optimism of modernity. But an adequate account of the self and of personhood cannot stop with its situatedness in some instantaneous moment within processes of shifting flux. Selfhood discovers its identity and personhood within a larger purposive narrative which allows room for agency, responsibility and hope. Even if postmodernity fragments the self and society into multiple role-performances, and dissolves truth into the conventions or power-interests of different or competing communities, the future may nevertheless hold out the possibility of reintegration on the basis of promise. Here two major dialogue partners are Paul Ricoeur and Jürgen Moltmann. The notion that the self draws its full personhood from a dialectic of self-identity and relation to the 'other' rightly finds expression in their work. Moltmann, together with Pannenberg and others, also rightly grounds this principle in the personhood of God as Trinity.

I introduce the heart of this argument in Part I, and expound it fully in more theological terms in Part IV. No more need be said about these central concerns. However, a brief word of explanation about Parts II and III respectively may be in order.

One reader of the manuscript found Part II the only relatively 'difficult' part. In technical terms it offers a 'hermeneutic of selfhood'. But part of its practical thrust can be briefly illustrated. When I teach Schleiermacher to undergraduate classes, I usually draw a contrast between his admission that he felt fully at ease with his thoughts only in social contexts, and the attempts of Descartes to establish self-knowledge in isolated reflection, sealed off from the world. Crises of identity, especially in late-teenage years, I then suggest, may in many cases become more readily resolved by entering fully into the to and fro of university life, than by brooding about 'who I am' in the solitude of a study bedrom. Who or what we 'are' often emerges only as we interact with others.

In more philosophical terms, this may place a question mark against rationalist or purely empiricist approaches to selfhood. We need a hermeneutic of selfhood. Interaction with others provides material for 'telling our story', and for mutual 'listening'. In turn, Christian identity locates self-identity within the larger story of God's dealings with the world. Here, as Ricoeur so clearly shows, notions of history, memory, promise, and accountability indicate aspects of a stable continuity of identity and selfhood amidst empirical change.

All this stands in the sharpest possible contrast to Cupitt's varied standpoints discussed in Part III. Indeed, if his later claims were valid, Part II as well as Parts I and IV would fall, since even the self would lose its past and future, swallowed up by the postmodern 'instantaneousness' of the disposable cup and fast food.

I have always tried to write fairly and constructively, without undue polemic. I do not doubt for one moment the genuineness of the concerns which motivate the Sea of Faith writers to write as they do, but I believe that they underrate the difficulties of their approach. I am grateful for discussions in the Diocese of Leicester which have enabled me to appreciate some of the positive concerns behind this movement, even if most of their arguments do not convince me. Part of the purpose of this study is to try to correct some of the distorted impressions of 'theism' which have encouraged undue overreactions against authentic Trinitarian theology.

I offer my most profound thanks to three groups of people for their understanding and support in this work. First, I wish to dedicate this study to Rosemary, Stephen, Amanda, David, Linda and Martin. The variety of my writing commitments has meant that I have spent less time with them than they had a right to expect. My wife, Rosemary, has once again given without stint of her time and support to help this work forward in many practical ways.

Second, in the University of Nottingham I have appreciated the opportunity to work alongside colleagues and students in the Departments of Philosophy and of Critical Theory. Philosophers warn us that too much emphasis on social context threatens to reduce truth to mere social history. Critical theorists warn us that a social power agenda may seek to disguise itself as a universal truth-claim. Theology, I believe, seeks to situate itself between these two ends of the spectrum, heeding the warnings of each. God is Alpha and Omega; but Jesus became a first-century Jew.

Writing commitments, especially in term time, bring additional pressures to my office, and with these Mrs Mary Elmer has coped admirably. I learn much from my research students. Of these, particular mention should be made of meticulous assistance from Mr Rick Berchiolli. I am also grateful for the constructive and happy atmosphere in the Department of Theology, of which I am privileged to be Head. This is conducive to collaborative research and discussion.

Third, I am deeply grateful to Dr Iain R. Torrance, as well as to his co-editor Professor Alasdair I. C. Heron, for honouring me by inviting me to present this work as the first in the new annual series of *Scottish Journal of Theology Lectures*. It was a delight to deliver these in the University of Aberdeen, where I have several times been welcomed over many years and have many friends. I hold the Department of Divinity at Aberdeen in great affection and esteem. Finally, I owe a further debt of thanks to the publishers T&T Clark of Edinburgh, and to Mr Jon Pott and others of Eerdmans, Grand Rapids, USA.

ANTHONY C. THISELTON
Department of Theology
University of Nottingham
March 1995

PART I

MEANING, MANIPULATION
AND TRUTH

I

God as Self-Affirming Illusion? Manipulation, Truth and Language

THE English political philosopher Thomas Hobbes (1588–1679) well knew that we can play tricks with truth by using language in particular ways. In his *Leviathan* (1651) he discusses the status of claims to receive private revelations of God's will. A person might claim, for example, 'God spoke to me in a dream', and expect others to act on such a claim. Hobbes observes, however, 'to say that God hath spoken to him in a dream is no more than to say that he dreamed that God spoke to him'.[1] The first form of the proposition appears to claim the status of a solemn oracle, perhaps to legitimate some belief or action. The second, we might speculate, could amount to no more than a regretful reflection on how much cheese may wisely be eaten immediately before retiring to bed.

Hobbes writes a short section on dreams towards the beginning of his *Leviathan*. Dreams, he argues, can hardly constitute serious communications, since within a dream nothing whatever seems 'absurd'. Dreams arise as 'phantoms' of past sensations which remain incoherent, because no 'end' or specific purpose seems to guide them coherently.[2] Hence to appeal to dreams as vehicles of truth may deceive both the self and others. Hobbes therefore attacks such appeals as entirely unsupported grounds for belief. Although he accepts that we cannot exclude the possibility that God may speak through dreams, as a matter of principle, Hobbes concludes that in everyday life this kind of claim 'has not force'.[3]

In other discussions of language, Hobbes extends his analysis of deceptive uses of language which may hide truth. Disguise may occur, for example, when speakers use 'inconstant signification'. Here they slide from one meaning to another. Speakers may also employ 'names that signify nothing'. We assert nothing whatever if we assert some quality, for example, about a 'round quadrilateral'.[4] Deception,

---

[1] Thomas Hobbes, *Leviathan*, ed. M. Oakeshott (Oxford: Blackwell, 1960), Pt. III, ch. 32, 243.
[2] Hobbes, *Leviathan*, I, ch. 2, 10–11.
[3] Hobbes, *Leviathan*, III, ch. 32, 243.
[4] Hobbes, *Leviathan*, I, ch. 4, 19–25.

3

however, can too easily lead to the possibility of manipulation. Sometimes clergy, Hobbes observes, speak with 'fraudulent intent'.[5]

Hobbes lived during a period when English Royalists and Parliamentarians sought to legitimate their respective political philosophies by seeking to validate their claims with reference to the will of God. Those who appealed to a theological doctrine of 'the right of kings' argued on different grounds from those of Hobbes's own Royalist sympathies. He himself expressed these in terms of a philosophy of social contract, not by an appeal to God's will. On the other side, Parliamentarians sought to legitimate a more egalitarian view by appealing to the doctrine of the priesthood of all believers.

In this respect parallels emerge with John Locke (1632–1704). It is easy to overlook the context of Locke's well-known maxim of 1690 that 'reason must be our last judge and guide in everything'.[6] Locke opposed equally the manipulatory use of the Bible by authoritarian Anglican bishops and the deceptive and often manipulatory claims of 'enthusiasts' to know God's will privately. Those whom he calls 'enthusiasts' try, Locke argues, to legitimate as 'truths' what amount to the 'ungrounded fancies of a man's own brain, and assume them for a foundation both of opinion and conduct'.[7] Peter Nidditch and especially Henning Graf Reventlow demonstrate that Locke was a scrupulous exegete of the Bible. His purpose was to recover the 'plain meaning' of the text from otherwise manipulative uses.[8]

It is a mistake merely to ascribe to Hobbes the seeds of 'atheism' in England, as David Berman carefully points out.[9] Likewise, even if he overestimates the role of reason within an empiricist frame, Locke's appeals to 'reasonableness' as Reventlow stresses, reflect a serious religious concern that Christian truth should be neither manipulated nor counterfeited by institutional or 'private' interests.

We cannot claim the same concerns for the German philosopher Friedrich Nietzsche (1844–1900). He shares with Hobbes a serious distrust of 'empty' language, which pretends to convey 'universal' truths. But Nietzsche attacks *all* religious belief, and in particular its universal misuse of language about truth as a disguise for its interests.

---

[5] Hobbes, *Leviathan*, I, ch. 2, 12; I, ch. 6, 35; I, ch. 12 (on religion); and IV, ch. 43–4 and 46–7, 435–59.

[6] John Locke, *An Essay Concerning Human Understanding* (London: Collins, 1964), Bk. IV, ch. 19 'On Enthusiasm', sect. 14, 432.

[7] Locke, *Essay*, IV, ch. 19, sect. 3, 429.

[8] Henning Graf Reventlow, *The Authority of the Bible and the Rise of the Modern World* (Eng. London: SCM, 1984), 259; cf. 243–85, Cf. further P. H. Nidditch, *The Locke Newsletter* 9 (1978), 15–19.

[9] David Berman, *A History of Atheism in Britain from Hobbes to Russell* (London and New York: Routledge, 1988 and 1990), 57. Cf. further F. S. McNeilly, *The Anatomy of Leviathan* (London: Macmillan, 1968).

In the *Notebooks* of 1873, Nietzsche writes: 'What is truth? A mobile army of metaphors, metonyms and anthropomorphisms.'[10] Especially in religion, Nietzsche urges, people use 'errors' for their own advantage, self-interest, or power. Some promote erroneous 'lies' merely from sheer personal need. In this sense, Nietzsche exclaims: *Truth is that kind of error* without which a certain species of living cannot exist. The value of Life is ultimately decisive.'[11] Nietzsche goes further. He includes even 'facts' here. He writes: 'All that exists consists of *interpretations*.'[12] 'Truths are illusions we have forgotten are illusions.'[13]

Nietzsche continues to attack the truth-status of both philosophy and theology as resting on metaphor and manipulation. They deal with 'fundamental errors' but as if these were 'fundamental truths'. The theme becomes more developed in his *Human, All-Too-Human* of 1878, and in *The Twilight of the Idols* (1889) and *The Antichrist* (published later in 1895).[14] Theology can offer only a manipulative tool by means of which the weak, the insecure, and the vulnerable may try to cope with life. It offers them anodyne illusions.

At worst, illusions of legitimacy as supposed 'truth' serve a power-hungry ecclesial priesthood or religious leadership. By claiming that they promote 'truths', they seduce the gullible and credulous into following where they lead.

How can such deception and manipulation be sustained? In Nietzsche's view three major factors give weight to the illusions. Together they serve to convey a seductive credibility to claims about God and about truth.

First, language, especially metaphor, provides the raw material for disguise. Nietzsche addresses the problem of language as that which constructs false 'idols', as 'universal truths'. A key work here is *The Twilight of the Idols*. No doubt, as Walter Kaufmann suggests, Nietzsche's identification of 'four great errors' in this work reflects 'the four idols' exposed by Francis Bacon.[15] Nietzsche declares: 'I fear we shall never be rid of God, so long as we still believe in grammar.'[16]

---

[10] Friedrich Nietzsche, 'On Truth and Lie in an Extra-Moral Sense', traditional translation (as above) in Walter Kaufmann (ed.), *The Portable Nietzsche* (New York: Viking Press, 1968 (1954)), 46; translated as 'movable host' in Daniel Breazeale (ed.), *Philosophy and Truth. Selections from Nietzsche's Notebooks of the Early 1870's* (New Jersey: Humanities Press, and Sussex: Harvester Press, 1979), 84.

[11] Friedrich Nietzsche, *The Complete Works of Friedrich Nietzsche*, 18 vols., ed. O. Levy (Eng. London: Allen & Unwin, 1909–13) [henceforward abbreviated as *Works*], vol. 15: *The Will to Power*, vol. 2, 20, aphorism 493 (his italics).

[12] Nietzsche, *Works*, vol. 15: *The Will to Power*, vol. 2, 12, aphorism 481 (his italics).

[13] Nietzsche, 'On Truth and Lie', loc. cit.

[14] Nietzsche, *Works*, vols. 6 & 7: *Human, All-Too-Human* (2 vols.), vol. 1, esp. aphorisms 1–9 and vol. 2, aphorisms 20, 28, 32, et al. (References to the other works appear below.)

[15] Kaufmann, 'Editor's Preface', *The Portable Nietzsche*, 463–4.

[16] Nietzsche, *Works*, vol. 12: *The Twilight of the Idols*, 22, aphorism 5.

Language appears to imply that theistic belief depends on 'reason'. But this invites the response which Nietzsche describes in the words of his sub-title *How to Philosophize with the Hammer*. Hammers are needed to destroy 'idols'.

Elsewhere Nietzsche comments: 'We are still constantly led astray by words ... Language contains a hidden philosophical mythology, which, how ever careful we may be, breaks out afresh at every moment.'[17] He speaks of 'the spell of certain grammatical functions'.[18] Indeed in *The Twilight of the Idols* he exclaims: '"Reason" in language! – oh what a deceptive old witch it has been!'[19] Ludwig Wittgenstein (1889–1951) would speak in due course of philosophy as 'a battle against the bewitchment of our intelligence by means of language', and of being 'held captive' by a linguistic 'picture'.[20] Even in his earlier work, *The Tractatus*, Wittgenstein observed that 'language disguises thought'.[21] Prior to Wittgenstein, Fritz Mauthner (1849–1923) stressed with equal force the capacity of language to generate illusions.

Second, Nietzsche aims to unmask supposed issues of truth as issues of value and issues of power. In *The Will to Power* he writes: 'Knowledge works as an *instrument* of power.'[22] Explicitly dissenting from Darwin's notions of 'survival' as mere perpetuation, Nietzsche observes: 'Where there is a struggle, it is a struggle for power.'[23] Even a value-system, namely 'morality' serves primarily as 'a means of preserving the community', not as any universal imperative or truth-claim.[24]

In *The Antichrist* Nietzsche attacks the motivations that underlie the truth-claims of Christian theology. Among ordinary theistic believers, these often take the form of desire for comfort, security, self-importance or self-affirmation. Nietzsche writes: 'The "salvation of the soul" – in plain English "the world revolves around me".'[25] But among priests, theologians, and church leaders the motivation is more sinister: 'A theologian, a priest, or a pope, not only errs but actually lies with every word that he utters.'[26] Nietzsche believes with Marx that Christian faith

[17] Nietzsche, *Works*, vol. 7: *Human, All-Too-Human*, vol. 2, pt. ii, 'The Wanderer', 192, aphorism 11.
[18] Nietzsche, *Works*, vol. 12: *Beyond Good and Evil*, 'Prejudices of Philosophers', 29, aphorism 20.
[19] Nietzsche, *Works*, vol. 16: *The Twilight of the Idols*, 22, aphorism 5.
[20] Ludwig Wittgenstein, *Philosophical Investigations* (German and Eng., Oxford: Blackwell [1967] 2nd edn. 1958), sects. 109, 115.
[21] Ludwig Wittgenstein, *Tractatus Logico-Philosophicus* (German and Eng., London: Routledge & Kegan Paul, 1961), 4.002.
[22] Nietzsche, *Works*, vol. 15: *The Will to Power*, vol. 2, 11, aphorism 480 (his italics).
[23] Nietzsche, *Works*, vol. 16: *The Twilight of the Idols*, 71, aphorism 14.
[24] Nietzsche, *Works*, vol. 7: *Human, All-Too-Human*, vol. 2, 221, aphorism 44.
[25] Nietzsche, *Works*, vol. 16: *The Antichrist. An Attempted Criticism of Christianity*, 186, aphorism 43.
[26] Ibid. 177, aphorism 38.

6

becomes 'repressive', and with Feuerbach that it diminishes humanness. It propagates 'vicious frauds . . . systems of cruelty on the strength of which the priest became and remained master'.[27]

Where a falsehood 'serves a purpose', the priest may appeal to the 'Will of God' or to 'Revelation of God'.[28] The priest is 'the *professional denier* . . . Truth has already been turned topsy-turvy'.[29] Even among ordinary Christians, '"beautiful feelings" . . . "the heaving breast" [become] the bellows of divinity'.[30] Nietzsche insists: 'Supreme axiom: "God forgiveth him that repenteth" – in plain English: him that sub-mitteth himself to the priest.'[31] He concludes: 'Transvaluation of all values!'[32]

Third, Nietzsche, has declared: 'All that exists consists of *inter-pretations*.'[33] There are no 'givens', not even as raw data awaiting categorization or ordering by the human mind. He has radicalized Kant and Fichte.

Interpretations of interpretations, however, readily lend them-selves as tools of self-interest, deception and manipulation. We confine ourselves to one example from Nietzsche, namely his attack on Paul. We have access now to very different approaches to Paul by J. Munck (1954), K. Stendahl (1963), E. P. Sanders (1977), J. D. G. Dunn (1990), and N. T. Wright (1991) from the one-sided portrait of Paul found in radical nineteenth-century Lutheranism on which Nietzsche based his attack.[34] Nietzsche interprets Paul as tormented by his inability to keep the Jewish Law. Hence a theology which abrogated the law appeared to serve his own deepest personal interests. Nietzsche interprets Paul as 'a man with a mind full of superstition and cunning'.[35] Paul, he wishes to argue, could not fulfill the Law. But in coming to terms with Jesus of Nazareth, 'his mind was suddenly enlightened . . . "Here is my means of escape . . . I have the destroyer of the Law in my hands!" . . . Morality itself was blown away, annihilated . . . "I am above the Law", thinks Paul'.[36]

---

[27] Ibid. 213, aphorism 54.

[28] Ibid. aphorism 55.

[29] Ibid. 134, aphorism 8 (his italics).

[30] Ibid. 138, aphorism 12.

[31] Ibid. 161, aphorism 26 (his italics).

[32] Ibid. 231, aphorism 62.

[33] Nietzsche, *Works*, vol. 15: *The Will to Power*, vol. 2, 12, aphorism 481.

[34] Cf. J. Munck, *Paul and the Salvation of Mankind* (Eng. London: SCM, 1959), 11–35; K. Stendahl, 'Paul and the Introspective Conscience of the West', rp. from *Harvard Theological Review* (1963) in *Paul among Jews and Gentiles and Other Essays* (London: SCM, 1977, and Philadelphia: Fortress Press, 1976); E. P. Sanders, *Paul and Palestinian Judaism* (London: SCM, 1977); J. D. G. Dunn, *Jesus, Paul and the Law: Studies in Mark and Galatians* (London: SPCK, 1990); N. T. Wright, *The Climax of the Covenant: Christ and the Law in Pauline Theology* (Edinburgh: T&T Clark, and Philadelphia: Fortress Press, 1991).

[35] Nietzsche, *Works*, vol. 9: *The Dawn of Day*, 67, aphorism 68; 66–71.

[36] Ibid. 68–70, aphorism 68.

Thus it came about, Nietzsche concludes, that Paul 'was the first Christian'.[37]

Nietzsche insists, therefore, that Paul's claims about 'truth', like those of later generations of Christians, rest at least partly on *manipulative interpretations of texts*. He writes: 'He who has interpreted a passage in an author "more profoundly" than was intended, has not interpreted the author but obscured him . . . They [Christian interpreters] often alter the text to suit their purpose.'[38] Pilate's question 'What is truth?', Nietzsche concludes, 'is now gleefully brought on the scene as an advocate of Christ.[39] He offers a parody of the opening of the Gospel of John: 'In the beginning was the nonsense, and the nonsense was with God, and the nonsense was God.'[40]

How relevant are Nietzsche's criticisms to the world of today? First, the notion that religion has more to do with value and power than with truth arises with regularity in English parish life, and perhaps no less in Scotland and North America. When he spoke of 'truth' as '*that kind of error* without which a particular kind of being cannot exist', Nietzsche anticipated a view, widespread among a certain type of self-confident male today that religion serves primarily to comfort vulnerable people.[41]

In the view of a certain type of man, characteristically such people include women. We may imagine such a macho figure watching football on television on a Saturday afternoon. The doorbell rings and to his barely suppressed irritation he finds a parish minister on the doorstep. By instant reflex he mutters: 'I'll fetch the wife.' This does not spring from his desire to return to football, for this was forgotten in the surprise of the moment. It reflects the *underlying assumption* that anything to do with religion serves merely to provide comfort and affirmation to lesser mortals. On this basis he views it as part of his wife's domain, not his.

Even requests for infant baptism sometimes entail a presupposition that truth remains subordinate to issues of value or power. An educated intellectual couple may explicitly seek to distance themselves from 'believing the creeds' or from 'all that'. But at a barely conscious pre-intellectual level they may feel that baptism offers some unspecified value or power which their child may (just possibly) need. Whether certain claims are true does not seem to enter the picture.

The relevance of Nietzsche's critiques for today appears even more clearly in the academic and intellectual climate which surrounds contemporary theology. One of the major intellectual debates of today

---

[37] Ibid. 71, aphorism 68.
[38] Nietzsche, *Works*, vol. 7: *Human, All-Too-Human*, vol. 2, ii, 'The Wanderer', 197, aphorism 17.
[39] Ibid. i, 16, aphorism 8.
[40] Ibid. i, 20, aphorism 22.
[41] Nietzsche, *Works*, vol. 15: *The Will to Power*, vol. 2, 20, aphorism 493 (his italics).

concerns an alleged shift from the attitudes of 'modernity' to those of postmodernism. If the challenge of postmodernism invites the transposition of issues of truth and argument into questions of power and rhetoric this becomes a fundamental issue for theology. Hence we must look more closely at postmodernism.

2

Postmodernism, Modernity and the Postmodern Self

THE term 'the postmodern self' denotes the predicament of the human self and society which has been caught up in the attitudes and suspicions of postmodernism. But to speak of 'the postmodern self' also leaves open the fundamental intellectual question, which is much debated, about whether postmodernism has *overtaken and eclipsed 'modernity'*, or whether it merely reflects a *specific phase*, perhaps even a degenerate phase, *of modernity*. On the other hand, it also implies a serious engagement with the attitudes, assumptions, and perceptions that permeate outlooks which are included within a postmodern stance towards truth, rationality, manipulation and selfhood.

A working distinction between 'postmodernism' and 'the postmodern self' emerges in Norman K. Denzin's *Images of Postmodern Society* (1991).[1] Postmodernism implies a *shattering of innocent confidence in the capacity of the self to control its own destiny*. It signals a loss of trust in global strategies of social planning, and in universal criteria of rationality. It often carries with it emotional by-products of 'anger, alienation, anxiety, . . . racism and sexism'.[2] In the wake of the collapse of traditional values or universal criteria, the 'postmodern self' becomes 'the self who embodies the multiple contradictions of post-modernism, while experiencing itself through the everyday performances of gender, class, and racially-linked social identities'.[3]

Whether or not we agree with J. Habermas in doubting whether postmodernity brings 'the end of modernity', we cannot recover the lost innocence which characterized the self of modernity, let alone that of the pre-modern.[4] The postmodern self faces life and society with

---

[1] Norman K. Denzin, *Images of Postmodern Society. Social Theory and Contemporary Cinema* (London: Sage Publications, 1991), vii. See further David Harvey, *The Condition of Postmodernity. An Enquiry into the Origins of Cultural Change* (Oxford: Blackwell, 2nd edn. 1989), esp. 3–118.

[2] Denzin, *Images of Postmodern Society*, loc. cit.

[3] Ibid.

[4] Classic studies on this issue include J. Habermas, *The Philosophical Discourse of Modernity* (Eng. New York: Political Press, 1988); Richard J. Bernstein (ed.), *Habermas and Modernity* (Cambridge: Polity Press, 1985), esp. 1–34, 125–39, 161–216; J.-F. Lyotard, *The Postmodern Explained to Children. Correspondence 1982–1985* (Eng.

suspicion rather than trust. The modern self retained a basic optimism about the capacities of human reason, governmental or social strategies and scientific achievement, to shape the world for the general advancement of human society. But such optimism omits too many factors to provide hope for the postmodern self.

The postmodern self follows Nietzsche and Freud in viewing claims to truth largely as devices which serve to legitimate power-interests. *Disguise covers everything. Hence a culture of distrust and suspicion emerges.* Even allegedly 'factual' reports of achievements may be suspected of embodying manipulative editing to protect the interests of some person or group. Hence bureaucracy initiates vast monitoring systems. But here even the monitors are suspected of having interests which, in turn, invite further processes of monitoring. In Part IV we explore these issues further with reference to Foucault.

Yet bureaucracy also brings into focus the self-contradictory character of the postmodern self. On one side it arises because of suspicions about competing manipulative interests. Yet on the other side it claims to retain a supposedly impartial role as arbitrator for the common good, remaining 'above' the competing interests. To the ordinary worker, however, the bureaucrats themselves may appear also to be engaged in empire-building and even in seeking to control or dominate the enterprises or institutions for whose benefit and service they originated. Hence the sense of anger and conflict which they were designed to mitigate and to retrain now escalates and proliferates. The postmodern self perceives itself as having lost control as active agent, and as having been transformed into a passive victim of competing groups. Everyone seems to be at the mercy of someone else's vested interests for power.

Mass advertising has contributed much to the collapse of confidence in claims to truth, along with power-seeking in party-politics. People suspect that here 'truth' disguises only the desire for success and domination. So thin has become the disguise that some advertisements achieve their success by witty self-mockery, conceding that their 'truth-claims' are not truth-claims at all. We know that a beer which 'reaches the parts which other beers cannot reach' gently mocks the whole process of asserting claims at face value. We *know* that the 'claim' has nothing whatever to do with physiology.

In matters of race, class, gender and professional guilds, however, the gloves are off. For what *counts as true* for one group is often disparaged as a *manipulative disguise to legitimate power-claims* by another group. If different groups choose to adopt different *criteria of truth* to determine what *counts* as true, or even *what counts as a meaningful truth-claim*, rational argument and dialogue become

London: Turnaround, 1992), 9–26 and 87–100. A further useful source is R. J. Bernstein, *The New Constellation. The Ethical-Political Horizons of Modernity/Post-modernity* (Cambridge: Polity Press, 1991).

undermined by recurring appeals to what one group counts as axioms, but seem far from axiomatic for another. At this point argument becomes transposed into rhetoric. Rhetoric then comes to rely on force, seduction, or manipulation.

Two consequences emerge for theology. Both are explored throughout this book. First, some religious people not only use manipulation in place of truth, but may eventually come to believe sincerely in the truth of their own inherited religious rhetoric, even if it may have served initially to further some power-interest. Second, to be manipulated is to be treated as less than a personal self. As Vincent Brümmer stresses in his writings, we do not seek to manipulate someone whom we genuinely respect and love as an Other in their own right.[5] Yet respect for the other *as 'Other'*, as a unique agent or active personal subject, stands at the heart of the Christian gospel.

Equally, this also constitutes the heart of concerns about interpretation or, more strictly, hermeneutics, from Schleiermacher and Dilthey to Gadamer and Ricoeur. We trace these concerns and their implications especially in Part II of this study. For Schleiermacher and for Dilthey, we shall see, genuine 'understanding' of a text or of another human person arises only when we seek to *'step out of our own frame'*.[6] We need to *renounce those prior categorizations and stereotypifications with which we begin*. In Gadamer's language, we renounce the manipulative 'control' epitomized by 'scientific method', and allow ourselves to enter unpredicted avenues into which mutual listening and genuine conversation leads.[7] In Ricoeur's terminology, we explore new worlds of possibility.[8]

Later we shall look more closely at the work of Roland Barthes, Michel Foucault, Jacques Derrida, and others. At an intellectual level such thinkers provide much of the force behind postmodernism, especially in literary and critical theory. We shall also note that a Christian account of human nature accepts the capacity of the self for self-deception and its readiness to use strategies of manipulation.

The term 'heart' (*kardia*) closely approaches in the Pauline letters Freudian notions of the hidden depths which lie below the threshold of conscious awareness. The things of the heart, Bultmann rightly

[5] Vincent Brümmer, *What are We Doing When We Pray? A Philosophical Inquiry* (London: SCM, 1984), 1–15, 74–113; *Speaking of a Personal God* (Cambridge: Cambridge University Press, 1992), 83–9, 115–27; and *The Model of Love: A Study in Philosophical Theology* (Cambridge: Cambridge University Press, 1993).

[6] F. D. E. Schleiermacher, *Hermeneutics. The Handwritten Manuscripts*, ed. H. Kimmerle (Eng. Missoula: Scholars Press, 1977), 42, 109.

[7] Hans-Georg Gadamer, *Truth and Method* (2nd Eng. edn. from 5th German edn., London: Sheed & Ward, 1993), esp. 362–79 (1st Eng. edn. 1975, 325–41) *et passim*.

[8] For a succinct retrospective account and prospective questioning, cf. Paul Ricoeur, *Time and Narrative* (Eng. 3 vols., Chicago: Chicago University Press, 1984–8), vol. 3, 253–61; cf. vol. 2, 100–60.

comments, 'need not penetrate into the field of consciousness at all, but may designate the hidden tendency of the self'.[9] Uses of 'flesh' (*sarx*) in Paul as describing the human self in pursuit of self-interests are confirmed by Bultmann, J. A. T. Robinson and Robert Jewett.[10] Thus Gal. 6:12, Bultmann writes, may allude to a 'secret motive hidden even from themselves'.[11] Motivations of the heart may remain 'darkened' (Rom. 1:21).

At the same time, the New Testament writers perceive self-deception and manipulation as incompatible in principle with the new creation, and subject to change and transformation. 'Maturity to the measure of the full stature of Christ' (Eph. 4:13) entails an abandonment of 'immature' strategies of 'trickery . . . craftiness in deceitful scheming [in favour of] speaking the truth in love' (4:14, 15). Loving respect for the personhood of 'the other' by truthful speech is part of 'growing up' (4:15). 'Darkened' understanding is self-defeating, for it ends in 'futility' (4:17). When at the advent the 'sleeper awakes' (Eph. 5:14), the tattered remnants of all the former deceits and illusions will fall away, like forgotten dreams in the solid day (5:8–14; 1 Thess. 5:4–8; Rom. 13:11–12).

Christian theology, then, cannot be said to be compatible with the transvaluation of questions about truth into questions about value or power as an ultimate principle. But it entirely coheres with Christian theology to accept that this transvaluation *frequently takes place* where self-interest still holds sway even among otherwise sincere believers. There remains much to learn in this respect from Barthes, Foucault and Derrida.

Roland Barthes (1915–80) exposes the manipulative power-interests which often underlie the 'mythologies' of the second half of the twentieth century. In his *Mythologies* (French, 1957; English, 1972) he unmasks what we too often perceive as 'natural' or 'given' as socially contrived. Many manipulative devices appear to be natural 'truths'.[12] Photographs in popular magazines, for example, do more than portray the object which appears to be depicted. By the use of perspective, light and shadow, proportion, angle, and so forth, the 'signs' (in the sense used in sign-theory) may be multidimensional. At one level they seem simply to portray a commercial product, but at another level they commend it by associating it with success, sex, or prestige.

Barthes's 'de-naturalizing' of what might otherwise be taken for granted goes deeper. He exposes to view coded signals about middle-

---

[9] Rudolf Bultmann, *Theology of the New Testament* (Eng. 2 vols., London: SCM, 1952 and 1955), vol. 1, 225; cf. 220–7.

[10] Robert Jewett, *Paul's Anthropological Terms. A Study of their Use in Conflict Settings* (Leiden: Brill, 1971), 95–104; cf. A. C. Thiselton, 'The Meaning of *Sarx* in 1 Cor. 5:5', *Scottish Journal of Theology* 26 (1973), 204–28.

[11] Bultmann, *Theology of the New Testament*, vol. 1, 224.

[12] Roland Barthes, *Mythologies* (Eng. London: Cape, 1972), e.g. 91–3.

class values, about imperialism, about power-interests, as part of a sign-system which generates far more than the 'obvious' meaning. His goal is to unmask hidden power-interests, whether political, social, or commercial. The 'objectivity' of the sign as an innocent truth-claim about a single state of affairs proves to be illusory. Postmodernity means, above all, loss of innocence, especially any innocence which perceives the contrived as 'natural'. Barthes observes: 'I resented seeing Nature and History confused at every turn.'[13] He develops these principles as an explicit theory of signs in the *Elements of Semiology* (French, 1964; English, 1967).[14] Here 'signs' includes the meaning-systems of clothes, furniture, food, and other 'messages' from seemingly innocent matrices.

Jacques Derrida (b. 1930) explicitly acknowledges his indebtedness to the principle of suspicion in Nietzsche, as well as to 'forces' in Freud, the work of Husserl, and 'situatedness' and '*Destruktion*' in Heidegger.[15] Indeed in his well-known long essay 'White Mythology' (1971) resonances with Nietzsche are unmistakable: 'Metaphysics – the white mythology . . . reflects the culture of the West: the white man takes his own mythology . . . for the universal form of that he must still wish to call Reason.'[16] The history of Western philosophy, Derrida concludes, largely rests on a confusion between 'so-called philosophical metaphors' and the presupposition that these represent truths which constitute 'the solution of important problems'.[17]

Like Barthes, Derrida attempts to underpin this, supposedly in his earlier work, with a theory of signs drawn initially from Saussure's notion of the dependence of meaning on 'difference'.[18] Neither language nor truth is 'item-centred', but is generated by a shifting flux of variables. Hence meaning (and thereby truth-claims) never reaches 'closure': 'difference' becomes 'deferral'.[19] Meaning is always postponed, in the sense that new meanings constantly overtake it as new interests and new cultural frames repeatedly change its multi-level currencies. Caputo rightly observes: 'Derrida does not overthrow hermeneutics but makes

[13] Ibid. 11.

[14] Roland Barthes, *Elements of Semiology* (Eng. London: Cape, 1967).

[15] Jacques Derrida, *Of Grammatology* (Eng. Baltimore: Johns Hopkins University Press, 1976), xxi (Translator's Preface by G. C. Spivak); cf. his *Writing and Difference* (Eng. London: Routledge & Kegan Paul, 1978), 278–93.

[16] J. Derrida, 'White Mythology: Metaphor in the Text of Philosophy', in his *Margins of Philosophy* (Eng. New York and London: Harvester Wheatsheaf, 1982), 213; cf. 207–72.

[17] Ibid. 228.

[18] I use 'supposedly' in the light of my critique in *New Horizons in Hermeneutics. The Theory and Practice of Transforming Biblical Reading* (London: HarperCollins, and Grand Rapids: Zondervan, 1992), 82–132.

[19] J. Derrida, *Speech and Phenomena and Other Essays on Husserl's Theory of Signs* (Eng. Evanston: North Western University Press, 1973), 135–41; cf. also 129–60, esp. 130.

it more radical.'[20] For this follows Nietzsche's view that there are only 'interpretations' and nothing else.[21]

In Part IV we shall trace further 'unmaskings' of the 'natural' as social habit or disguised power-interests in Michel Foucault (1926–84). His work on 'madness', for example, demonstrates that what 'madness' seemed to consist in has largely depended on shifts in social assumptions between the ancient world, the nineteenth century and today. His later work explores relations between knowledge and power, especially institutional power in the penal system or in medicine.[22]

In his introduction to G. Vattimo, The End of Modernity (Italian, 1985; English, 1988), J. R. Snyder observes that the writings of Nietzsche lie behind not only Barthes, Derrida and Foucault, but also Lacan, Deleuze, Baudrillard and Lyotard.[23] He explains: 'The project of nihilism is to unmask all systems of reason as systems of persuasion.'[24] In other words, issues of truth become issues of rhetoric. Snyder continues: 'All thought that pretends to discern truth is but an expression of the will-to-power – even to domination – of those making the truth-claims over those who are being addressed by them.'[25]

Jean-François Lyotard rejects not only the possibility of 'universal' truth, but even the very notion of 'theory' as a construct of 'modernity' (other than in a purely local, ad hoc, functional sense). In his book ironically entitled The Postmodern Explained to Children (French, 1986; English, 1992), he not only declares 'war on totality', but, like Derrida, insists that we cannot grasp reality, because it slips by before we can catch hold of it. Don Cupitt, we shall note in Part III, makes wide use of this principle. In this sense, truth is not even 'presentable'.[26]

These perspectives constitute the most serious and urgent challenge to theology, in comparison with which the old-style attacks from 'common-sense positivism' appear relatively naïve. Theology has more at stake than perhaps any other discipline because, although philosophy and some other disciplines share the same loss of truth, theology serves to establish critically-informed trust, whereas the postmodern perspective rests on suspicion. Theology seeks to recover elements of the authentic and the genuine from among the chaff of self-interest, manipulation, and power-claims. It would also become problematic to claim that at the heart of Christian theology stands the paradigm-case of non-manipulative love, namely the theology of the cross and

[20] John D. Caputo, Radical Hermeneutics (Bloomington: Indiana University Press, 1989), 4.
[21] Nietzsche, Works, vol. 15: The Will to Power, vol. 2, 12, aphorism 481.
[22] Michel Foucault, Discipline and Punish (Eng. New York: Pantheon, 1977), 190.
[23] Gianni Vattimo, The End of Modernity. Nihilism and Hermeneutics in Post-modern Culture (Eng. Cambridge: Polity Press, 1988 and 1991), xii–xiii.
[24] Ibid. xii.
[25] Ibid.; cf. 1–13, 134–8, 176–80, where Vattimo discusses Gadamer and Nietzsche.
[26] Ibid.; Lyotard, The Postmodern Explained to Children, 24.

the free gift of resurrection if all that exists is manipulative interpretation.

We cannot reply to these claims, however, simply by appealing to the 'weakness' of the cross. For Nietzsche such a response would merely confirm his suspicions about the nature of Christianity. He writes: 'Christianity has sided with everything weak, low, and botched; it made an ideal out of *antagonism* towards all the preservation instincts of strong life.'[27] In Nietzsche's view, the God of Christianity degenerated into the *contradiction of life*, 'instead of being its . . . eternal Yes! In God a declaration of hostility towards life . . . the will to nothingness sanctified . . .'[28]

---

[27] Nietzsche, *Works*, vol. 16: *The Antichrist*, 130, aphorisms 5 and 6, 131, aphorism 7.

[28] Ibid. 146, aphorism 18.

3

Do All Controlling Models in Religion Serve Manipulative Purposes?

NIETZSCHE has brought a double charge. Christian claims to truth, he asserts, disguise power-bids; and religious faith breeds insipid mediocrity. Both claims find a powerful response in the writings of Dietrich Bonhoeffer (1906–45). Bonhoeffer attacked notions of Christian belief which appeared to offer comfort and self-affirmation while the believer simply lets the world go by as it is. He equally challenged an interpretation of God and of Christian discipleship which settles merely for passive resignation and mediocrity, or entails manipulative interests.

This is no accident. His close friend Eberhard Bethge tells us that Bonhoeffer read very carefully the entire corpus of Nietzsche's writings and was influenced by them.[1] Bonhoeffer's work, however, in these two respects simply reflects the New Testament writings. We may note first of all how these anticipate what Bonhoeffer translates into twentieth-century terms.

The Gospel of John explicitly identifies the desire for personal status and power as a fundamental obstacle to believing in Jesus as the Christ. Jesus exclaims: 'How can you believe when you accept glory (Greek, *doxa*) from another?' (John 5:44). *Doxa* carries with it notions of 'reputation', 'opinion', or in this context social and religious prestige and influence.

The Matthean denunciation of pharisaic leadership, which some interpret as a thinly-veiled warning to Christian leaders more generally, includes an explicit rejection of the use of 'religion' to gain 'places of honour . . . the best seats . . . being seen by others' (Matt. 23:5, 6).[2]

---

[1] Eberhard Bethge's Preface to vol. 3 of Dietrich Bonhoeffer, *Gesammelte Schriften*, 5 vols. (Munich: Kaiser, 1958–66); cf. E. Bethge, *Dietrich Bonhoeffer: Theologian, Christian, Contemporary* (Eng. London: Collins, 1970), 84–5, 773; and 'The Challenge of Dietrich Bonhoeffer's Life and Theology', *The Chicago Theological Register* (Feb. 1961), 4.

[2] Cf. David Garland, *The Intention of Matthew 23* (Leiden: Brill, 1979), esp. 62–3, 116 and 214. For more recent approaches, cf. further Richard A. Edwards, *Matthew's Story of Jesus* (Philadelphia: Fortress, 1985), and F. W. Burnett, 'Exposing the Anti-Jewish Ideology of Matthew's Implied Author: Its Characterization of God as Father', *Semeia 59: Ideological Criticism of Biblical Texts* (1992), 155–91.

The Jesus of Matthew does not mince his words. Those religious leaders who revel in titles of respect and power (23:7) are 'snakes' (23:33). Like whitewashed tombs, they seek to disguise their own degenerative rottenness, while simultaneously warning people away from 'religion' (23:27). Authentic religious leadership and faith finds expression in self-giving service of others (23:11).

The Pauline writings expound these themes in detail. Recently much attention has been given to Paul's 'Narrenrede' ('I am speaking as a fool') in 2 Cor. 11:21 – 12:10. At the end, as at the beginning, he says 'I have been a fool! You forced me to it' (12:10).[3] It is generally agreed that the issue behind these twenty-three verses arises from the manipulative strategies of rival leaders or 'false apostles' at Corinth. Should Paul exert his own leadership by following the same methods? He had already made it clear in earlier correspondence that self-assertion and reliance on the purely causal force of rhetoric stood at odds with the message of the cross (1 Cor. 1:18 – 2:5). Paul recalls: 'I came to you in weakness . . . My speech and my proclamation were not with plausible words of "wisdom"' (2:3, 4). Yet the Corinthians still seem to expect that genuine leaders will show qualities that impress, whether by 'signs', by rhetorical power, by some institutional pedigree or credentials, or by some trait of character that commands submissive response.

For Paul himself, as E. Käsemann, C. K. Barrett, R. P. Martin and many others rightly argue, such principles or appeals remain incompatible with authentic or 'legitimate' apostleship.[4] Yet for the sake of Corinthian expectations, partly tongue-in-cheek Paul adopts a rhetorical form or style of 'boasting' of credentials to establish and legitimate his 'power', while in practice he deconstructs or undermines the game of power-play. As he declares in 2 Cor. 11:30: 'If I must boast, I will boast of the things that show my weakness.' E. A. Judge, followed by S. H. Travis, shows delightfully that Paul reverses the claim to fame and honour accorded to a Roman soldier who has the courage and daring to be 'first over the wall' in the storming of a besieged city.[5]

---

[3] For example, J. Zmijewski, *Der Stil der paulinischen 'Narrenrede'* (Cologne and Bonn: Hanstein, 1978); C. K. Barrett, 'Boasting (*kauchasthai* k.t.l.) in the Pauline Epistles', in A. Vanhoye (ed.), *L'Apôtre Paul – Personalité, style et conception du ministère* (Leuven: Leuven University, 1986), 363–8; J. P. Sampley, 'Paul, his Opponents in 2 Corinthians 10–13 and the Rhetorical Handbooks', in J. Neusner et al. (eds.), *The Social World of Formative Christianity* (Philadelphia: Fortress, 1988), 162–77.

[4] E. Käsemann, 'Die Legitimät des Apostels: eine Untersuchung zu II Korinther 10–13', *Zeitschrift für die neutestamentliche Wissenschaft* 41 (1942), 33–71; C. K. Barrett, *The Signs of an Apostle* (London: Epworth Press, 1970); R. P. Martin, *2 Corinthians* (Dallas: Word, 1986, and Milton Keynes: Word, 1991), 326–424.

[5] E. A. Judge, 'The Conflict of Educational Aims in New Testament Thought', *Journal of Christian Education* 9 (1966), 32–45, and further in 'Paul's Boasting in Relation to Contemporary Professional Practice', *Australian Biblical Review* 16 (1968), 37–50; S. H. Travis, 'Paul's Boasting in 2 Corinthians 10–12', *Studia Evangelica* 6 (1973), 527–32. Cf. Livy 23:18.

Paul 'boasts' that he, too, was 'first over the wall' – but unceremoniously in the reverse direction to escape in a fish basket to secure a quick exit from arrest: 'I was let down in a basket through a window in the wall, and escaped' (11:33); what bravery! Even if we accept that some opponents already cited this incident as disqualifying Paul for leadership, this does not undermine the broader principle that he recites his 'humiliations' as his 'qualifications'.[6] Apostleship depends on identification with the message of the cross, not with religious triumphalism.

By contrast, the 'false' apostles (11:13) use deceit and seduction (11:3, 13, 15), demand 'submission' and exercise domination: they 'make slaves of you, prey on you, put on airs' (11:20) and 'you submit to it readily enough' (11:4). The 'false apostles' are precisely true to type in the context of Nietzsche's analysis. But Paul does not fit this type. Even the 'weakness' and list of 'sufferings' which, against his will, he enumerates, are not qualities of passive mediocrity or unhealthy masochism. He escapes when he can, but endures without complaint those afflictions which become inevitable if he is to share in the self-giving that reflects the principle of the cross. This is venturesome and courageous service for the sake of others: 'I will most gladly spend and be spent for you' (12:15).

To be sure, two or three writers offer a very different account of Paul. Later in this study we shall consider the views of Graham Shaw that Paul uses manipulation for authoritarian purposes, and explore the claims of Elizabeth A. Castelli and Stephen D. Moore which link Paul with Foucault's analysis of 'institutional' and 'pastoral' power. But we reserve these discussions to later sections.

The two principles of non-manipulative service and a boldness that is far from servile come together vigorously in Martin Luther (1483–1546). Especially in *The Heidelberg Disputation* of 1518 he places in contrast a triumphalist, manipulative, 'theology of glory', and a self-giving, truthful, 'theology of the cross'. He comments: 'The theologian of glory says bad is good, and good is bad. The theologian of the cross calls them by their proper name.'[7] The one deserves the title 'theologian' who comprehends God not through power-seeking or a search for self-affirmation, but in receiving judgement and grace through the cross. The seeker after self and power 'prefers works to sufferings; and glory, to a cross'.[8]

We should not interpret what it is to 'prefer sufferings', however, in the way proposed by Nietzsche as servility or the 'slave morality' of Christians. Indeed, Luther quite explicitly opposes those 'fanatics' or 'enthusiasts' who 'select their own cross . . . making their suffering

---

[6] R. P. Martin, *2 Corinthians*, 384.
[7] Martin Luther, 'The Heidelberg Disputation', in *Luther: Early Theological Works*, ed. J. Atkinson (London: SCM, 1962), 291, Thesis 21.
[8] Luther, loc. cit., Proof 21.

meritorious'.[9] This would transpose it into a bid (even if an illusory bid) for power. There is nothing of a servile, lie-down-to-die, insipid, or bland character in Christian faith for Luther. In his Preface to Romans he declares: 'Faith is a living, daring, confidence in God's grace, so sure . . . that a man would stake his life upon it . . . [It] makes men glad and bold . . . ready and glad, without compulsion, to do good to everyone, to serve everyone, to suffer everything in love and praise to God who has shown him this grace.'[10]

Dietrich Bonhoeffer takes up these profound interpretations of God as known through the cross and applies them to the confusions of our own century. For Bonhoeffer, belief in God is no hallucinatory anodyne which merely helps people to cope with discomforts, insecurities, or difficulties. Christian theology has nothing to do with the consumers' wishes to purchase power or comfort.

Bonhoeffer writes: 'If it is I who say where God will be, I will always find there a [false] God who in some way corresponds to me, is agreeable to me, fits in with my nature. But if it is God who says where He will be . . . that place is the cross of Christ.'[11] This, he urges, is why the beatitudes in the Sermon on the Mount do not declare 'blessed are the powerful', but 'blessed are those who mourn', 'blessed are the poor'. That this has nothing to do with manipulative interests is demonstrated by the parallel 'Blessed are the pure in heart'.[12]

Bonhoeffer elucidates this principle further in *The Cost of Discipleship*. Here he attacks those who transpose a gospel which demands glad but costly discipleship into a commerce of 'cheap grace . . . sold on the market like a cheapjack's wares'.[13] Cheap grace is precisely what Nietzsche characterizes as a self-affirming illusion. Bonhoeffer writes: 'Cheap grace means the justification of sin without the justification of the sinner . . . the world goes on in the same old way . . . Cheap grace is the preaching of forgiveness without requiring repentance, baptism without church discipline, Communion without confession . . . grace without the cross, grace without Jesus Christ.'[14] For the first disciples grace was bound up with obedience to the call of Jesus to follow him in the everyday world.

This theme lies behind Bonhoeffer's equally well-known passage in his *Letters and Papers from Prison* written fromTegel about ten months before his execution. Christians, he writes, must live for others without

[9] Martin Luther, 'Sermon at Coberg on Cross and Suffering' (1530), in *Luther's Works*, vol. 51 (Philadelphia: Fortress, 1959), 199.

[10] Martin Luther, 'Preface to the Epistle of St. Paul to the Romans', in *Luther's Works*, vol. 35 (Philadelphia: Fortress, 1960), 370–1.

[11] Dietrich Bonhoeffer, *Meditating on the Word* (Eng. Cambridge, Mass: Cowley Publications, 1986), 45.

[12] Ibid. Cf. D. Bonhoeffer, *The Cost of Discipleship* (Eng. London: SCM (unabridged edn.) 1959), 93–176.

[13] Ibid. 35.

[14] Ibid. 35–6; cf. 37–47.

resort to the notion of God as some 'useful' crutch to soften reality, or to reduce the cost of service. On 16 July 1944 he wrote: 'Before God and with God we live without God. God lets himself be pushed out of the world on to the cross . . . Christ helps us, not by virtue of his omnipotence, but by virtue of his weakness and suffering.'[15]

E. Bethge, to whom this letter was personally written, explains in his theological biography of Bonhoeffer: 'The Christian listens to Feuerbach and Nietzsche – with a good conscience . . . They, for example, warn the Church against becoming a chemist's shop to minister to heavenly needs, leaving the world to its own desires.'[16] It is as if Bonhoeffer said to Nietzsche from his Nazi prison: 'But not all Christians are as you suggest. For even if you are right about "religion" as a human construct, authentic Christian faith lies in identification with the Christ who neither sought power by manipulation, nor was "weak" in the sense of being bland, conformist, or world-denying. He was "the man for others".'[17]

Thus Bonhoeffer writes further to Bethge that *metanoia* [Greek, repentance; Hebrew, turning] is 'not in the first place thinking about one's needs, problems, sins, and fears, but allowing oneself to be caught up into the way of Jesus'.[18] Faith does not '*use*' God, either as a pretext for legitimating one's wishes, or to 'explain' gaps in certain intellectual problems.[19] Biblical faith is controlled by the model not of 'religiosity' but of the Christ who goes to the cross 'for the other'.[20]

Bonhoeffer drives another nail into the coffin of Nietzsche's critique of all Christian faith when he turns to attack mistaken strategies on the part of clergy and leaders. Here he attacks, equally, liberalism on one side and pietist strands of Lutheranism and Methodism on the other.

The evangelistic strategy of liberalism remains flawed, he asserts, because 'it conceded to the world the right to determine Christ's place in the world'.[21] But no less the strategy of outreach proposed by pietists, namely 'despair or Jesus' rests on a mistake.[22] Bonhoeffer views this as a manipulative strategy which depends for its success in projecting the world into an infantile regression into an immature dependency-state. Almost echoing Nietzsche, he complains: 'They set themselves to drive people to inward despair and then the game is in their hands . . . And whom does it touch? A small number of people who regard themselves

---

[15] D. Bonhoeffer, *Letters and Papers from Prison* (Eng. enlarged edn.) (London: SCM, 1971), 360–1 (also 3rd edn. Eng. 1967, 196; 1953 edn., 121).
[16] Bethge, *Dietrich Bonhoeffer*, 773.
[17] Bonhoeffer, *Letters and Papers* (enlarged 1971 edn.) 381–2 (my italics).
[18] Ibid. 361 (18 July 1944).
[19] Ibid. 360 (16 July).
[20] Ibid. 361 (16 July).
[21] Ibid. 327 (8 June).
[22] Ibid.

as the most important thing in the world, and who therefore like to busy themselves with themselves.'[23]

It is important to sift the wheat from the chaff at this point. On one side, on the basis of such proclamation it becomes scarcely surprising if many churches become havens for self-centred, self-preoccupied religious lives. In Bonhoeffer's eyes this is 'like an attempt to put a grown-up man back into adolescence'.[24] On the other side, however, Gerhard Ebeling wishes to distinguish between his right expression of concern (with Luther) that believing faith is centred on Christ, rather than on some 'inner state' of the self, from a less judicious, over-hasty dismissal of experiences of human plight. Ebeling does not undervalue Bonhoeffer's approach, but wonders whether his importance is recognized 'in spite of' rather than 'because of' some of these reflections from his Tegel prison.[25]

If we heed Ebeling's careful warning, however, Bonhoeffer's main argument stands. Moreover Bonhoeffer attacks all manipulative strategies, even if they have good intentions behind them. For, Bonhoeffer reflects, this 'attack by Christian apologetic on the adulthood of the world' becomes 'ignoble, because it amounts to an attempt to exploit man's weakness' and thereby 'unchristian'.[26] Bonhoeffer's positive alternative comes to the fore in earlier writings, including his *Ethics*. Everything hinges on the demonstration in the public domain of everyday life of 'this really lived love of God in Jesus Christ'.[27] The strategy depends not on 'ideals or programmes' but on '*Ecce homo*'.[28] It is 'to be caught up into the way of Jesus Christ'.[29]

The very notion of defining the 'identity' of Christian discipleship as 'the way of Jesus Christ' anticipates the even more powerful writings by Jürgen Moltmann (b. 1926). We shall postpone our main discussion of Moltmann until Part IV. For the present we may note that Moltmann distinguishes authentic Christian hope equally from 'presumption' and from 'the sin of despair'.[30] As our argument progresses, we shall see that while the former reflects tendencies in over-optimistic 'modernity', the latter threatens to damage the more pessimistic postmodern self.

[23] Ibid. 326–7.
[24] Ibid. 327.
[25] Gerhard Ebeling, *Word and Faith* (Eng. London: SCM, 1963), 101 (his italics); cf. 98–161.
[26] Bonhoeffer, *Letters and Papers*, 327.
[27] D. Bonhoeffer, *Ethics* (London: SCM, 1955 (1965 edn.)), 70.
[28] Ibid.
[29] Bonhoeffer, *Letters and Papers*, 361. In addition to Bethge's works, see also John A. Phillips, *Christ for Us in the Theology of Dietrich Bonhoeffer* (New York: Harper & Row, 1967), esp. 71–106, 183–99, 222–48; John D. Godsey, *The Theology of Dietrich Bonhoeffer* (London: SCM, 1960), esp. 248–82; A. Dumas, *Dietrich Bonhoeffer: Theologian of Reality* (London: SCM, 1971), esp. 163–280; and the introductory anthology of selected extracts, John de Gruchy (ed.), *Dietrich Bonhoeffer: Witness to Jesus Christ* (London: Collins, 1988).
[30] J. Moltmann, *Theology of Hope* (Eng. London: SCM, 1967), 22–5.

Moltmann, like Bonhoeffer, emphatically rejects any Christian withdrawal from the world. Faith is not genuine which 'can wear the face of smiling resignation' or can become merely 'bourgeois Christianity'.[31] Further, the close conjunction of the cross and the resurrection addresses both Nietzsche's assertion that 'God is dead', and Bonhoeffer's language about 'God-forsakenness'.[32] Far from becoming a manipulative tool to gain security, the truth proclaimed in the cross calls the people of God to leave the security of 'the camp', and to go forth as the 'exodus church', bearing 'the reproach of Christ' as defenceless pilgrims (Heb. 13:13, 14).[33]

In *The Crucified God* Moltmann rejects the notion of the church as 'a social ghetto' which provides artificial affirmation and power by withdrawing from anything alien or threatening. Self-justification and self-deification must be abandoned.[34] Like Bonhoeffer, he insists that 'Christian identity can be understood only as an act of identification with the crucified Christ'.[35] In *The Way of Jesus Christ* Moltmann sees the rejection of power as characterizing those 'who have borne "the abuse of Christ"' (Heb. 11:26).[36]

Might this now fall victim to Nietzsche's opposite criticism concerning 'a slave mentality'? Far from it; for we have already noted that in Moltmann's theology passivity, mediocrity, or 'the face of smiling resignation' finds no place. He explicitly includes examples of Christians whose suffering for others could never be described as 'passive' rather than as brave. Bonhoeffer, for example, 'was not overwhelmed passively by persecution, suffering, and death. He returned voluntarily to Germany in 1939. He became involved in political resistance knowing exactly what he was doing, and it was a deliberate act of choice when he became a "traitor" to a regime which had shown its contempt for human beings.'[37]

Moltmann's recent work *The Spirit of Life* carries a sub-title which, in effect, meets Nietzsche head on: *A Universal Affirmation* (German, 1991; English, 1992). Here Moltmann explicitly rejects the two-storey dualism which Nietzsche and Heidegger ascribe to Christianity as 'Platonism for the people'.[38] He cuts the ground from under the feet of those who interpret the God of the resurrection as 'world-denying'. For he rejects the Kantian premise that leads either some theologians

---

[31] Ibid. 24.

[32] Ibid. 166, 167, 197–216.

[33] Ibid. 304–38.

[34] J. Moltmann, *The Crucified God. The Cross of Christ as the Foundation and Criticism of Christian Theology* (Eng. London: SCM, 1974), 27, 28.

[35] Ibid. 19.

[36] J. Moltmann, *The Way of Jesus Christ. Christology in Messianic Dimensions* (Eng. London: SCM, 1990), 210.

[37] Ibid. 201.

[38] J. Moltmann, *The Spirit of Life. A Universal Affirmation* (Eng. London: SCM, 1992), 8–10.

to interpret God as 'within the self', or others to interpret him as 'outside' the world as 'Other'.[39] Relationality and otherness constitute a two-sided dialectic. Here the wholeness of life is affirmed not by some autonomous self, but in the reciprocity of mutual self-giving and mutual 'interpenetration' of love. The early Fathers expressed this mutual regard for the other through the language of *'perichoresis'* and we explore this in Part IV.[40] Contrary to Nietzsche's notions of 'love', Moltmann asserts: 'Love makes life worth living.'[41] We shall later explore more deeply Moltmann's 'Yes' to life on the basis of promise.

[39] Ibid. 5–8, 31–8.
[40] Ibid. 10–14, 47–51, 58–77, 114–22.
[41] Ibid. 259.

4

The Rhetoric of Theological Models and Currencies of Meaning

WE do not claim that our use of Luther, Bonhoeffer and Moltmann offers a definitive 'answer' to the critiques of Nietzsche and his postmodern successors, although possible directions of some valid responses may have been provisionally indicated. But it is at least arguable on the basis of these theological observations that claims about the transvaluation of all claims to truth into power-questions are not necessarily applicable to *all* instantiations of Christian faith.

It is one task of theology, among others, to attempt to disentangle manipulative power-bids from non-manipulative truth-claims, and to distinguish evidence, argument, or valid testimony from modes of rhetoric which rely on seduction, disguised force, or illegitimate appeals to privilege.

This is by no means to imply some superior or patronizing judgementalism on the part of theologians. For, as Karl Barth and others have repeatedly stressed, theology remains an intensively self-critical discipline, always rigorously assessing the grounds, scope, and limits of the theologian's own access to understanding.[1] Indeed, if religious testimony may be thought of as narrative, theology handles transcendental issues about a possible basis on which truth-claims implicit in narrative may be tested and understood.

If many theologians reject as inadequate a purely functional or pragmatic view of truth, this is not in order to reinstate some metaphysical imperialism. The opposite is the case. To reject a purely functional approach to truth invites us to endorse the comments on truth made by Simone Weil. She observes: 'The need of truth is more sacred than any other need.'[2] To offer to a fellow human being 'spurious provender' in the name of truth is no less morally culpable than for a railway official to allow a fatal accident to occur through irresponsibility or negligence.[3] Ordinary people are too busy and too tired at the end

---

[1] Karl Barth, *Church Dogmatics*, I/1, *The Doctrine of the Word of God*, Part 1 (Eng. Edinburgh: T&T Clark, 1975), esp. sects. 1–3.
[2] Simone Weil, 'Truth', in *The Need for Roots. Prelude to a Declaration of Duties towards Mankind* (Eng. London: Routledge & Kegan Paul, 1952), 35.
[3] Ibid.

of a hard working day to take time to check the validity of speculative or rash truth-claims, and usually have no access to the kind of libraries that might enable them to do so if they could. This is one reason why documentation of sources remains morally obligatory for very serious works.

This angle of vision further entails *enlargement of mind* as well as moral constraint. In his seminal and still important work of 1852, *The Idea of a University*, John Henry Newman argues that a university education diminishes both human persons and the university if its goals are set at the functional level of communicating mere information and techniques for restricted purposes only. Today's supposed knowledge might be tomorrow's out-dated hypothesis. However, to promote independent critical judgement through a meeting of minds which entails mutual growth and change enlarges the horizons of both the student and the teacher. Newman rightly concludes that the goal of university education includes 'freedom from littleness and prejudice'.[4]

The term 'enlargement' occurs repeatedly in Newman's chapter on the relation between knowledge and learning. 'Expansion of mind' constitutes the human goal for which 'knowledge' offers an instrument. Newman stresses 'intellectual enlargement', 'a power of judging', 'accurate vision and comprehension of all things, as far as the finite mind can embrace them'.[5]

Language about 'enlargement of mind' and 'independent judgement', however, might well appear to backfire in the light of the critical analyses of the human predicament within a pre-given situatedness in history and language, offered by Nietzsche, Derrida and Lyotard. We recall Derrida's insistent thesis that 'metaphysical' metaphor 'has turned everything upside down'.[6] This apparent 'largeness' may prove to be deceptive. People de-contextualize and re-contextualize metaphors that have become embedded in our language, and re-activate them as truth-claims to legitimate power-interests. Wittgenstein, looking back on what drove his concerns in his earlier work, observes: 'A *picture* held us captive. And we could not get outside it, for it lay in our language and language seemed to repeat it to us inexorably.'[7] Wittgenstein bequeaths the aphorism: 'A whole cloud of philosophy condensed into a drop of grammar.'[8]

The later Wittgenstein might be perceived as casting doubt, however, on the Nietzschean assumption that *all* controlling models in *all* theology *necessarily* function as disguised power-bids. Arguably the sweeping

---

[4] John Henry Newman, *The Idea of a University* (New York and London: Longmans, Green & Co., 1947), 123.
[5] Ibid. 115, 116, 117, 118, 123; cf. 110–33.
[6] Derrida, *Margins of Philosophy*, 212.
[7] Wittgenstein, *Philosophical Investigations*, sect. 115 (his italics).
[8] Ibid. II. xi, 222e.

generalizations of Nietzsche and Derrida about language fall under Wittgenstein's condemnation of 'the contemptuous attitude towards the particular case'.[9]

The work of Ian T. Ramsey (1915–72) sheds some light on this point. Ramsey was one among many Christian philosophers of religion who recognized that controlling models offer organizing power and integrating vision but also potentially destructive seduction in religion.[10] Pictures and metaphors can monopolize attention and thereby distort rational judgement. Thus pictures of God as judge can, for example, damage the guilt-obsessed, while pictures of God as lover can inflate the over-confident. Hence Ramsey stressed that *isolated* or *single* controlling models could seduce, distort, or deceive. He refused, however, to reject models as necessarily deceptive. He proposed two key safeguards. First, models, symbols, or pictures should be used in *plurality*, in *multiform* clusters.[11] Second, models should be *qualified* by other language which serves to cancel off unwanted or manipulative resonances.[12] Such models retain the power to disclose truth and (as Tillich also claims) 'to open up new levels of reality'.[13] But they need not elude disciplined, self-critical thought.

A variety of models which operate together provides what Ramsey calls 'checks and balances'. Moreover, whereas for Derrida the chain of semiosis (sign-generated signification) never reaches 'closure', for Ramsey models used in religion, like models used in the natural sciences, need to reach some anchorage in what he calls 'an empirical placing' in the everyday world. He readily concedes that without such placing in the public world, models may fly off into mere fantasy.

Ramsey is aware that the functions of 'qualifiers' may easily be misinterpreted. One example which postdates Ramsey's work comes from writers of the 'Sea of Faith' perspective whom we discuss in Part III. For Ramsey himself, the addition of the qualifier 'all' to the model 'powerful' when applied to God serves precisely to underline its uniqueness in this setting: God is all-powerful (Greek, *pantokratōr*, Rev. 16:14; 1 Clem. 60:4; 3 Macc. 6:2) in a sense logically different from that of possessing power to the *n*th degree. But whereas this logic

---

[9] L. Wittgenstein, *The Blue and Brown Books. Preliminary Studies for the Philosphical Investigations* (Oxford: Blackwell, 2nd edn. 1969), 18.

[10] Ian T. Ramsey, *Religious Language. An Empirical Placing of Theological Phrases* (London: SCM, 1957); *Models and Mystery* (Oxford: Oxford University Press, 1964); *Christian Discourse. Some Logical Explorations* (Oxford: Oxford University Press, 1965); and *Words about God* (London: SCM, 1971).

[11] The theme runs through all four works cited above, but cf. esp. *Religious Language*, 92–100.

[12] Ibid. 57–92 *et passim*.

[13] Paul Tillich, 'The Meaning and Justification of Religious Symbols', in Sydney Hook (ed.), *Religious Experience and Truth* (New York: New York University, 1961), 3ff.; and *Theology of Culture* (New York: Galaxy Books, 1964), 56. Cf. I. T. Ramsey, *Religious Language*, 54–7 *et passim*.

is taken up and well understood by such philosophical theologians as Gijsbert Van den Brink, Marcel Sarot, and their former doctoral mentor Vincent Brümmer, writers such as Don Cupitt, Graham Shaw and Anthony Freeman treat the qualifier as merely *intensifying* rather than *re-directing* the application of the model.[14]

Van den Brink examines 'the cumulative tradition'.[15] He takes up the arguments of Peter Geach that *Almightiness* differs in its linguistic and logical currency from *omnipotence*.[16] *Almighty* occurs some seventy times in the Septuagint, and reflects the Hebrew. It remains 'not only authentically Christian but also in our time indispensable for Christianity' communicating the meaning of 'God's having power over all things'.[17] By contrast, *omnipotence* drew its currency from later scholastic re-interpretations of the Latin *omnipotens*, coming to mean 'being able to do all things'. This, according to Geach, belongs to the realm of 'metaphysical luggage that can be abandoned with relief'.[18]

Van den Brink draws careful logical distinctions between, for example, notions of 'A-power (power as authority), B-power (power as back-up), and C-power (power as capacity)'.[19] In Wittgenstein's terminology, he does not discuss the model in the abstract, as if it were 'like an engine idling'.[20] He asks how models and qualifiers operate in language-games which constitute their 'original home'.[21] Thereby he is able to indicate directions in which manipulatory, idolatrous, or grossly anthropomorphic interpretations, as against others, come to be included within theology.

By contrast, Anthony Freeman and Graham Shaw try to insist that models of divine power remain *necessarily* manipulative and illusory unless we recognize that 'God' is a way of talking about oneself in religious terms. Freeman writes: 'Any power he has is that which we ourselves supply by using him as a focus and symbol for our own energies.'[22] But for him this is no loss: 'Do I really want to be like a

---

[14] Gijsbert Van den Brink, *Almighty God. A Study in the Doctrine of Divine Omnipotence* (Kampen: Kok Pharos, 1993); Marcel Sarot, *God, Passibility and Corporeality* (Kampen: Kok Pharos, 1992); Vincent Brümmer, *Speaking of a Personal God* (Cambridge: Cambridge University Press, 1992). (On Cupitt, Freeman and Shaw, see below.)

[15] Van den Brink, *Almighty God*, 43–4.

[16] P. T. Geach, 'Omnipotence', *Philosophy* 43 (1973), 7–20, and Van den Brink, *Almighty God*, 46–8; cf. further 159–203.

[17] Van den Brink, *Almighty God*, 46.

[18] Geach, loc. cit. 5; Van den Brink, *Almighty God*, 47.

[19] Van den Brink, *Almighty God*, 49; cf. 50–115 on historical theology, 116–203 on conceptual analysis, and 204–75 on evaluation.

[20] Wittgenstein, *Philosophical Investigations*, sect. 132.

[21] Ibid. sect. 116.

[22] Anthony Freeman, *God in Us. A Case for Christian Humanism* (London: SCM, 1993), 41.

lifeless coin, someone else's plaything to lose and find? Do I even want to be like a helpless lamb, dependent on a shepherd?'[23] We shall return to Freeman and this type of claim in Part III.

Graham Shaw examines manipulation as his central theme in *The Cost of Authority. Manipulation and Freedom in the New Testament* (1983) and in its sequel *God in Our Hands* (1987). Shaw views Paul and Mark with different eyes from those with which I have interpreted Paul in the present study. Both writers, he claims, are shamelessly manipulative. In the context of Mark he appeals to what all literary theorists know about the role of any creative author: the author writes from a 'point of view' which provides the coherence of the narrative plot. This remains the case whether or not the voice of the author, as a speaker within the world of the narrative, does not come onto the stage, but only writes the script. Shaw judges that Mark ecclesializes Jesus: we either have to reject Jesus as an enigma, or else share in the church's understanding of Jesus. Hence, Shaw writes: 'We may even look back rather wistfully at the undisguised egotism of Paul's letters: the self-assertion of Mark's Gospel is considerably more devious.'[24] More broadly, 'God' is the mainpulative device of the powerful.[25]

Shaw begins *God in Our Hands* by rehearsing the conclusions of his earlier book. In theism, 'the only function of that God is to deter change; he is the classic ally of the privileged and powerful'.[26] Appeals to 'God' become manipulative because this 'distracts attention from the speaker'.[27] Beliefs about God 'have exercised enormous power'.[28] Prayer to an 'almighty God' can certainly entail 'the possibility of self-deception'.[29] Shaw comments: 'The reverence and docility which accompany prayer give dangerous opportunities for unscrupulous manipulation.'[30] Appeals to an 'all-knowing' God trap people in a 'floodlit concentration camp', especially if 'God's representatives . . . seem to posses some access to the omniscience with which they credited him.'[31] But for Shaw divine 'power' is even more seductive. He writes: 'It may be doubted whether the power of God has ever been celebrated by people who did not hope to participate in it.'[32]

Shaw concludes that non-manipulatory models depend on a human desire for peace, not for power, for which 'God' may then be 'used' as a focus of reconciling and liberating human value. 'The God in whom

[23] Ibid.; cf. 26–8.
[24] Graham Shaw, *The Cost of Authority. Manipulation and Freedom in the New Testament* (London: SCM, 1983), 257.
[25] Ibid. 283.
[26] Graham Shaw, *God in Our Hands* (London: SCM, 1987), x.
[27] Ibid. xiii.
[28] Ibid. xv.
[29] Ibid. 2.
[30] Ibid. 15.
[31] Ibid. 31, 47.
[32] Ibid. 59.

I believe lives in the consciousness of his worshippers. In Mark's words, he is not an objective reality but merely an intentional object, that is, exists only in the believer's mind . . . Religion is not concerned with power, but with the consciousness of peace.'[33]

Shaw is convincing in his warnings about the potential of religious language for manipulation and illusion. But he is mistaken in his over-simplistic polarization of 'realist' and 'non-realist' interpretations of God, as we shall explain further in Part III. Like Van den Brink, whose discussion is more rigorous and sophisticated, we need more patiently to *look* at the *variety of particular cases* which together reflect certain patterns of what Wittgenstein calls 'overlapping and criss-crossing'.[34] Some particular cases reflect self-giving service in creative love; others, manipulation in the interests of power.

A critical evaluation of controlling models is essential not least because of the social consequences which such models bring for society as a whole. Destructive effects may occur when a nominally religious nation adopts a picture of the nation as 'the chosen people of God' and it becomes a controlling model for action. The medieval crusades, the *Vortrekkers* of South Africa, or armed conflict between extreme Israelis and Muslim fundamentalists, might spring to mind as possible instances. Relatively few nations or religions can claim to be entirely blameless in their use of religious models to legitimate political self-interest. In Part IV we discuss this in more detail, with some reference to Niebuhr.

Few issues could also demonstrate more clearly the public role of a critical theology in the universities of a nation. A critique of religious language does not merely address people's private hobbies; it addresses issues that may lead to peace or to war, to destruction or to healing in society as a whole. We explore issues of society further in Part IV.

---

[33] Ibid. 240, 241.
[34] Wittgenstein, *Philosophical Investigations*, sect. 66.

5

Language, Truth and Life in
Theology and Postmodernity

THE work of the later Wittgenstein offers one point of meeting for
dialogue between the claims of Christian theology and perceptions
of the postmodern self. Christian theology attempts to make *more than
merely 'local' truth-claims* which collapse into power-bids about *values*.
On the other hand in the perceptions of the postmodern self, everything
addresses issues only within a localized context, and may seem to count
as meaningful or truthful *only in relation to goals and projects already
established within this pre-given social context*.

At first sight Wittgenstein appears to corroborate the postmodern
perspective. He writes, 'Don't say "There must be something common"
. . . Look and see whether there is.'[1] He refuses to speak of the 'essence'
of language, or of meaning, or of truth.[2] What counts as 'meaning', as
'thinking', or as 'true', depends on the nature of the situation that gives
rise to a specific agenda of questions. Even a primitive theory of meaning
works for a small model-language-game, as in the example of a list of
instructions from 'Wittgenstein's builders'.[3]

A number of writers, notably Richard Rorty, interpret Wittgenstein
in a radically pluralized and functional way. According to Rorty,
Wittgenstein came to believe that 'philosophy does not study a subject
called "language", nor does it offer a theory of how meaning is possible
– it offers only what Wittgenstein calls "reminders for a particular
purpose" . . . a pragmatic point of view'.[4] What 'counts as' meaningful
or true is always context-specific and purpose-specific. According to
Rorty, 'meaning' and 'truth' become only linguistic strategies for
'coping' with life as we find it.[5]

To be fair to Rorty, he rightly criticizes the reading of Wittgenstein
adopted by Lyotard, which is even more radically relativistic. Lyotard

---

[1] Wittgenstein, *Philosophical Investigations*, sect. 66.
[2] Ibid. sect. 65; cf. sects. 136–7, 327–40.
[3] Ibid. sects. 2, 3.
[4] Richard Rorty, *Essays on Heidegger and Others. Philosophical Papers*, vol. 2
(Cambridge: Cambridge University Press, 1991), 62, 65.
[5] Richard Rorty, *Philosophy and the Mirror of Nature* (Princeton: Princeton University
Press, 1979), 356.

falls into the well-known trap of perceiving Wittgenstein as proposing, in effect, 'autonomous' language-games, or localized linguistic activities the criteria for which remain incommensurable or incapable of 'translation'. Against Lyotard, Rorty rejects the view that Wittgenstein offers only 'islets of language' between which no bridges can be constructed.[6] He concedes: 'I see him as recommending the construction of causeways which will, in time, make the archipelago in question continuous with the mainland.'[7] I query here only the word 'construction', since Wittgenstein speaks of linguistic activities-in-context (language-games) as 'overlapping and criss-crossing' already, as pre-given phenomena.[8] Indeed in many cases (even if not in all) Wittgenstein sees 'the common behaviour of humankind' as 'the system of reference by means of which we interpret an unknown language'.[9]

Jane Heal and Richard Bernstein perceptively question Rorty's reading of Wittgenstein, just as Georgia Warnke queries his relativist reading of Gadamer. Heal rightly observes that to reject the notion of a 'representational' account of language and truth which 'mirrors nature' remains a different issue from espousing Rorty's neo-pragmatism as the only alternative. She writes: 'Rorty believes that Wittgenstein, among others, had an outlook similar to his own . . . This is not an accurate reading of Wittgenstein . . . To say that judgements are bound up with, interdependent with, concerns and projects is not to *subordinate* the notion of judgement and fact to that of project' (her italics).[10] Her comment identifies the key issue.

In two excellent books Richard J. Bernstein also incisively exposes the consequences of Rorty's approach. He explores the consequences of what may be called 'the end of philosophy' and of 'rationality'.[11] I have put forward a number of such criticisms in *New Horizons in Hermeneutics*, and also offered a reading of Wittgenstein that accords with them in *The Two Horizons*.[12]

---

[6] Richard Rorty, *Objectivity, Relativism and Truth. Philsophical Papers*, vol. 1 (Cambridge: Cambridge University Press, 1991), 215–16.

[7] Ibid. 216.

[8] Wittgenstein, *Philosophical Investigations*, sect. 66.

[9] Ibid. sect. 206.

[10] Jane Heal, 'Pragmatism and Choosing to Believe', in Alan R. Malachowski (ed.), *Reading Rorty: Critical Responses to 'Philosophy and the Mirror of Nature' and Beyond* (Oxford: Blackwell, 1990), 101, 113; cf. 101–14. On Rorty's reading of Gadamer, see G. Warnke, *Gadamer. Hermeneutics, Tradition and Reason* (Cambridge: Polity Press, 1987).

[11] Richard J. Bernstein, *Beyond Objectivism and Relativism. Science, Hermeneutics, and Praxis* (Philadelphia: University of Pennsylvania Press, 1991 (1983)), 197–207; and *The New Constellation. The Ethical–Political Horizons of Modernity/Postmodernity* (Cambridge: Polity Press, 1991), 15–30, 230–92.

[12] Anthony C. Thiselton, *New Horizons in Hermeneutics* (London: HarperCollins, and Grand Rapids: Zondervan, 1992), 393–405, 440–1, 544–9; and *The Two Horizons. New Testament Hermeneutics and Philosophical Description* (Carlisle and Exeter: Paternoster Press and Grand Rapids: Eerdmans, 1980 (rp. 1993) [also in Korean]), 24–50 and esp. 357–85; cf. further 386–438.

Wittgenstein's appeal in many cases to 'the common behaviour of humankind', and in other cases to identifiable behaviour in the public domain within given traditions or contexts provides what in *The Blue Book* he calls the 'backing' for the paper currency of language.[13] Where human behaviour is insufficiently public, patterned and stable to provide such 'backing', the currency becomes 'soft'. It cannot be cashed outside a very limited context or tradition. But where human beings exhibit, for example, consistent care and respect, we can learn the exchange-rate of the currency of 'I love you', by 'watching' how the consequent 'language-game' is played.[14]

Wittgenstein compares the grammar of 'love' with the 'pain-behaviour' that gives currency to expressions of pain. It makes sense to complain of searing pain, and then to cry out in relief: 'Oh, it's all right, it's gone off now.' But how would a husband or a wife react if their spouse ardently declared: 'I love you so passionately', and added a couple of moments later: 'Oh, it's all right, it's gone off now'?[15] Wittgenstein asks: 'Could someone have a feeling of ardent love or hope for the space of one second *no matter what* preceded or followed this second?' (his italics).[16] Wittgenstein observes in the *Zettel* concerning varieties of meanings: 'What determines our judgement, our concepts, and reactions is not what *one* man is doing *now*, an individual action, but the whole hurly-burly of human actions, the background against which we see any action.'[17]

This is the backing against which Wittgenstein measures the currency of language which is often employed in religion. He notes, again in the *Zettel*: 'Only someone who can reflect on the past can repent.'[18] 'Joy is manifested in facial expressions, in behaviour.'[19]

Parallels emerge in the biblical writings. Indeed, significantly behaviour and life stand behind the meanings of 'true' or 'false' in many contexts. Many have claimed that whereas the so-called 'Greek' view of truth remained largely theoretical, the so-called 'Hebrew' view was practical, and related to life. In 1978 I argued in detail that while this represents an oversimplification of the evidence, the issue calls attention to an important point. The relation between linguistic

---

[13] Wittgenstein, *The Blue and the Brown Books*, 48–55; cf. *Zettel* (German and Eng. Oxford: Blackwell, 1967), sects. 143 and 145. On the relationship between language and life in Wittgenstein, see especially Dallas M. High, *Language, Persons and Belief* (New York: Oxford University Press, 1967), 44–55, 96–126, 133–84, esp. 140–6; and Cyril Barrett, *Wittgenstein on Ethics and Religious Belief* (Oxford: Blackwell, 1991), 111–44, 254–8.

[14] Wittgenstein, *Philosophical Investigations*, sect. 54.

[15] Wittgenstein, *Zettel*, sect. 504.

[16] Wittgenstein, *Philosophical Investigations*, sect. 583; cf. *Zettel*, 53–68.

[17] Wittgenstein, *Zettel*, sect. 567.

[18] Ibid. sect. 519.

[19] Ibid. sects. 486, 487.

currency, truth, and life holds a firm place in both traditions, although especially in the biblical writings.[20]

'Truth' occupies a major place in the Gospel of John.[21] In the Prologue (John 1:1–18) that which might otherwise remain remote or even unthinkable finds stable expression in the person, words, and deeds, of Jesus Christ as the divine *Logos*. Language about 'truth' comes to be associated with 'life' and with 'light' (John 1:3, 4, 8, 9, 14). It is unfortunate, in my view, that in John 1:9 the Greek word *photizō* has usually been translated as 'enlightens' everyone (NEB and NRSV). The Greek word *photizō* more usually means to shed light *upon* something, or to show it up for what it is. This coheres with the context in the Prologue that the truth of the embodied word discloses reality for what it is.

Because the eternal word has become contextually enfleshed, truth in John achieves a comprehensible focus, intertwining word and deed in a specific life-world.[22] In Wittgensteinian terminology the deeds of Jesus give transactional currency to the meaning and truth of his words. Hence he himself may be called 'truth' (John 14:16), since the personal 'backing' of his deeds gives meaning and credibility to his words.

The Johannine writings lay emphasis not simply on speaking the truth but also on doing it. 'He who does the truth (Greek, *ho de poiōn tēn alētheian*) comes to the light' (John 3:21). Similarly in John's First Epistle, the credibility and intelligibility of the community's truth-claims depend on this match of word and deed: 'if we say we have fellowship with Christ and walk in darkness, we lie and are not doing the truth' (1 John 1:6). An excellent study by D. Neufeld expounds this as an issue of speech-acts.[23]

The major Pauline epistles also use 'truth' in its expected sense, in semantic opposition to error, falsehood or deceit (Rom. 1:25; 9:1; 2 Cor. 7:14). But equally characteristic of Paul is the notion that truth entails a match of word and deed, of language and life. This gives claims to truth their credibility and 'backing' (2 Cor. 4:2; 6:4–7). When Paul rejects the charge of manipulative 'cunning methods' (4:2), a variety of aspects of Paul's life-style come into question. Paul's 'list of trials' in 6:4–10 recall our earlier considera-

---

[20] Anthony C. Thiselton, 'Truth, *alētheia*', in Colin Brown (ed.), *The New International Dictionary of New Testament Theology*, 3 vols. (vol. 3, Exeter: Paternoster Press, 1978), 874–902.

[21] Nearly half of the 109 of the Greek words for 'truth' in the New Testament occur in the Johannine writings, while 17 of 26 adjectival forms and 23 out of 28 occurrences of *alēthinos* occur in Johannine literature.

[22] In the above article I have compared the exegetical comments of C. K. Barrett, R. E. Brown, R. Bultmann, B. Lindars, R. Schnackenburg and others.

[23] D. Neufeld, *Reconceiving Texts as Speech Acts. An Analysis of 1 John* (Leiden: Brill, 1994), esp. 37–60.

tion of his 'boasting in weakness' (2 Cor. 11:21 – 12:10). These hardships suggest neither 'power-interests' nor Nietzsche's 'weakness of mediocrity'.[24] 'Love of truth' leads to salvation (2 Thess. 2:10). Openness to truth, wherever it may lead, furthers the gospel (2 Cor. 13:8). Paul can do nothing outside the realm of truth.[25] Purity of life constitutes part of the grammar of truth (1 Cor. 5:8).

Ephesians, which is often viewed as a summary of Pauline theology whether by Paul or by a Pauline disciple, stresses no less the relation between truth in word and corresponding backing in life. To 'put away' falsehood entails dealing truthfully and honestly with others in social commerce (Eph. 4:24, 25). 'To speak the truth in love' does not mean hurtful 'frankness' with a manipulative veneer, but grounds truthful speech in a stable attitude of respect and concern for the other (4:15).

The Pastoral Epistles include an example to which I have paid very detailed attention in a recent article.[26] I am not permitted space to set out the details here. However, in my view the commentators have missed the point of the sentence, 'It was one of them, their very own prophets, who said, "Cretans are always liars, vicious brutes, lazy gluttons." That testimony is true' (Titus 1:12, 13). Almost every commentator tries to find some 'excuse' for a judgemental stereotypification of Cretans as liars. Some argue that 'This testimony is true' reflects either the opinion of the writer based on experience, or a consensus behind such stereotypification in the ancient world. But the author can hardly fail to have been aware that in Greek logic the paradox of the liar posed a familiar dilemma. If a habitual liar says, 'Everything that I say is a lie', is this true or false? If we add, 'this testimony is true', are we corroborating its truth or its falsity?

All this shows, as the writer well knows, that the paradox is neither true nor false but self-defeating. But self-defeating paradoxes perform other functions at a different level, whether in Greek philosophy or in modern mathematical logic. They invite us to view the 'claim' from another angle. In practice, the aim of the writer has nothing to do with assassinating the character of Cretans, but with demonstrating a lack of logical symmetry between first-person testimony and third-person statement. The former draws its currency in certain cases from the stance and personal history of the speaker. Here the writer disparages the

[24] This passage is discussed in detail later with reference, on one side, to the work of E. A. Judge and S. H. Travis, and in a different direction to the claims of E. A. Castelli and S. D. Moore, who relate Paul's claims to Foucault's critique of power interests by manipulation. Cf. also J.-F. Collange, *Enigmes de la deuxième épitre de Paul aux Corinthiens* (Cambridge: Cambridge University Press, 1972), 281–301; Martin, *2 Corinthians*, 75–8.

[25] G. P. Wiles, *Paul's Intercessory Prayers* (Cambridge: Cambridge University Press, 1974), 246.

[26] Anthony C. Thiselton, 'The Logical Role of the Liar Paradox in Titus 1:12, 13: A Dissent from the Commentaries in the Light of Philosophical and Logical Analysis', *Biblical Interpretation* 2 (1994), 207–23.

value of endless verbal rhetoric. This can be self-defeating unless the speaker lives a blameless life which gives his or her speech operative currency. Hence this proposition is a meta-statement about self-defeating language and also an injunction to focus on the kind of life-style urged throughout the epistle to give validity to the witness of the church and of its elders. In my article I offer reasons why Patristic exegesis set subsequent interpretation on the wrong track.

We conclude that 'truth' in the biblical writings is more complex, subtle, and richly diverse in emphasis than alleged differences between 'Greek' and 'Hebraic' notions of truth suggest. W. Pannenberg rightly perceives that they do not characteristically view truth as 'timeless' or abstract. 'The truth of God must prove itself anew.'[27] Truth 'proves itself in relationships and thus has personal character'.[28]

Meaning in theological or religious discourse, I have elsewhere argued, depends on how stretches of language draw their currency from regular, observable, patterns of behaviour in life.[29] The later Wittgenstein demonstrates this principle with a host of memorable examples. The notion of 'giving', to cite one case-study, remains central to language about God. But what giving amounts to, in terms of its cash-currency, must make some difference in the public domain. Thus Wittgenstein asks: 'Why can't my right hand give my left hand money? My right hand can put it into my left hand. My right hand can write a deed of gift and my left hand a receipt. – But the further practical consequences would not be those of a gift. When the left hand has taken the money . . . we shall ask: "Well, and what of it?"' (German, 'Nun, und was weiter?').[30]

Norman Malcom recalls how one day Wittgenstein 'gave' him every tree that they passed on their walk on condition that Malcom would never mark them, remove them, or do anything of substance to them. Gifts can be given only by those who own them in the first place, and the transfer of property brings about a change of situation. Otherwise the word has no effective meaning.[31]

Wittgenstein also applies this principle to *believing*, *expecting* and *loving*. It makes sense, he concedes, to say: 'He believes it, but it is false.' But how could it make sense to utter the words: '*I believe it*, but it is false'? This is because my relation to my words is different from

[27] W. Pannenberg, 'What is Truth?', in *Basic Questions in Theology*, vol. 2 (Eng. London: SCM, 1971), 8; cf. 1–27.

[28] Ibid. 9. Cf. Gen. 42:16; Ps. 57:3; Zech. 8:8, 16, 17.

[29] Anthony C. Thiselton, *Language, Liturgy and Meaning* (Nottingham: Grove Liturgical Studies 2, 1975, 2nd edn. 1986), 3–21; *The Two Horizons*, 370–85, 392–401, 411–15; and *New Horizons in Hermeneutics*, 146–8, 325–8 (cf. 328–38), 400–4, 444, 541–6, 549, 601.

[30] Wittgenstein, *Philosophical Investigations*, sect. 268.

[31] Recounted in N. Malcolm (with G. H. von Wright), *Ludwig Wittgenstein. A Memoir* (Oxford: Oxford University Press, 1958, 2nd edn. 1984).

other people's.[32] In this sense, creeds may involve both a cognitive truth-context and simultaneously a self-involving stance of 'nailing one's colours to the mast'.[33]

Similarly what it is to expect is to be cashed out in the public domain. If I am expecting a friend to visit me, I may perhaps move old newspapers into the bin, wash up the tea things, and so forth. This is one reason why it may be injudicious to make too much of whether the final coming of Christ was 'expected' during the life-span of the first generation. 'Expecting' depends for its currency not on mental calculations about chronology, but in living in an appropriate state of readiness for the event. Does one stop 'expecting' the *parousia* when one falls asleep and 'mental states' have largely closed down? This 'tension' is more apparent than real. Gilbert Ryle demonstrates that logical tensions arise when we try to use a mixture of existential 'participant' language and logical or cosmic 'observer' language.[34]

In Wittgenstein's phraseology 'the surroundings' of language give it at least part of its currency.[35] Without any special pleading for theology, we may suggest that for Derrida texts can never reach stable 'closure' because, unlike Wittgenstein, he fails to recognize the stability of linguistic 'markers' offered by human behaviour in the public domain. After all, he explores mainly 'literary' meaning. It was not for nothing that Irenaeus and other early Fathers passionately opposed the gnostic attempt to construe the cross as an *intra-linguistic* entity; as an *idea* rather than *an event in the public domain*.[36] Very recently both R. Lundin and F. Watson have offered incisive critiques of the 'gnostic' and anti-theological character of intralinguistic approaches in post-modernism.[37] All that we earlier noted about costly discipleship and active venture in Luther, Bonhoeffer and Moltmann applies pre-eminently to the ministry of Jesus. In as far as the church down the centuries has 'backed' this currency with genuinely derivative patterns of life and service, this tradition constitutes a frame of reference for stable interpretations of the language of Christian theology.

---

[32] Wittgenstein, *Philsophical Investigations*, II. x, 190, 192.

[33] This double emphasis is affirmed concerning creeds and confessions in the New Testament by Vernon H. Neufeld, *The Earliest Confessions* (Leiden: Brill, 1963), in a useful but neglected study.

[34] Gilbert Ryle, *Dilemmas* (Cambridge: Cambridge University Press, 1966 (1954)), esp. 36–53.

[35] Wittgenstein, *Philosophical Investigations*, sect. 583.

[36] Irenaeus, *Adversus Haereses*, I.9.2; 11.1; II.5.2; 27.

[37] Roger Lundin, *The Culture of Interpretation. Christian Faith and the Postmodern World* (Grand Rapids: Eerdmans, 1993), 76–103; and Francis Watson, *Text, Church and World. Biblical Interpretation in Theological Perspective* (Edinburgh: T&T Clark, 1994), 79–153.

6

Non-Manipulative Interpretation and Truth as Relational

ONLY just below the surface of this entire discussion lie issues about interpretation, or in a more precise sense, hermeneutics. At one end of the spectrum Betti, Gadamer and Ricoeur regard hermeneutical enquiry as fundamental for the protection of truth against manipulation. At the other end of the spectrum Rorty, Derrida and Lyotard claim almost the reverse: hermeneutics and rhetoric largely displace rational argument because nothing can escape deceit and manipulation or at least 'interests'.

Hermeneutics, as it is understood today, takes full account of the problem of pre-given human situatedness within history and society as the postmodern self perceives it. But the first set of writers see hermeneutics as a means to restore mutual respect and understanding between different cultural contexts and different traditions; while the second set of writers associate hermeneutics with what Rorty calls a means of 'coping'. If, in Rorty's view, hermeneutics *serves* prior interests, in Betti's view it *constrains* prior interests. If in Gadamer's view, hermeneutics *serves* 'openness' and 'conversation', for Derrida it *constrains* any search for meaning which we can catch before it moves on. In the words of Roland Barthes: 'the Text cannot stop; it is an *irreducible* plurality'.[1]

The major pioneer of the modern discipline of hermeneutics was Friedrich Schleiermacher (1768–1834). His hermeneutics sought to address the challenge left by Kant's *Critique of Pure Reason*: on what basis is truth and meaning possible, given the limits to the scope of pure reason that Kant had exposed? Schleiermacher worked out a theory of understanding which depended on an interaction between two poles: the inter-personal, divinatory, *relational* dimension which Schleiermacher associated with the feminine principle; and the critical, comparative dimension which, rightly or wrongly, he associated with the masculine.[2] The former facilitates creative understanding; the latter

---

[1] Roland Barthes, 'From Work to Test', in J. V. Harari (ed.), *Textual Strategies* (Ithaca: Cornell University Press, 1979), 76; cf. 73–81 (his italics).
[2] Schleiermacher, *Hermeneutics*, 150.

facilitates critical knowledge. It is therefore possible to formulate a theology in terms which go beyond the merely intellectual or abstract to include the inter-personal and relational, without sacrificing rational critical testing.

In our own century Karl Barth, who in a number of specific respects vigorously attacked Schleiermacher, also shared the latter's conviction that theology can remain rigorously self-critical while insisting that God is more than an object or a construct of abstract rational thought. Understanding of God remains *relational*. To the question: 'Who is God?' Barth replies: 'It is He who gives Himself to humanity as Trinity . . . He makes himself over as *Spiritus sanctus*.'[3] God's most distinctive quality is not his absoluteness but his self-imparting in sovereign love, freely given.

Hermeneutical enquiry, as it was developed after Schleiermacher and finds expression today in such theorists as Betti and Ricoeur aims (among other tasks) to understand persons as persons, and not as mere objects. But the discipline also invites simultaneously a hermeneutic of critical evaluation. In the language of the discipline, a hermeneutic of suspicion operates alongside a hermeneutic of creative understanding.

Here theology can perhaps contribute something in the university in dialogue with law, medicine, and the social sciences. We expand this theme in detail in Part II. For in these disciplines, as also in theology, the 'scientific' axis of comparison, typology, and testing needs to be held together with issues of distinctive personal history and agency. Human persons and indeed God are more than examples of categories or objects of cause-effect analysis. God and human persons choose, love and give.

Hence Betti insists on the importance of hermeneutics for almost all disciplines within the university. He declares: 'nothing is of greater importance to humankind than living in mutual understanding with one's fellow human beings'.[4] But this dimension is, in Betti's words, fundamentally different from the physical. To equate personal understanding with scientific knowledge of a physical object would be like claiming to understand a Beethoven symphony by mapping its sound-waves on an oscilloscope. But this combination of critical enquiry and hermeneutical understanding calls for 'patience, tolerance, openness and respect for the Other'.[5]

To these issues we now turn in Part II. Like the postmodern self, Christian theology understands the relativities and constraints of historical situatedness. For Jesus of Nazareth was enfleshed historically in the context of first-century Judaism in the Graeco-Roman world.

---

[3] Barth, *Church Dogmatics*, I/1, sect. 12, 489.

[4] Emilio Betti, *Die Hermeneutik als allgemeine Methodik der Geisteswissenschaften*, 2nd edn. (Tübingen: Mohr, 1972), 7.

[5] Emilio Betti, *Allgemeine Auslegungslehre als Methodik der Geisteswissenschaften* (Tübingen: Mohr, 1967), 21; cf. 158, 211–13.

Nevertheless, contrary to the expectations of the postmodern self, the cross of Christ in principle shatters the boundaries and conflicts between Jew and Gentile, female and male, free person and slave. Moreover the resurrection holds out the promise of hope from beyond the boundaries of the historical situatedness of the postmodern self in its predicament of constraint.

The claims to truth put forward in Christian theology, therefore, call for love where there is conflict, for service where there are power-interests, and for trust where there is suspicion. Our remaining pages explore the grounds and implications of these large claims, beginning with a necessary consideration of the hermeneutics of human selfhood.

PART II

INTERPRETING TEXTS AND INTERPRETING THE SELF

7

Respecting the Other:
Transcending Prior Categories and the
Limits of Empirical Method

THE theory of interpretation, or hermeneutics, began historically
as critical reflection on the nature of the interpretation of
texts. With the work of Schleiermacher and especially Dilthey,
however, hermeneutics also embraced the interpretation and understanding of human persons, or of that which is 'Other' in human
life.

It may seem surprising when we discover that 'hermeneutics' finds
a place within a volume entitled *New Words: A Dictionary of
Neologisms since 1960*. After all, J. C. Dannhauer probably first
used the term in his *Hermeneutica Sacra* of 1654. But second
thoughts are invited when we discover that the editor defines
hermeneutics in its new use since 1965 as 'the theory and method of
interpreting meaningful human action'.[1] He concedes that in the era
before printed texts, hermeneutics concerned textual variants and
philology. But the 'new' use is different: 'its use subsequently developed
to deal with the way in which lived human experience is studied by
looking both at individuals and at the world-view of which they are a
part'.[2]

Reflection on the interpretation of texts, then, has led on to a
hermeneutics of lived experience. This phrase might well have been
taken directly from the extensive writings of Wilhelm Dilthey (1833–
1911), especially from his essays of 1900 and 1911. For him 'life'
(*Leben*) takes the place occupied by 'mind' or 'spirit' (*Geist*) in
Hegel. Dilthey observes concerning the empiricism and idealism of
the Enlightenment period: 'No real blood runs in the veins of the
knowing subject that Locke, Hume and Kant constructed.'[3] Hence
Dilthey's hermeneutics becomes important not only for the history
of philosophy, but also for cultural studies and for theology. As

---

[1] Jonothon Green, *New Words. A Dictionary of Neologisms since 1960* (London:
Bloomsbury Publications, 1993), 126.
[2] Green, *New Words*, loc. cit.
[3] Wilhelm Dilthey, *Gesammelte Schriften*, 12 vols. (Leipzig and Berlin: Teubner, 1962),
vol. 5, 4; cf. also vol. 1, xvii, 217.

Zygmunt Bauman has demonstrated, his thought becomes a strong influence in subsequent social science.[4]

Bauman shows how many of Dilthey's concerns relate to the study of social life in Karl Marx, Max Weber, Karl Mannheim, Talcott Parsons, Alfred Schütz and to recent writers in social ethnography.[5] Finally, in the work of Paul Ricoeur and in other recent writers we reach a hermeneutic of selfhood and of human action.

This introduces a main thesis. A close relationship of analogy and interaction may be proposed between hermeneutics of texts and hermeneutics of selfhood and of human life. *Lessons learned in developments in one area may often become a resource for theoretical developments in the other.*

The story here begins not with Dilthey, but with Friedrich Schleiermacher (1768–1834), whom we introduced at the end of the previous section. Schleiermacher, as Kimmerle and Gadamer have underlined, aimed to disengage hermeneutics from remaining a mere service discipline.[6] Up to this point in the history of thought it had served simply to validate or to explain some prior understanding of a text at which an interpreter or community of interpreters had already arrived. In theology this amounted to formulating 'rules' on the basis of which some expected interpretation of the biblical writings could be defended as rational, valid or 'natural'.

This does not imply that the Reformers, for example, approached the Bible with closed minds. It implies only that hermeneutics became a court of appeal for deciding between various views already held on different sides, rather than being concerned with the very possibility of reaching any view in the first place. By contrast, in his *Hermeneutics: The Handwritten Manuscripts* Schleiermacher writes: 'Hermeneutics is part of the art of thinking.'[7]

Schleiermacher was heavily influenced by Christian pietism, by the spirit of Romanticism and by the transcendental philosophy of Kant. The term 'transcendental' distinguishes Kant's concern to ask on what

---

[4] Zygmunt Bauman, *Hermeneutics and Social Science. Approaches to Understanding* (London: Hutchinson, 1978).

[5] Dilthey's influence is explicitly acknowledged by Heidegger and Bultmann, and demonstrable in Weber, Troeltsch, Mannheim, Schütz, Gadamer, Ricoeur and Habermas. Cf. further, David Klemm (ed.), *Hermeneutical Inquiry*, 2 vols. (Atlanta: Scholars Press, 1986), vol. 1, 90.

[6] F. D. E. Schleiermacher, *Hermeneutics: The Handwritten Manuscripts* (Eng. Missoula: Scholars Press, 1977), edited by Heinz Kimmerle (German: *Hermeneutik: Abhandlung der Heidelberger Akademie der Wissenschaften*, Heidelberg: Carl Winter, 1959), who expands the issues further in his 'Hermeneutical Theory or Ontological Hermeneutics', in *Journal for Theology and the Church, 4: History and Hermeneutics* (Tübingen: Mohr, and New York: Harper & Row, 1967), 107–21. See also H.-G. Gadamer, *Truth and Method* (2nd Eng. edn. from 5th German edn., London: Sheed & Ward, 1993), 173–9.

[7] Schleiermacher, *Hermeneutics*, 97.

basis knowledge might be possible at all, in contrast to the more limited concerns of his predecessors to ask how we know what we think we know. In a parallel way, Schleiermacher asks not how, or what we may understand, but how the very process of understanding becomes possible.

Accepting Kant's challenge, Schleiermacher asks not simply what theology may say, but on what basis theology and theological understanding becomes possible. Nevertheless, consistent with his double affinity with pietism and Romanticism, none of this is simply a matter of abstract reason. All understanding is rooted in the concrete diversity of human life, including experiences of immediacy and what he called a 'divinatory' (*divinatorische*) method of apprehending that which eludes reason alone.[8] 'Intuition' remains a poor second-best as a synonym for 'divination', since it encourages Hegel's well-known criticism that his less-than-rational dog could more readily 'feel' dependency or relationality than many humans. The issue here is that of *immediacy and relationality* as against *conceptual distance*.

It is no coincidence that Schleiermacher stresses what is often today taken for granted about *inter-subjectivity* in understanding. He reflects his own temperament and character when he writes that for the exercise of creative thought he needs 'the presence of some loved one . . . so that there may follow the sharing of it with another'. 'In solitude the springs of my soul dry up.'[9] With his warm outgoing nature, Schleiermacher's model of understanding texts, life and selfhood was construed more closely along the lines of empathy between two friends, than the solitary exercise on which Descartes embarked in order to discover the respective scope of doubt and knowledge.

Descartes stands at the opposite end of the spectrum from hermeneutics. William Temple, even if with some extravagance, described Descartes' action of withdrawal for solitary reflection as 'the most disastrous moment in the history of Europe'.[10] Paul Ricoeur has consistently demonstrated the problematic nature of what he calls 'the Cartesian *cogito*', and in systematic theology Helmut Thielicke adds his voice to the criticisms.[11]

---

[8] Schleiermacher, *Hermeneutics*, 150 (German: *Werke*, vol. 4, Aalen: Scientia Verlag, 1967, from 2nd edn. Leipzig, 1928, 153).

[9] Cf. Bernard M. G. Reardon's comments and extract from Schleiermacher in his *Religious Thought in the Nineteenth Century* (Cambridge: Cambridge University Press, 1986), 20.

[10] William Temple, *Nature, Man and God* (London: Macmillan, 1934, and 1940), 57.

[11] Most recently, Paul Ricoeur, *Oneself as Another* (Eng. Chicago: University of Chicago Press, 1992), 4–16; also in several essays in *The Conflict of Interpretations – Essays in Hermeneutics* (Evanston: Northwestern University Press, 1976), cf. also *Hermeneutics and the Human Sciences* (Cambridge: Cambridge University Press, 1981). Cf. Helmut Thielicke, *The Evangelical Faith* (Eng. 3 vols., Grand Rapids: Eerdmans, 1974–82), vol. 1, 40ff. and vol. 3, 4–5.

Relationality, then, is part of the process which makes understanding possible. It is significant for our subject that Schleiermacher's earlier writings from 1799 to 1810 reflect some degree of influence from the philosophy of Friedrich W. J. von Schelling (1775–1854). In his early period from 1797 to 1810 Schelling was concerned with how consciousness emerged as *consciousness of the self*. He concluded that the fundamental element lay in the self's awareness of a contrast between self and not-self, or between the Self and the Other.

Specialist discussions of the influence of Schelling on Schleiermacher are offered by Hermann Suskind and Richard Brandt among others.[12] Brandt observes that, for Schelling: 'Nature is an organic system whose "end" is self-consciousness.'[13] Like other Romantics, Schelling moved away from the moralism of Kant and Fichte, to stress the pluriformity and creativity of nature. Thus he paved the way for the notion that encountering the strange, the alien, the unfamiliar, the different, in short the Other, is a pre-condition for interpreting and understanding persons and selfhood.

Gadamer rightly perceives this to be central to the hermeneutics of Schleiermacher and of Dilthey. He writes: 'Schleiermacher's idea of a universal hermeneutics starts from this: that the experience of the alien and the possibility of misunderstanding is universal . . . In a new and universal sense, alienation is inextricably given with the individuality of the Thou.'[14]

Schleiermacher applied this principle simultaneously to the interpretation of texts and to the understanding of selfhood. In his view, we become hermeneutically aware when we encounter a text or another self *before* we have taken the step of subsuming the alien or Other within our own horizons of the familiar and pigeon-holed it within the prior categorizations of our expectations.

Schleiermacher's criticism of previous hermeneutics, whether Catholic or Protestant, or the philological interpretation of classical literature (as by Wolf and Ast), was that in each case the mode of enquiry presupposed a prior understanding rather than establishing the basis for its possibility. In Gadamer's words, hermeneutical awareness of the particularity of texts or of life or of human selves cannot arise until we have come to experience what it is to encounter the Other 'within a hitherto unknown horizon'.[15]

To apply the point, before I ever seek to know how a text relates to me, or how another person's experience relates to mine, it is not good enough simply to approach that text or person with supposedly value-

---

[12] Hermann Suskind, *Der Einfluss Schellings auf die Entwicklung vom Schleiermachers System* (Tübingen: Mohr, 1909); Richard B. Brandt, *The Philosophy of Schleiermacher* (New York and London: Harper, 1941), 56–70.

[13] Brandt, *The Philosophy of Schleiermacher*, 59–60.

[14] Gadamer, *Truth and Method* (revised edn.), 179.

[15] Ibid.

neutral *observation*. For then, as Hume and Kant perceived, we shall at once begin to impose upon what we seek to understand prior categories of thought and stereotypification. The *first* requirement is *respect for the otherness of the Other as Other*. This invites *not observation but listening*.[16]

Here we see how profoundly hermeneutical approaches to texts differ from positivist, rationalist or empirical enquiry. We also see how closely biblical studies, for example, relates to pastoral counselling. *Both entail ability to listen, before rushing in*.[17] Both require respect for 'the Other'.

In Christian theology we often describe approaching the biblical text as *listening in reverent expectancy*, while we view approaching another human *self* as considering their unique personal identity and personal history with care, with attentive respect, or with what the New Testament writers call *agapē*. This means *creative regard for the Other; it is a love prompted by will, not by prior 'like-mindedness'*. In Schleiermacher's own words, all understanding, including the interpretation of texts, involves stepping 'out of one's own frame of mind'.[18] Does not this distinguish human care and love from supposedly value-neutral 'observation'? Mere observation reduces texts and human selfhood to mainly passive objects, subject to our own mental manipulation. Is this so-called scientific approach not, in the end, a defeat for the very goal of openness which we associate with scientific method?

---

[16] This issue also emerges in Betti, *Die Hermeneutik als Allgemeine Methodik der Geisteswissenschaften*, 2nd edn., 6–9.

[17] The comparison is introduced in Thiselton, *New Horizons in Hermeneutics*, 558–9.

[18] Schleiermacher, *Hermeneutics*, 42, 109.

8

Biblical Texts and
Pastoral Hermeneutics:
History, Science and Personhood

EMILIO BETTI identifies this hermeneutical respect for the 'otherness' of the text and of other selves as *Other* as central for the humanities, for the social sciences, and indeed for politics and for all human life. Hermeneutics, he urges, trains human beings in 'openness' (*Aufgeschlossenheit*) and 'receptiveness' (*Empfänglichkeit*).[1] What can be more important, he asks, if humankind is to live together in mutual understanding? Hermeneutics demands patience, tolerance, and a willingness to understand the other as something more than a projection of one's own prior assumptions. The Other is not an object to be manipulated in accordance with one's own stereotypes and interests. In Martin Buber's language: 'Relation is reciprocity . . . The language of objects catches only one corner of actual life.'[2] On the same kind of basis Betti wishes to see hermeneutics incorporated into all academic disciplines which relate to persons.

A growing literature now rightly calls for hermeneutical theory to occupy an obligatory place in pastoral theology. One such study is Charles V. Gerkin's book entitled *The Living Human Document: Re-visioning Pastoral Counselling in a Hermeneutical Mode*. Gerkin points out that 'the "story" of an individual life begins with the earliest experience of being a self separate from other selves'.[3] But the story in terms of which another self perceives its own uniqueness as a human agent, character, and self 'itself is, of course, an interpretation of experience'.[4]

In this sense, we might say the task of understanding the Other in pastoral counselling entails interpreting interpretation. Often the one who is being counselled hopes that the counsellor may serve as a catalyst to make sense out of what has threatened to become senseless. Here, Gerkin rightly declares: 'It is important to avoid, at all costs, the temptation to stereotype or take for granted.'[5] In this context he alludes

---

[1] Betti, *Allgemeine Auslegungslehre also Methodik der Geisteswissenschaften*, 21.
[2] Martin Buber, *I and Thou* (Eng. New York: Scribner, 1970), 67, 69.
[3] Charles V. Gerkin, *The Living Human Document. Re-visioning Pastoral Counseling in a Hermeneutical Mode* (Nashville: Abingdon Press, 1984, rp. 1991), 20.
[4] Gerkin, *The Living Human Document*, 26.
[5] Ibid. 27.

to the work of Anton Boisen in clinical pastoral education and to Schleiermacher and Dilthey in hermeneutics. Describing selfhood in this context as 'text', he observes: 'The individual human text demanded a hearing on its own merit.'[6]

Many will probably be aware of certain clergy or pastors who not only pigeon-hole every member of their congregation, but transparently address their sermons to these pigeon-holed constructs. For the listeners it is easy as well as often valid to disclaim association with such a pre-constructed pigeon-hole. Thereby the sermon engages only with unreal constructs created by the preacher. Further, a biblical exposition which does not do justice to the *otherness* of biblical texts reduces everything to the bland, dull, and predictable. The cutting edge of the text is assimilated into some repeated hobby-horse of the preacher.

Most of us also know clergy, pastors, or counsellors who will begin to tell us some pre-given 'solution' before we have even finished telling our story. Far from trying to interpret our own interpretation of our selfhood and story, they assume that nothing hidden lies behind our own words. Moreover little respect for human selfhood in its opaqueness and otherness seems to lie behind theirs. This issue will carry us forward in due course to consider the hermeneutics of suspicion in Freud and in Paul Ricoeur. Just as Gerkin, therefore, explores Schleiermacher and Dilthey for pastoral theology, so Donald Capps looks to the hermeneutics of Paul Ricoeur in his book *Pastoral Care and Hermeneutics*.[7]

We have noted that Schleiermacher writes: 'In interpretation one may be able to step out of one's own frame of mind.'[8] We also heeded his warning against charting mere 'sub-divisions' of a text atomistically, as if it were only an object of scientific enquiry.[9] Nevertheless, he does not dispense with all rational control and scientific criteria. Interpretation, he declares in 1819,

> involves two methods: a divinatory and a comparative. The two should never be separated. By leading the interpreter to transform himself, so to speak, into the author, the divinatory method seeks to gain an immediate comprehension of the author *as an individual*. The comparative method proceeds by *subsuming the author under a general type*. It then tries to find his distinctive traits by comparing him with others of the same general type. Divinatory knowledge is the feminine strength in *knowing people*; *comparative knowledge*, the masculine. Each method refers back to the other.[10]

[6] Ibid. 38.
[7] Donald Capps, *Pastoral Care and Hermeneutics* (Philadelphia: Fortress, 1984), esp. 15–36 which concerns Ricoeur.
[8] Schleiermacher, *Hermeneutics*, 42.
[9] Ibid. 44.
[10] Ibid. 150 (my italics).

Does not this begin to erode away all that we have said about stereotyping and the limits of generalization? Not at all. For part of Schleiermacher's most distinctive genius lay in his perceiving how these two dimensions are woven inextricably together. Dilthey takes this up, although with more bias towards the general and scientific. It collapses in Heidegger and Gadamer for whom the scientific becomes lost in the hermeneutical. But the balance is restored in Paul Ricoeur as a dialectic of explanation and understanding. Finally, Habermas gives the whole a sociological application in terms of 'system' (science) and 'life-world' (hermeneutics).

In everyday life, we may draw on the analogy of the General Medical Practitioner's consulting room. When I enter his or her surgery as a patient, I tell my own story. The GP recognizes this as a combination of two sets of factors. On one side my story fits general patterns which are described in medical textbooks. On the other side it includes personal nuances and interpretive glosses which may either turn out to be irrelevant or else of the utmost importance. The doctor who is a good listener will need to determine whether, for example, if certain symptoms point to depression, this may be a purely clinical phenomenon arising almost entirely in origin from neurological and chemical imbalance, or partly a matter of individual agency, responsibility, or vulnerability. Responsible selfhood may invite therapy of a kind which entails more prolonged dialogue and interpretation. This may continue until it reaches what Schleiermacher, Fuchs, and especially Gadamer call 'shared understanding' or 'full rapport' (*Einverständnis*).[11]

Here we see one more parallel or analogy between textual interpretation and the hermeneutics of selfhood. Schleiermacher rightly believed that no short-cut could be taken which avoided historical reconstruction for the understanding of texts. In the case of New Testament texts, this entailed viewing them comparatively alongside other texts in the Graeco-Roman world. The interpreter can no more avoid asking questions about the author, genre, first readers, purpose, style and language of the text than a medical student can effectively practise medicine merely by 'listening to the patient' with no knowledge of anatomy, physiology, or biochemistry. Indeed Schleiermacher effectively places what we call 'New Testament Introduction' as a proper coherent rigorous discipline (*Wissenschaft*) in the service of hermeneutics. But this remains inseparable from the 'divinatory' dimension of understanding. We also need to *listen* to texts and persons as *they* speak.

Schleiermacher's concern to reach 'behind' the text has been widely misunderstood. He has been accused of a 'genetic fallacy'; of being unduly concerned with 'origins', as one of the key factors which lie behind a text and lead to the production of its 'meaning'. But

[11] Gadamer, *Truth and Method* (revised edn.), 180 (1st Eng. edn., 158).

Schleiermacher's concern is not antiquarian or primarily causal. He anticipates the maxim which the later Wittgenstein articulates in his *Zettel*: 'Only in the stream of thought and life do words have meaning.'[12]

To be sure, Schleiermacher shares the Romanticist view inherited from Herder that texts constitute a kind of 'deposit' left behind by the creative vision of the human spirit that produced them. But he explicitly states that what we regard as 'prior' in hermeneutics remains only a matter of *heuristic strategy*. When all has been said, he insists in his *Compendium*: 'Only historical interpretation can do justice to the rootedness of the New Testament authors in their time and place.'[13]

We must therefore reconsider the criticism of many contemporary literary theorists that Schleiermacher remains more interested in textual origins than in textual effects. The very reverse is the case. Only understanding texts and selfhood in *their otherness and alienness* can make it possible for them to address us in ways that avoid readings already domesticated and made bland by our construing them *as products of our own world*. Precisely the same principle applies to the hermeneutics of selfhood. Here the impact of feminism and ethnography have made literary theorists more sensitive to the problem. Schleiermacher's call for the historical or comparative dimension is precisely to *allow* texts and persons to enter present understanding *as themselves* and not as some construct of our own devising.

Yet if scientific observation were to operate on its own, once again we should slide back into subsuming texts and persons into the artificial constructs of prior categorization. Schleiermacher's famous essay *Christmas Eve* of 1806 (*Die Weinachtsfeier* is also translated under the title of *The Celebration of Christmas*), shows where his heart lies in this matter.[14] When the men and women return from church, the men 'celebrate' Christmas by the 'masculine' principle of debating the conceptual problems of the incarnation; the women articulate the 'feminine' or 'divinatory' understanding of the whole by singing hymns of praise to Jesus Christ.

The contrast between the comparative and the divinatory is also connected with two more features in Schleiermacher's hermeneutics. First, Schleiermacher in effect anticipated the fundamental distinction later formulated by Ferdinand de Saussure between language as patterned system or reservoir (Saussure's *la langue*) and specific speaker-generated utterances performed in time and history (Saussure's *la parole*). I have put forward this argument in full detail elsewhere.[15] Schleiermacher contrasts 'language with its possibilities' (the developing system to be studied by 'scientific' linguistics) and its specific uses or

[12] Wittgenstein, *Zettel*, sect. 173.
[13] Schleiermacher, *Hermeneutics*, 104.
[14] F. D. E. Schleiermacher, *Christmas Eve: Dialogue on the Incarnation* (Eng. Richmond: John Knox, 1967).
[15] Thiselton, *New Horizons in Hermeneutics*, 217–19, 232.

instantiations 'in the thinking of the speaker' (the 'performance' or speech-act which invites divinatory as well as comparative understanding).[16]

Second, Schleiermacher develops the principle of the hermeneutical circle. In the words of Schleiermacher's *Academy Addresses on Hermeneutics* (1829), 'Just as the whole is understood from the parts, so the parts can be understood from the whole.' This principle, explored by Ast, is 'uncontestable'.[17] Indeed Dilthey traces the origins of this version of the hermeneutical circle to Flacius in his *Clavis Scripturae Sacrae* of 1567. He quotes Flacius as asserting: 'The individual parts of a whole become comprehendible through their relation to the whole and the other parts.'[18]

We may distinguish from this, however, a second, more complex, version of the hermeneutical circle in Schleiermacher, which may also be applied to a hermeneutics of the self. Here the initial preliminary understanding or 'pre-understanding' (*Vorverständnis*) with which we approach the text or person to be understood becomes modified, corrected, and refined as that which we seek to understand 'speaks back', in turn, to the interpreter. Schleiermacher states that all understanding begins with 'a preliminary knowledge of the subject matter'.[19] In his later work (1819) he adds: 'Only in the case of insignificant texts are we satisfied with what we understand on our first reading.'[20] In 1829 he concludes that this demands 'moving forward slowly'. Understanding remains 'always provisional'.[21]

How does this apply to the understanding of selfhood? David Hume's view of the self according to which I can 'catch only a succession of perceptions' is shallow in its empiricist method. It is as if Hume's *empirical method* not only missed 'the personal', 'the divinatory', and the 'strange', but also remained satisfied with 'a *preliminary* understanding', and a pre-understanding only of '*the parts*'. In an understanding of 'the whole', the analogy, Dilthey and Ricoeur propose, is more like perceiving a temporal 'plot'. Character, identity, and plot lie beneath apparently separate acts, events, or perceptions, which make up the story *together as a whole*. But to appreciate the fundamental importance of this point we need to move beyond Schleiermacher. Dilthey perceives the crucial significance of time and temporality.

---

[16] Schleiermacher, *Hermeneutics*, 97–9.

[17] Ibid. 198.

[18] W. Dilthey, 'The Development of Hermeneutics' (1900) in *Gesammelte Schriften*, vol. 7; Eng. in H. P. Rickman (ed.), *W. Dilthey: Selected Writings* (Cambridge: Cambridge University Press, 1976), 246–63, and part extract in David E. Klemm (ed.), *Hermeneutical Inquiry*, 2 vols. (Atlanta: Scholars Press, 1986), vol. 1, 93–105; cf. sect. 3, in Klemm, 99–100. We should note, however, that Flacius made this point as a *theological* point about the wholeness and unity of scripture as the context for interpreting individual passages.

[19] Schleiermacher, *Hermeneutics*, 59.

[20] Ibid. 113.

[21] Ibid. 198.

9

A Temporal Hermeneutic of the Self through the 'Detour' of Texts as 'Other'

WILHELM DILTHEY (1833–1911) cherished an ambition, following the work of Hegel, to formulate a critique of historical reason which would rival Kant's *Critique of Pure Reason* (1781) and *Critique of Practical Reason* (1788) in importance. Just as Kant perceived the basic role of 'categories' for all thought, Dilthey stressed the fundamental part played by coherence or 'interconnectedness' (*Zusammenhang*) for hermeneutics or 'historical understanding'. The process of fitting together isolated pieces of the jigsaw of life intelligibly constituted not some timeless logical abstraction, but depended on the temporal flow of life (*Leben*) and life-experience (*Erlebnis*) as a condition of meaning.

Dilthey addresses these issues in terms of selfhood as well as texts. In his 'Draft for a Critique of Historical Reason' he expounds the key theme of 'the lived experience (*Erlebnis*) of time'.[1] Within this temporal context the self faces the *future* under the hermeneutical mode of *hope*. Here, selfhood assumes an *active agency*, hoping actively to shape events in accordance with *possibility* which has not yet become constrained and limited to the actual. Also within the context of time, the self also recalls the *past* under the hermeneutical mode of *memory*. But here the self perceives itself as *passive*. For the chance to shape events has passed by, and the self finds itself powerless as it reflects on 'what might have been'. Dilthey explicitly relates this to 'interconnectedness' (*Zusammenhang*) in a way which transposes Schleiermacher's emphasis on 'the whole' into a temporal frame. Meaning and interpretation presuppose the temporal whole of 'memories' (*Erinnerungen*) and 'possibilities of the future' (*Möglichkeiten der Zukunft*).[2]

---

[1] Dilthey, *Gesammelte Schriften*, vol. 7, 233–4: 'How words have meaning, the means by which they signify something . . . is the special manner of relationship which . . . the parts have to the whole (*zum Ganzen*) . . . in recollections and possibilities of the future (*Möglichkeiten der Zukunft*).'

[2] Dilthey, loc. cit. See further 'Draft for a Critique of Historical Reason', in *Selected Writings*, 208–12, also rp. in Kurt Mueller-Vollmer (ed.), *The Hermeneutics Reader* (Oxford: Blackwell, 1986), 149–52.

This constitutes an advance which contains within it a decisive critique of Hume's scepticism about the self. It will eventually become developed as a complex but satisfying interpretation of self in Paul Ricoeur's *Time and Narrative*, and his impressive work *Oneself as Another*. As Ricoeur argues, the notion of self as a narrative text embodying narrative plot, personal agency, and future accountability convincingly offers a better account of selfhood than can be offered by positivists, or empiricists, or naturalistic theorists. He does not need to appeal to distinctively Christian belief-systems.[3] His work also seriously challenges postmodern selfhood as merely a passive 'point' generated by natural or social forces.

In his earlier work, Dilthey anticipates David Klemm's belief that the heart of hermeneutics is *'understanding'* the other precisely as 'Other'.[4] But increasingly as his thought develops, Dilthey moves away from Schleiermacher's emphasis on 'the Other' to stress the universality and 'sameness' of human nature. It is this principle which seduces him into seeking what Gadamer so intensely rejects, namely a 'universal method of understanding'.

These issues remain closely relevant to everyday life. A brief reference to George Ridding, first Bishop of Southwell, will show their immediate relevance to pastoral theology. Ridding was Bishop from 1884 to 1904, almost the precise period when Dilthey was Professor at Berlin (1882–1907). In a litany which he composed for their Retreats, Ridding invited his clergy to pray: 'Give us true knowledge of our people *in their differences from us and in their likenesses to us,* that we may deal with their *real selves,* measuring their feelings by our own, but patiently considering their varied lives and thoughts and circumstances.'[5]

Dilthey believes that to understand selves 'in their differences from us', we need to undertake what Ricoeur later terms 'a detour'. The detour entails listening to, and appreciating, the 'otherness' which may be discerned in written texts. Texts represent the objectified self-expression of another self. Dilthey rejects both bare empiricism and also concerns about inaccessible 'private' mental states. (This may remind us of Wittgenstein.) Texts constitute self-expression in the public domain. Selfhood may be understood most sensitively and adequately in its interconnectedness with social institutions and patterns in the public world which, Dilthey insists, include texts. The self achieves its selfhood amidst the institutionalized social systems of family, nation, education and texts.

---

[3] Paul Ricoeur, *Time and Narrative* (Eng. 3 vols., Chicago: University of Chicago Press, 1984–8), and *Oneself as Another,* 23–5, where Ricoeur explains why his particular version of the Gifford lectures is offered without the theological comments and additions put forward in the Lectures.

[4] Klemm, *Hermeneutical Inquiry,* vol. 1, 1.

[5] George Ridding, *A Litany of Remembrance Compiled for Retreats and Quiet Days for his Clergy* (London: Allen & Unwin, rp. 1959), 7 (my italics).

One hermeneutical pole arises from 'life as the interweaving of all humankind'.[6] The other pole of hermeneutics perceives the self as unique. Hermeneutical enquiry and understanding entails 're-living' (*nacherleben*) the life experience (*Erlebnis*) of the other, by stepping into the shoes of the other in 'transposition' (*Hineinversetzen*) to arrive at 'empathy' (*Einverständnis*).[7] In his most widely celebrated maxim Dilthey declares: 'Understanding (*Verstehen*) is the rediscovery of the I in the Thou.'[8] In order to underline this 'public' dimension which entails detour, Dilthey further observes: 'Not through interpretation [only] but through history do we come to know ourselves.'[9] Contrary to Descartes' rationalism and Hume's sceptical empiricism, we find what H. A. Hodges calls 'an appreciative understanding of the meaning and value of the unique individual'.[10]

All the same, Gadamer accuses Dilthey of two fundamental failures. First, he falls back into the Enlightenment preoccupation with 'science' and with 'method'. Gadamer believes that this defeats his own hermeneutics by making too much of the supposedly objective and universal in human life. Second, he accords priority to consciousness and the subjectivity of the self, rather than the traditions and pre-judgements that make subjectivity and consciousness what they are. Texts and institutions, for Gadamer, are more than mere self expression.[11] Gadamer claims: 'Dilthey wants to say that historical reason calls for the same kind of justification as pure reason.'[12] 'He was always attempting to legitimate the knowledge of what was historically conditioned as an achievement of objective science.'[13]

Gadamer's emphasis on pre-judgement as prior to subjectivity and consciousness remains in principle valid. But he also overstates the matter. In certain respects Dilthey himself seems to agree that 'the focus of subjectivity is a distorting mirror'.[14] That is why Dilthey moves beyond 'interpretation' by means of a 'detour' into texts and institutions. But it gives too many hostages to postmodern selfhood when Gadamer continues in his next sentence: 'The self-awareness of the individual is only a flickering in the closed circuits of historical life.'[15]

None of this effectively challenges the point that Dilthey understands human selfhood in a temporal and historical sense. In theological terms, human beings remain part of the creation and share certain trans-

[6] Dilthey, *Gesammelte Schriften*, vol. 7, 131; *Selected Writings*, 178.
[7] Dilthey, *Gesammelte Schriften*, vol. 7, 216; *Selected Writings*, 226–7.
[8] Dilthey, *Gesammelte Schriften*, vol. 7, 191; *Selected Writings*, 208.
[9] Dilthey, *Selected Writings*, 279.
[10] H. A. Hodges, *The Philosophy of Wilhelm Dilthey* (London: Routledge & Kegan Paul, 1952), xiv.
[11] Gadamer, *Truth and Method* (revd. edn.), 218–42 (1st Eng. edn., 192–214).
[12] Ibid. 219 (1st Eng. edn., 194).
[13] Ibid. 231 (1st Eng. edn., 204).
[14] Ibid. 276 (1st Eng. edn., 245).
[15] Ibid. 276–7 (1st Eng. edn., 245).

contextual characteristics, as Dilthey sees. Yet the human self is also unique, because the story of each human self remains unique. Hence, as Howard Tuttle observes in his critical study of Dilthey, hermeneutical understanding of the self includes 'individual gestures, words, art, textual interpretation, society, historical eras, biographical data. Empathetic projection of oneself into the sorrow caused by the death of another's father', Tuttle adds, is neither a value-neutral, objective, enquiry, nor is it merely 'private' in the sense of being purely psychologistic.[16]

The 'inner' is reached through interpreting the symbolic content of texts and institutions in the public world, against the background of which the self achieves, expresses and communicates its distinctive identity. Meaning in the public world is largely perceived in relation to some 'effect' (*Wirkung*).[17] Thus Dilthey prepares the ground for Gadamer's notion of a 'history of effects' (*Wirkungsgeschichte*) or 'effective history'. This stands in contrast to a bare succession of data in rationalism or in empiricism. Interpretations of selfhood must go beyond these.

---

[16] Howard N. Tuttle, *Wilhelm Dilthey's Philosophy of Historical Understanding. A Critical Analysis* (Leiden: Brill, 1969), 11–14, 35–7, 45–54.
[17] Ibid. 50.

10

Five Ways in which
Textual Reading Interprets the Self

W<small>E</small> may distinguish between five different senses and contexts in which selfhood and self-identity reaches understanding through encounter with texts.

1. In an obvious sense a reader comes to understand something of the *author of a text* through textual interpretation. Even if we do not know the name of the author, it is customary in biblical studies to speak of 'the writer' or 'the redactor' or even 'the source'. On this basis we can discuss their distinctive perspectives and theology as expressed or implied in the texts. Formalist and postmodernist objections to the place often accorded to this model do not destroy the capacity of texts to illuminate life and human selfhood.

2. In a distinctively theological sense the biblical text, as actually or potentially the word of God, may be said to address the selfhood of the reader with transforming effects. It thereby gives the self an identity and significance as the recipient of loving and transforming address. In this sense it 'names' the self.

Karl Barth pre-eminently formulates such a theological hermeneutic, based on the valid principle that God's 'word' is not to be abstracted from God's own loving, self-imparting, holy presence. Thus Barth asserts: 'God's word is itself God's act.'[1] Barth anticipates an approach to language that, since the work of J. L. Austin and John Searle, has come to be known as speech-act theory. Thus he sees the word of God as performing acts of promise, election, call, disclosure and bestowal of life.[2] Expressed through the text of scripture, the word may enact performance as 'a promise . . . a judgement, a claim on man by which God binds man to Himself . . . The promise of God is not as such an empty pledge . . . It is the transposing of man into the wholly new state of one who has accepted and appropriated the promise'.[3] We explore these themes further in Part IV.

This stands a long way from the empiricist model of 'scrutinizing the text as an object of enquiry'. Rather, the text addresses, confronts,

[1] Barth, *Church Dogmatics*, I/1, 147.
[2] Ibid. 148.
[3] Ibid. 150.

and challenges the reader's selfhood. Robert Funk, discussing Fuchs, comments: 'The direction of flow between the interpreter and text that has dominated modern biblical criticism from its inception is reversed, and . . . hermeneutics is now understood as the effort to allow God to address man through the medium of the text.'[4]

3. Such a hermeneutical principle nevertheless does not depend exclusively on Christian theology. If Dilthey is right, an encounter with texts becomes a necessary condition for the process of understanding what otherwise remains opaque in one's own selfhood. Some writers, among whom may be included Bultmann, Fuchs, Ebeling and Funk oscillate between working out this principle as one of Christian theology, and as a principle demanded by purely philosophical hermeneutics. Thus in a memorable statement Ernst Fuchs declares: 'The texts must translate us (*uns übersetzen*) before we can translate them.'[5] '*The truth has ourselves as its object*'(his italics).[6] Likewise Ebeling insists: '*The text . . . becomes a hermeneutical aid in the understanding of present experience.*'[7]

Funk illustrates this principle in his interpretation of the parable of the Prodigal Son (Luke 15:11–32). The welcome which the father in the story accords to the wastrel invites wider indignation than only from the dutiful elder son. All hearers or readers who are governed in their attitudes primarily by moralism and a passion about their 'rights' share his indignation. By contrast, those who know too well that their lives are marked by failure and who long for some new start rejoice with the younger son. Funk observes: 'The word of grace and the deed of grace divide the audience into younger sons and elder sons – into sinners and pharisees.'[8] Alluding again to Fuchs he adds: '*One does not interpret the parable*; the parable interprets him . . . It is man and not God who is on trial'.[9]

We need not point out, I hope, that these first, second and third approaches are not mutually exclusive. This appears clearly in the context of Bultmann's hermeneutics. On one side he insists that we cannot even comprehend a text of music, for example, if we are tone deaf or have no understanding whatever of what it is to interpret marks

[4] Robert W. Funk, *Language, Hermeneutic and Word of God* (New York: Harper & Row, 1966), 11.

[5] Ernst Fuchs, 'The Hermeneutical Problem', in James M. Robinson (ed.), *The Future of our Religious Past. Essays in Honour of Rudolf Bultmann* (London: SCM, 1971), 277, cf. 267–78; German, 'Zum Hermeneutischen Problem', in E. Dinkler (ed.), *Zeit und Geschichte. Dankesgabe an Rudolf zum 80 Geburtstag* (Tübingen: Mohr, 1964), 365, cf. 357–66.

[6] E. Fuchs,'The New Testament and the Hermeneutical Problem', in James M. Robinson and J. B. Cobb Jr. (eds.), *New Frontiers in Theology: II, The New Hermeneutic* (New York: Harper & Row, 1964), 143.

[7] G. Ebeling, *Word and Faith* (Eng. London: SCM, 1963), 33.

[8] Funk, *Language, Hermeneutic and Word of God*, 16–17.

[9] Ibid. (his italics).

on a stave as notes of variable pitch and duration. Could we understand a mathematical text if we have no understanding, respectively, of processes of calculation?[10] On the other hand, he equally stresses that biblical texts place a 'claim' *upon* the reader. Sometimes, in the context of his Lutheran theology, Bultmann sees this as a distinctively 'gospel' or kerygmatic claim. But at other times he expounds the approach as part of a merely general hermeneutic drawn from Dilthey and the earlier Heidegger, which applies equally to the interpretation of any historical text.

Thus in his essay 'The Problem of Hermeneutics', Bultmann writes: 'The "most subjective" (*subjektiviste*) interpretation is . . . the "most objective" (*objektivste*), that is, only those who are stirred by the question of their own existence can hear the claim which the text makes.'[11] He declares: '*All* texts can, in fact, be understood in accordance with Dilthey's formulation, that is, as documents of "historical" personal life.'[12]

4. How different people have interpreted biblical texts may well tell us *even more about them* than about the texts themselves. (It is rather like asking: 'Do you like Beethoven?' The answer says more about the addressee than about Beethoven.) We discover what kind of people attempt to use biblical texts for manipulative purposes, whether consciously or unconsciously, and why they do it. Some may do this sincerely or insincerely, for purposes of self-interest or power, or out of misguided piety or sense of faithfulness.

Willard Swartley's collection of case-studies on interpretations of texts about 'slavery, sabbath, war and women' offers abundant instances. Swartley offers documented cases of those who argued for slavery on the grounds that in their view the abolitionists in 'modern wisdom presume to set aside the word of God'.[13] Swartley rightly notes that our own identification with, or dissociation from, aspects of this discussion provoke the questions: 'To what community do I belong?' and 'Who am I?'[14]

Within this frame of thought, Gerhard Ebeling entitled his Inaugural Lecture at Tübingen in 1947, 'Church History as the History of the Exposition of Holy Scripture'.[15] Ebeling explicitly compared traditions

[10] Rudolf Bultmann, 'The Problem of Hermeneutics', in *Essays Philosophical and Theological* (London: SCM, 1955), 242–5.

[11] Ibid. 256; German: *Glauben und Verstehen. Gesammelte Aufsätze* (4 vols., Tübingen: Mohr, 1964–5), vol. 2, 230. See further 'Is Exegesis without Presuppositions Possible?', in his *Existence and Faith* (London: Collins (Fontana) 1964), 342–51.

[12] R. Bultmann, 'The Problem of Hermeneutics', loc. cit. 240 (German, 216).

[13] Willard M. Swartley, *Slavery, Sabbath, War and Women. Case Issues in Biblical Interpretation* (Scottdale: Herald Press, 1983), 37, 53.

[14] Ibid. 63.

[15] Translated in Gerhard Ebeling, *The Word of God as Tradition. Historical Studies Interpreting the Divisions of Christianity* (Philadelphia: Fortress, 1968), 11–31.

within Reformed and Lutheran theology, Roman Catholicism, and Pentecostal 'enthusiast' outlooks with how, as interpreters, they read biblical texts.

More recently Karlfried Froelich has endorsed and further explored the approach of Ebeling as entirely proper to the distinctive work of the church historian. The 'understanding' of a biblical text, he insists, cannot stop short with reconstructing its own historical setting and the author's aim. He declares: 'Understanding must take into account the text's post-history and . . . the way in which the text itself can function *as a source of human self-interpretation* in a variety of contexts, and thus, through its historical interpretations, in participating in the *shaping* of life' (my italics).[16] Reception theory, often associated with H. R. Jauss, offers a major resource for hermeneutics in this respect.

5. This brings us to the final point. The central thesis in my volume *New Horizons in Hermeneutics* is that biblical reading has to do with transformation,[17] although this is not to be understood as excluding disclosure of some cognitive content. Indeed I have argued that authentic transformation, as against mere psychological reaction, presupposes disclosure that certain states of affairs are the case. For example, the claim that the pronouncements of Jesus 'liberate' is bound up with whether he speaks with the authority of God. But the transforming purpose of scripture entails a hermeneutics of the self. For interpretation may too easily remain in the realm of theory and the mere satisfaction of curiosity unless it also leads to a new understanding of the self's identity, responsibility, and future possibilities of change and growth. I have endorsed the observations of David Kelsey and Frances Young that the biblical writings, when they function as 'scripture', shape the *identities* of persons so decisively as to *transform* them. We shall return to these issues in Part IV.

---

[16] Karlfried Froehlich, 'Church History and the Bible', in Mark S. Burrows and Paul Rorem (eds.), *Biblical Hermeneutics in Historical Perspective. Studies in Honor of Karlfried Froehlich on his Sixtieth Birthday* (Grand Rapids: Eerdmans, 1991), 9; cf. 1–15, rp. from *Princeton Seminary Bulletin* n.s. 1 (1978), 213–24.

[17] The sub-title is *The Theory and Practice of Transforming Biblical Reading*, Chapter I includes 'The Capacity of Texts to Transform Readers', 31–5; and 'The Capacity of Readers to Transform Texts', 35–42.

II

Self-Deception and Sub-Text: Psychoanalysis, Suspicion and Conversation

DOES not much of the above come to grief in the light of Gadamer's observations that 'the focus of subjectivity is a distorting mirror', as against his view that Dilthey sees everything as 'self-reflection and autobiography'?[1] Does not the work of Ebeling and Froelich demonstrate that our interpretations of texts and self are hopelessly trapped within the presuppositions, pre-judgements or prejudices of the traditions to which we belong? We cannot gainsay Gadamer's insistence that these factors, more than our own derivative conscious judgements, largely predetermine what we *want* to hear or even are *able* to hear from texts. They condition what we can understand about our own selfhood. More profoundly the conclusions of Freud and Lacan about the opaqueness and deceptiveness of the self compound the problem.

Gadamer and Ricoeur, among others, are fully aware of these problems, but do not consider that they are insuperable. To be sure, they do call in question the credibility of the persistence of empiricist accounts of selfhood. It may well serve the interests of a self or society which values 'freedom' above responsibility to perceive the self as nothing other than a bundle of perceptions served by instrumental reason. Hume's view that reason is the slave of the passions, and that no stable core of selfhood can be perceived may well encourage a succession of disconnected goals, each centred only on the desire of the passing moment. But selfhood is more than Hume allows.

Ricoeur's strategy has perhaps more to offer than Gadamer's, but both deserve attention. Ricoeur rightly perceives that if the Freudian analysis of selfhood lies near the root of the problem, we may learn something from Freud's own procedures of interpretation. After all, if the deceptions, evasions and delusions of the self were utterly impenetrable, Freud could not even begin his work of psychoanalysis, let alone therapy.

Sigmund Freud (1856–1939) published his *Die Treumdeutung* in Vienna in 1900, translated as *The Interpretation of Dreams*.[2] The central

---

[1] Gadamer, *Truth and Method* (revised edn.), 276 (1st Eng. edn., 245).

[2] Sigmund Freud, *The Interpretation of Dreams* in *The Standard Edition of the Complete Psychological Works of Sigmund Freud* (London: Hogarth Press, 1953 onwards), vols. 4–5; published separately in 1955.

motif might be described as that of the relation between desire and language. Certainly Ricoeur views this as its central theme.[3] Naturally enough, this resonates with Ricoeur's own pilgrimage from work on the human will in *Freedom and Nature* and *Fallible Man* (French, 1949; English, 1966 and 1967), through work on symbols in *The Symbolism of Evil*, to hermeneutical enquiry (from 1965 onwards). Moreover Freud viewed dreams, as Ricoeur saw symbols, as expressions of 'double meaning'. Ricoeur recalls: 'The claim of psychoanalysis to explain symbols and myths as fruits of unconscious representations, as distorted expressions of the relation between libidinal impulses and repressive structures of the super-ego, compelled me to enlarge my first concept of hermeneutics beyond a mere semantic analysis of double-meaning expressions.'[4]

Dreams, Freud believes, represent expressions of human desires and wishes construed in disguised forms. The person who tries to 'interpret' the dream in such a way as to unmask the writer has two layers of opacity to overcome. First, the interpreter cannot gain access to the dream as such ('the dream-thoughts') but only to the dream as remembered and recounted ('the dream-content'). But in order to protect itself from the shock of discovering what it really wishes, the self re-orders, or more strictly dis-orders or scrambles, the dream-thoughts by omissions, displacements, reversals of characters or sequences, and so forth. In Freud's terminology, the censor effectively 'condenses' and 'displaces' what has been dreamed.

Second, even the dream as recounted may embody further levels of self-deception or conscious and unconscious manipulative editing. Sometimes an apparent sequence may merely reflect the 'over-determination' of a 'text' many times repeated under different guises. The interpreter seeks to interpret interpretation, to understand 'another text . . . beneath the text of consciousness'.[5]

Freud, Ricoeur concedes, makes it clear that 'the subject is never the subject one thinks it is'.[6] He has changed our understanding of the self. *But this serves only to press the claims and relevance of a hermeneutics of texts more sharply as an approach to interpreting the self.* Since the work of Nietzsche, Marx, and Freud, we have become aware that 'texts' are seldom what they may seem to be.

In more recent times Roland Barthes (1915–80) has exposed the double-layered meaning of much mass media communication and especially mass advertising in his book *Mythologies* (French, 1957; English, 1972). We introduced his work in Part I, and noted that

---

[3] Paul Ricoeur, *Freud and Philosophy. An Essay on Interpretation* (New Haven and London: Yale University Press, 1970), 5.

[4] Paul Ricoeur, *The Rule of Metaphor. Multi-disciplinary Studies of the Creation of Meaning in Language* (Eng. London: Kegan Paul, 1978), 318.

[5] Ricoeur, *Freud and Philosophy*, 392.

[6] Ibid. 420.

he develops the principles at a more technical level in his *Elements of Semiology* (French, 1964; English, 1967). Even apparently innocent choices of clothes or furniture may serve as a communicative sub-text of our life. At different stages in cultural history, for example, the wearing of a beard or of blue jeans may be only a matter of aesthetic or functional preference; at another time these may serve as signals of protest; at yet another time, as signals of conformity or even anonymity.[7] Jacques Derrida (b. 1930), as we have noted, attempts to urge in his 'White Mythology' (1971) that what purport to convey profound truth-claims in the texts of philosophy turn out to be only inherited metaphors now manipulated to serve given interests.

Ricoeur points out, however, that these very interpretations offered by Freud and others simply confirm that 'double-meanings' in texts simultaneously hide and reveal, conceal and disclose. Otherwise none of the 'masters of suspicion' could say anything about the 'texts' of selfhood. What is required, therefore, is neither naïve positivist enquiry, as if everything was value-neutral, nor mere openness in hermeneutical listening, as if the self did not often distort understanding for purposes of self-protection, manipulation, evasion, or power. He urges that we work with a 'hermeneutic of suspicion', alongside a more constructive 'hermeneutic of retrieval'. Hermeneutics may be summed up in the two principles: 'willingness to suspect', which destroys idols, and 'willingness to listen' which retrieves the power of symbols and communicative texts.

Pastoral counsellors are well aware that as clients have recounted the 'text' of a family argument, what a husband or wife may represent sincerely as the key issue which brought everything to a head does not constitute an issue of this kind at all. It is perhaps the last in a chain of petty grievances that together mask a larger sense of grievance caused by something perhaps too big and too painful even to have entered into the family conversation, let alone into the 'text' presented to the counsellor. But sympathetic unravelling in a non-threatening context may expose the raw nerve. Similarly, while he does not for one moment entertain Freud's anti-theistic world-view, Ricoeur sees his procedures as informing and resourcing a 'hermeneutic of suspicion', as the way for a positive 'retrieval'.

Gadamer (b. 1900) approaches these issues entirely differently, even if he shares Ricoeur's concern about the opaqueness of human consciousness. He rejects the whole notion of 'method' as imposing a scientific 'control' in advance of listening to what is to be understood. He deliberately swims against the stream not only of rationalism and empiricism, but even against the double emphasis in hermeneutics on '*explanation*' and '*understanding*' found in Droysen,

---

[7] Roland Barthes, *Elements of Semiology*.

Dilthey and Ricoeur. Karl-Otto Apel demonstrates the widespread influence of the double emphasis first of all in Droysen and Dilthey and their influence on Weber; then in the debate about science and human behaviour between Hempel and Popper; and finally in the work of G. E. M. Anscombe, Charles Taylor (1964) and G. H. von Wright (1972), all partly under the influence of Wittgenstein.[8] Ricoeur sees 'explanation' as a vital component of a hermeneutic of suspicion.

In his 'Afterword' to the third German edition of *Truth and Method* Gadamer ponders whether his attack on 'method', or 'explanation' came 'too late' to turn the tide.[9] He complains of Apel, Habermas, Betti and others: 'All they can think about are rules and their application . . . By contrast, I have pointed to "dialogue" . . . a dialectic of question and answer'.[10] For Gadamer *dialectic or conversation constitutes the only non-manipulatory mode of apprehending truth which does not pre-determine what counts as true in advance.*

Three factors help us to understand why Gadamer adopts this approach. First, in a brilliantly perceptive study Robert Sullivan directs our attention to the political significance of Gadamer's out-look especially from 1932 to 1942, after which his reservations about Nazism made it difficult for him to write until after 1945.[11] Sullivan points out that although they held much in common, Gadamer differed from his teacher Heidegger not only in a more critical attitude towards the rise of Nazism but also in a more positive evaluation of Plato. Whereas Heidegger followed Nietzsche in regarding Plato as initiating the degeneration of Western philosophy, Gadamer first wrote his dissertation on Plato under Hartmann and Heidegger, and then, from 1932 to 1942, published a series of studies on Plato's dialectic and ethics. Here he laid the foundation for his view that the openness of dialectic, of seeing *where the conversation leads*, serves the wisdom (*phronēsis*) of the city-state, as against the manipulative strategies of Nazi propagandists who used statements of rhetorical 'control' or 'method' (*technē*) to distort truth for self-interest. The result was a series of 'closed' statements, excluded from negotiation or critical discussion.[12]

Second, this is confirmed by Gadamer's recent appraisal of his own career in the *Frankfurter Allgemeine* in October 1989, in which he declares that his work on Plato's dialectic remains 'the most independent

---

[8] Karl-Otto Apel, *Understanding and Explanation. A Transcendental-Pragmatic Perspective* (Cambridge, Mass: MIT Press, 1984), 1–28.

[9] Gadamer, *Truth and Method* (revised edn.), 551.

[10] Ibid. 555, 556, 576.

[11] Robert R. Sullivan, *Political Hermeneutics. The Early Thinking of Hans-Georg Gadamer* (University Park: Pennsylvania State University Press, 1989), esp. 25–9, 140–6, 176–81.

[12] Ibid. 171, 177–8, 179.

part of all my philosophical work'.[13] His interest lay primarily in Plato's adoption of the 'Socratic question and the Socratic dialectic . . . There, dialectic means the art of leading a *conversation*'.[14]

Third, only dialectic is non-manipulatory, for only in 'conversation' can something genuinely new 'emerge' which does not reflect the prior manipulative interests of one or more of the speakers.[15] Gadamer comments (as we noted): 'Something comes to speak' which is 'not a possession *at the disposal of* one or other of the interlocutors . . . To reach an understanding in dialogue is not merely a matter of . . . successfully *asserting one's own point of view*, but being transformed into a communion (commonality) in which we do not remain what we were'.[16]

Understanding texts and selfhood cannot therefore, for Gadamer, remain a solitary affair. Part of the safeguard against self-deception and manipulation is the task of listening to other selves in mutuality and self-criticism. This belongs to that aspect of selfhood which has to do with intersubjectivity and more especially with moral and political responsibility in the context of community and traditions. We shall explore further how 'personhood' depends for what it is on a relationship of mutuality or reciprocity with 'the Other' in Part IV. It will be argued that, in theology, personhood is grounded in the nature of God-as-Trinity and in his self-imparting love. We shall refer especially to the work of Moltmann and of Pannenberg to substantiate this. A. I. McFadyen and F. Watson endorse this approach to personhood. McFadyen's 'basic conception of the person' depends on its 'relation with other personal centres, through commitment to others'.[17] Watson relates this especially to a theological understanding of persons as created in the image of God.[18]

---

[13] Reprinted and translated as 'Gadamer on Gadamer', in Hugh J. Silverman (ed.), *Gadamer and Hermeneutics* (London: Routledge, Chapman & Hall, 1991), 13–19; quotation on 13.

[14] Ibid. 16.

[15] Gadamer, *Truth and Method* (revised edn.), 369–79.

[16] Ibid. 378–9 (my italics).

[17] A. I. McFadyen, *The Call to Personhood. A Christian Theory of the Individual in Social Relationships* (Cambridge: Cambridge University Press, 1990), 9.

[18] F. Watson, *Text, Church and World* (Edinburgh: T&T Clark, 1994), 107–23, esp. 107–11.

12

Self-Identity within the Temporal Logic of Narrative Plot

THE crowning work which brings together many of the above considerations is Paul Ricoeur's work *Oneself as Another*. He himself regards this as applying many of his earlier works including *Time and Narrative* to a hermeneutics of the self. Ricoeur agrees with Dilthey that the hermeneutics of the self begins with a recognition of 'a primary trait of the self, namely its temporality'.[1] However, Dilthey did not follow through the full implications of this. Ricoeur continues: 'Identity in the sense of *ipse* implies no assertion concerning some unchanging core of the personality.'[2] In accordance with what has already been said about discovering the 'Other' or 'alien' as part of the self, for example through encounters with 'otherness' in texts, as Schleiermacher so long ago saw, self-hood presupposes what Ricoeur calls 'the dialectic of *self* and the *other than self*'.[3]

As Ricoeur's thought unfolds, the grossly simplistic character of Hume's notion of looking inside myself to perceive a succession of mental perceptions is thrown into relief by the insights of Nietzsche (and subsequently Freud) that 'everything that reaches our consciousness is utterly and completely adjusted, simplified, schematized, interpreted; the actual process of inner "perception" ... is absolutely concealed from us'. 'Where positivism says, "There are only facts"', Nietzsche says, 'there are no facts, only interpretations.'[4]

Ricoeur, however, does not see this as calling into question the reality of personal agency and personal identity. Taking up the argument of his *Time and Narrative*, vol. 3, he introduces the notion of 'narrative identity'.[5] Whereas for Descartes, for Locke and for Hume, either there are ideas, objects or essences, or there is nothing; for Ricoeur, by

[1] Paul Ricoeur, *Oneself as Another* (Eng. Chicago: Chicago University Press, 1992), 2.

[2] Ibid.

[3] Ibid. 3.

[4] Friedrich Nietzsche, *Works*, vol. 15: *The Will to Power*, vol. 2, 7, aphorism 477; and Ricoeur, *Oneself as Another*, 14–15.

[5] Ricoeur, *Oneself as Another*, 17; cf. his *Time and Narrative* (Eng. 3 vols., Chicago: Chicago University Press, 1984–8), vol. 3, esp. 235–40.

contrast, narrative opens up the notion of an entity who acts and suffers within a framework of continuity and change through the changes and continuities of time. Human action seems to carry with it not only initiation of change, which may rebound in changing the self, but also a continuity of accountability as the action of *this* self.

Narratives bring out this feature clearly. We trace the inscribing of actions and events on characters and even on physical appearance and social status. But the narrative traces the destiny and responsibility of 'the same' self amidst changes which may sometimes render it almost unrecognizable as this same self. For example, we set aside super-annuation for the benefit of some future self as a 'senior citizen' whom we may not recognize or even like, from our present perspective. But this self is still 'us'. Moreover, as Ricoeur points out, whatever the philosophical problems about retrospective memory, in the context of testimony or witness, we readily speak of a witness 'admitting' or 'falsely denying' some event or action separated in time. Even if this can never be more than a matter of trust and judgement, law courts and police expect witnesses to make responsible statements as the same 'self' as that which witnessed some long-past event.

Ricoeur readily recognizes that a theological understanding of witness, promise, and accountability strengthens his argument, but he does not wish his argument to be perceived as resting on special theological pleading.[6] What is fundamental in theology finds resonance in all human experience, namely the identity of the self through time as one who is loved and who loves. Theology could add 'in relation to God', or 'in the sight of God', but the principle otherwise still stands.

Ricoeur's hermeneutics addresses three distinct areas at this point. The first is the philosophy of mind. Hume believed that 'the mind never perceives any connection among distinct existences'. Therefore 'identity is nothing really belonging to these different perceptions, and uniting them together; but is merely a quality which *we* attribute to them, because of the union of their ideas in the *imagination* . . .'[7]

C. A. Campbell, Paul R. Clifford, and most recently Harold Noonan ask how (if Hume were correct) the self, as agent, comes to make sense of successions of isolated events in an ordered and intelligible pattern. Campbell asks, for example, why a self's perception of Big Ben's striking nine o'clock should not, on Hume's showing, be the same as a perception of its striking one o'clock, repeated nine times.[8] Similarly Paul Clifford speaks of the self's 'capacities for structural integra-tion . . . the ability to piece together various elements into an ordered

---

[6] Ricoeur, *Oneself as Another*, 24–5; cf. also 'Time Traversed', in *Time and Narrative*, vol. 2, 130–52.

[7] David Hume, *Treatise on Human Nature* (Oxford: Clarendon Press, 1897), I.iv.6, 260.

[8] C. A. Campbell, *On Selfhood and Godhood* (London: Allen & Unwin, and New York: Macmillan, 1957), 76–7; cf. 130–57 on self-activity.

whole'.[9] Harold Noonan guides us through an intricate maze of philosophical arguments to urge that 'continuant identity is compatible with more than one definition of the concept of a person'.[10] This may well be the case, but the temporal logic of narrative appears to offer a less 'closed' and generalized mode of 'ordering' and of 'making sense of the whole' than many of the models more usually employed in the philosophy of mind to explore self-identity and personhood.[11]

The notion of selfhood as temporal narrative addresses also a second area, namely that of pastoral theology and counselling. In his book *The Living Human Document. Re-visioning Pastoral Counselling in a Hermeneutical Mode*, Charles V. Gerkin, we noted, takes up Anton Boisen's model of the human being as a document or living text. Just as Schleiermacher and Gadamer insist that the 'otherness' of a text must be respected, so 'the individual human text demanded a hearing on its own merit'.[12] Too readily, Boisen argues, the pastor or counsellor wishes to 'explain' rather than 'to understand'. Too often a notion of 'reductive explanation' invites superficial 'therapy' before the pastor has even noticed that the person concerned may constitute a multi-layered text which cannot be 'understood' by the mere exercise of 'skills' which presuppose prior, stereotyped categories.[13] Gerkin explicitly appeals to Gadamer's model of dialogue and dialectic. Only in reciprocal listening and speaking may the hitherto unspoken but crucial new 'point' arise, which may have escaped the prior conscious horizons of both participants.[14] Understanding here moves beyond any technical inventory of both parties, to initiate *change*.

Further, a person who seeks assistance in understanding themselves in their self-identity has often suffered the impact of some disruptive event which has *shattered a hitherto presupposed meaning* ascribed to the self or life. Bereavement, serious illness, or deep disappointment may constitute such events. Gerkin rightly suggests that in such cases, a *re-casting* and *'re-ordering'* of the self in relation to a temporal past, present and future is of more importance than some more empirically-based 'pastoral therapy'. Hermeneutical awareness operates 'between

---

[9] Paul R. Clifford, *Interpreting Human Experience. A Philosophical Prologue to Theology* (London: Collins, 1971), 59.

[10] Harold Noonan, *Personal Identity* (London and New York: Routledge, 1989 (1991)), 252.

[11] The issue of agency also raises the well-known problem of freedom and predictability. Among a huge range of literature, cf. for example G. Van den Brink, *Almighty God. A Study in the Doctrine of Divine Omnipotence* (Kampen: Kok Pharos, 1993), 134–83, 214–26, 240–67; Alvin Plantinga, 'The Free Will Defence', in Max Black (ed.), *Philosophy in America* (London: Allen & Unwin, 1965), 204–20; and Linda T. Zagzebski, *The Dilemma of Freedom and Foreknowledge* (Oxford: Oxford University Press, 1991).

[12] Gerkin, *The Living Human Document*, 38.

[13] Ibid. 39–46.

[14] Ibid. 47.

the occurrence of those events and a language of meaning for those events'.[15] The 'unitary vision' which we associate with theology and the gospel of Christ may be discovered. But this may entail what Dilthey and Ricoeur call the 'detour' in which the self discovers a relation between its own memory of the past, its hopes for the future, and a larger narrative which constitutes the history of God's dealings with the world. This stretches forward into the future as promise, as we shall argue in Part IV.

Life may be understood, then, within the wider frame of temporal relation between the past, present and future.[16] Here Ricoeur's notion of narrative as projecting 'possibility' becomes part of the temporal logic of the narrative plot.[17] A plot has a beginning and an end; a pattern of tension and resolution, and often (according to whether it is a tragic or a comic plot), a downward or upward movement. The identity of 'the real self' emerges fully only *in relation to purposes which transcend the self*. Again, we shall explore this in Part IV.

Gerkin also rightly appeals to Moltmann, for the most profound theological interpretation of this phenomenon. He writes: 'The possibilities and limits of the human situation are defined by the limits of our human location within the history of God's life within himself in the times between creation and the fulfilment of God's Kingdom.' 'For Moltmann, the history of human life and the trinitarian history of God are closely intertwined.'[18] In Part IV we explore these themes explicitly with reference to promise, Christology and Trinity.

Ricoeur's hermeneutics of the self addresses not only the philosophy of mind and pastoral theology, but also a third area, namely sociological theory. Pressures of space confine us to considering a single approach by way of example. We select Richard Harvey Brown's *Society as Text* (1987).[19] Brown explores how social, economic, and political orders and the sign-worlds that belong to them serve to define the self and its identity.

In a specific 'situatedness' of roles and performances within such a linguistic and socio-economic order, for example, a person may perceive themselves as a 'company' man or woman. The 'sign-systems' of their clothes, furniture, house, car and so-forth define who they

---

[15] Ibid. 53; cf. 51–70.

[16] Ibid. 63; cf. W. Pannenberg, 'Eschatology and the Experience of Meaning', in *Basic Questions in Theology*, vol. 3, 192–210, and 'Hermeneutic and Universal History', ibid., vol. 1, 96–136.

[17] Ricoeur, *Time and Narrative*, vol. 1, 3, 52–90; vol. 2, 100–52; vol. 3, 60–156, 207–74, *et passim*.

[18] Gerkin, *The Living Human Document*, 66. Cf. J. Moltmann, *The Trinity and the Kingdom of God. The Doctrine of God* (Eng. London: SCM, 1981), esp. 21–60, 94–6; *The Spirit of Life*, esp. 229–67; and *History and the Triune God* (Eng. London: SCM, 1991), 125–65, 171–6.

[19] R. H. Brown, *Society as Text. Essays on Rhetoric, Reason and Reality* (Chicago and London: University of Chicago Press, 1987).

are. Following Hannah Arendt, Brown underlines the importance of speech as defining the relationality which forms part of the search for security.[20] Nevertheless this speech can readily become distorted. It can become subordinated to a sub-text of manipulative interests which redefine what is 'legitimate' or 'real' for the self in deceptive or illusory ways.

Even more fundamentally, however, a radical economic, political or social change can 'reconstitute' the identity of the self. If a senior manager loses his or her job, cannot maintain payments on the house or service debts, and ends up begging on the streets, the self and its identity become *reconstituted*. Here the similarities and differences between the perceptions of postmodern selfhood and Christian theology come to view. On one side, Christian theology endorses the realism of postmodernism that the human self can fall victim to forces which overwhelm it, damage it, imprison it and change it. This is nearer to the truth than the innocent confidence of the self of modernity that it can always remain 'in control'. On the other side, however, from the vantage point of Christian revelation and faith a far wider and larger range of inter-personal relations, worlds of language and external forces serve to change or to reconstitute self than those of social, political and economic forces alone. As David Kelsey, followed by Frances Young, reminds us, the promisory language of the biblical writings 'shape . . . identities so decisively as to transform them'.[21]

Like Ricoeur, Brown calls for a clearer place for moral agency and indeed for 'narrative plot' within social theory as offering a more adequate account of 'a social order of meaning'.[22] But Brown mentions Ricoeur only once; and Dilthey, only in passing.[23] Meanwhile part of Ricoeur's aim in *Oneself as Another* is simultaneously to reveal the limitations of empiricist and even postmodernist accounts of the self, and at the same time to stress the past and future action of the larger 'plot' which 'keeps the self from occupying the place of foundation' as it has in modernity since Descartes.[24] Just as, in personal terms, selfhood and personhood are what they are only in relation to 'the Other', even so, the very experiences of 'I want, I move, I do' acquire their meaning only against a larger background of a wider world and other selves which carry with it Ricoeur's principle that 'existing is resisting'.[25] *In summary, Ricoeur's profound achievement is to undermine equally the autonomous self which commands the centre of the stage in high*

[20] Ibid. 20, 25, 55–63.
[21] David H. Kelsey, *The Uses of Scripture in Recent Theology* (London: SCM, 1975), 90; and Frances Young, *The Art of Performance: Towards a Theology of Holy Scripture* (London: Darton, Longman & Todd, 1990), 173.
[22] Brown, *Society as Text*, 143–71.
[23] Ibid. 133, 134.
[24] Ricoeur, *Oneself as Another*, 318.
[25] Ibid. 321, 322.

modernity and the reduced, de-centred self of postmodernity. This comes closest to the self of scripture.

As against the self-interpretation of the postmodern self as mere flotsam, driven by the surface currents of the power-interests and language-worlds of society, a theology of promise, we argue in Part IV, *beckons from beyond* to invite new hope, new purpose, even 'resurrection'. For what else is *resurrection* but a reconstituted selfhood of the same *identity*, or a *reconstituted identity* for the '*same*' *self*? In Gerkin's words: 'the Holy Spirit creates hope where otherwise there is no reason for hope'. The Spirit makes possible 'a hermeneutic of hope and expectation'.[26] From the viewpoint of Christian theology, everything depends on divine promise and agency. Resurrection may be compared with awaking to a new dawn, with the tasks and glories of a new day, in the daylight of which the tatters of half-forgotten dreams of the night fall away (1 Cor. 15: 50–57; cf. 15: 35–49). All this is explored in Part IV.

However, how might the postmodern self fare if 'God' turns out to be no more than a human projection, as Kant and Feuerbach claimed? Even if the optimistc self of modernity whose goal is 'autonomy' might welcome such news, what hope could such a possibility leave for the postmodern self? This is the question which we now address in Part III.

---

[26] Gerkin, *The Living Human Document*, 69.

PART III

POSTMODERN GOD?
SEA OF FAITH
OR
ABYSS OF BABEL?

13

The Sea of Faith Network:
Interpreting God as a
Human Construct

THE term 'Sea of Faith' first came into prominence as the title of a
BBC television series presented by Don Cupitt in 1984. Cupitt (b.
1934) borrowed the term from Matthew Arnold's poem 'Dover Beach'
first published in 1867. Through analogical imagery Arnold portrayed
a 'Sea of Faith ... once ... at the full' which sounded out its
'melancholy, long, withdrawing roar' retreating to expose 'the naked
shingles of the world'.[1] The analogy represents the retreat of a faith
from the supposedly stable rocks and shores of a 'modern' nineteenth-
century world-view inspired by the rationalism of the eighteenth century
and the scientific achievements which it initiated. Cupitt argues that
traditional faith is in retreat, but does not lament it. We should note
that in 1984 Cupitt is attacking targets in the name of the 'modern'
(not postmodern) self. With Kant and Feuerbach he fears that 'theism'
may diminish the dignity of the confident modern self.

The television broadcasts were followed by a published version
produced in the same year under the same title, and recently a second
edition in 1994. Cupitt's broadcasts and books led to the convening of
a conference of those sympathetic with his approach in 1988. In 1989
a second conference agreed to meet annually under the name of 'the
Sea of Faith Network'.

The official membership application for 1993–4 sums up the key
point in its statement: 'Cupitt ... offered a vision for the future of
religious faith as entirely human, centred in spiritual and ethical activity.'
The Network not only 'explores' but also, more assertively, seeks 'to
promote religious faith as a human creation' (their italics).[2] In addition
to the main central annual conference, some twenty regional and local
support groups in Britain also meet more frequently.

The view of religion as a human creation, in which 'God' is subsumed
within human consciousness as a projection of value, finds further
explication in the Notes for Newcomers prepared for the third 'Sea of

---

[1] The poem by Matthew Arnold is quoted in full in Don Cupitt, *The Sea of Faith*
(London: BBC, 1984), 21; cf. also 7–12, 22–35.
[2] *Sea of Faith Application Network Form* 1993/4 from R. Pearse, Hon. Secretary,
Loughborough.

Faith' conference in 1990. One of the Network's major pioneers, David A. Hart, quotes an extract as a good definition of the 'non-realism' which he promotes in his book *Faith in Doubt: Non-realism and Christian Belief*. This is 'the view that there is nothing beyond or outside human beings, neither God nor some other notion like "Ultimate Reality" that gives life and meaning and purpose. We do that for ourselves!'[3]

Many (though not all) of the Sea of Faith Network are clergy. The issue of how such a view cohered with their ordination vows was raised in a broadcast on Easter Day in 1992. David Hart observes that as a result of this broadcast membership of the Network doubled over the remainder of the year.[4] It has apparently escaped notice, however, that by 1989 (indeed since 1986) Cupitt attacks his targets on quite different ground, namely in the name of postmodern views of language.

How serious and how unequivocal, then, is the declaration that faith, even God, is 'a human creation'? Anthony Freeman's book *God in Us. A Case for Christian Humanism* leaves us in little doubt. He examines the passage about idolatry in Isaiah 44:14–17. The biblical writer depicts a person who 'plants a cedar and the rain nourishes it. Then it becomes fuel for a man; he takes a part of it and warms himself . . . And the rest he makes into a god, his idol; and falls down to it and worships it; he prays to it and says, "Deliver me, for thou art my god!"'. But Freeman draws a surprising conclusion. He argues: 'The writer . . . failed to realise . . . how close his own case was to that of the pagan whom he was lampooning. The idol worshipper had constructed his idol with wood; our author made his God out of words: *that was the only difference*'.[5] Freeman suggests that the author could be lampooned by the very same logic: 'he makes a verbal image and falls down before it'.

Norman Whybray and Gerhard von Rad propose that this passage may well have been based on a satirical tract dating from as far back as Israel's early encounter with idolatry in the heathen world.[6] In terms suggested by the biblical traditions and our argument up to this point, Israel had begun to conceive of their covenant God, whose *identity* as Yahweh had begun to emerge in a series of redemptive acts and providential care, interpreted on the basis of recurring *patterns* capable of *narrative expression* within a *temporal* framework or '*plot*'.

Furthermore, to take up another of Ricoeur's points, the beginnings of a notion of an agent's commitments and responsibility, fundamental to the continuity of selfhood as active agent, became implicit in a

---

[3] David A. Hart, *Faith in Doubt: Non-realism and Christian Belief* (London: Mowbray, 1993), 7; cf. *Notes for Newcomers*, for Sea of Faith III Conference, 1990.

[4] Ibid. xiv, n. 2.

[5] Anthony Freeman, *God in Us. A Case for Christian Humanism* (London: SCM, 1993), 26 (his italics).

[6] Gerhard von Rad, *Wisdom in Israel* (Eng. London: SCM, 1972), 177–85; and R. N. Whybray, *Isaiah 40–66* (London: Oliphants (New Century), 1975), 98–9.

relationship of covenant. This entailed a logic of promise and faith-fulness.

Nevertheless, in his common subsuming of heathen idols and the God of Isaiah and the wilderness wanderings under the heading 'human construct', Freeman can find *no criterion of identity* for distinguishing between the idolatrous constructs which Isaiah 44 attacks, and the God of Israel. Both are simply 'constructs'. Hence Freeman insists: 'To ask, "Do you believe in God?" is rather like asking "How long is a piece of string?" . . . in any case I need to be rid of the idea of god in order to make room for a new one.'[7] But having discarded Isaiah's God as a mere human projection, he finds no criterion to distinguish between the 'projections' of Canaanite polytheism, covenantal biblical relationality, post-Kantian modernity, and post-Nietzschian post-modernity.

Cupitt has retained a life-long interest in Immanuel Kant (1724–1804), and Kant's philosophy features decisively in Cupitt's career as a thinker. Kant anticipated Feuerbach and Freud in interpreting 'God' as a human projection. God represents an internal objectification of what we experience as the categorical imperative of moral obligation. We interpret this sense of duty impinging upon us as divine, as some external 'command of God', when it is merely the inner conflict which paves the way for a free decision to act responsibly. Kant described the 'Enlightenment' as the age in which humankind had reached sufficient maturity to take responsibility for its own free decisions, without sheltering under the notion of 'obeying' divine commands, in the traditions of the church.

Hence Cupitt declares in his book *Taking Leave of God* (1980):

> The modern concern for the autonomy of the individual human spirit, and the closely related concern for the autonomy of purely religious values and claims, make it no longer possible for us to have quite the original prophetic experience of being summoned by an alien almighty and commanding will . . . For us God is no longer a distant person over against us.[8]

Since we should not interpret the experience of the moral imperative as a divine 'command', there cannot be any notion of 'God has spoken', of *ipse dixit*.

Cupitt explains: 'Rather, God *is* the religious requirement personified, and his attributes are a kind of projection of the main features as we experience them.'[9] But this opens the possibility, once its implications have been grasped, for the Kantian invitation to Enlightenment, adult, 'autonomy'. In these terms, Cupitt writes: 'The unconditional religious

[7] Freeman, *God in Us*, 15.
[8] Don Cupitt, *Taking Leave of God* (New York: Crossroad, and London: SCM, 1980), 85.
[9] Ibid.

requirement . . . is an autonomous inner imperative.'[10] 'I do not suppose God to be an objectified individual over and above the religious requirement.'[11]

The first few pages of *Taking Leave of God* extol the theme of 'autonomy' with reference also to Buddhism. The nineteenth-century hostility towards 'religion', Cupitt argues, was more specifically directed against *dependency* than against spiritual *values*. Freud and the Enlightenment had too hastily equated religion with 'dependency'.[12] But the equation 'is sufficiently refuted by the mention of Buddhism, which has no trace of dependency'.[13] Cupitt asks: 'What is integrity?' and answers: 'It is one's *autonomy*'.[14] Kant, he argues, succeeded in holding together a notion of moral freedom and the presupposition of 'God' not by a notion of a God of inter-personal relations but by '*internalization*' which made possible 'radical autonomy'. This entails in turn, 'the internalization of meanings and values'.[15] Cupitt agrees with Kant that talk of 'providence' has effectively lost its currency.[16] Similarly, 'spirituality' becomes a matter of 'internalized *a priori* principles, freely adopted and self-imposed', of which Buddhism offers a paradigmatic example. We may recall that Kant described prayer, in any traditional sense of the term, as 'a superstitious illusion'. For Kant 'rational' faith (*reiner Vernunftglaube*) perceived prayer as to do only with 'ourselves' while the faith of church practice (*Kirchenglaube*) too easily degenerates into fetish faith and superstitious attempts at manipulation.[17]

This precisely matches Anthony Freeman's view of the implications of his 'Christian humanism' for prayer: 'I do not actually believe there is anyone "out there" listening to me . . . I was talking to myself.'[18] In Freeman's system 'God' becomes a symbolic focus of selfhood 'useful' for a 'religious' person.[19]

Four years after the publication of *Taking Leave of God* Don Cupitt repeats his 'non-realist' version of Kantian philosophy in the conclusion to his series *The Sea of Faith*, which is added to the broadcast material as an afterword. He asserts: 'God (and this is a definition) is the sum of

---

[10] Ibid. 94.
[11] Ibid. 87.
[12] Ibid. 2.
[13] Ibid. 4.
[14] Ibid. 5 (his italics).
[15] Ibid. 6.
[16] Ibid. 9.
[17] Immanuel Kant, *Religion Within the Limits of Reason Alone* (Eng. New York: Harper & Row, 1960), 181–5; see further, Helmut Gollwitzer, *The Existence of God as Confessed by Faith* (Eng. London: SCM, 1965), 73, Vincent Brümmer, *What are We Doing When We Pray?* (London: SCM, 1984), 16–19 and R. Harries, *The Real God* (London: Mowbray, 1994), 33–7.
[18] Freeman, *God in Us*, 52.
[19] Ibid. 76.

our *values*, representing to us this ideal unity . . . mythologically . . . portrayed as an objective being because ancient thought tended to personify values.'[20] The latter comment picks up Hegel's contrast between religious 'representations' (*Vorstellungen*) and the role of 'concept' (*Begriff*) in a critical philosophy.

Within only a year, however, in his book *Only Human* (1985) Cupitt will include one or two scattered references to Jacques Derrida.[21] This will indicate that he is beginning to discover French postmodernism. *Life Lines* (1986) then contains a number of references to Derrida, passing allusions to Roland Barthes and some references to Michel Foucault.[22] Within three years, *The Long Legged Fly* (1987) then engages more fully with the implications of Derrida's radicalization of Heidegger and his critique of a 'metaphysics of presence'.[23] By this stage all talk of God as an internal symbol or focus for 'unifying' a value system, will have vanished. In French postmodernist philosophy and socio-literary theory, there *is* no 'centre' or 'unity'. Everything is shifting, as every stable meaning is 'deferred' and 'erased' in an ever-moving, never-ending flux. *There is now no 'autonomous', courageous, active self, within which 'God' can be 'internalized'.*

This brings us back, still more radically, to the earlier question about *criteria*. Cupitt's conscious turn towards Derrida, Foucault, and French postmodernism compounds this difficulty still further. For these thinkers language and meaning have neither foundation nor centre. If, as Saussure and Wittgenstein propose, language may be compared with pieces and moves in chess, then, according to Derrida, the world of language is 'a bottomless chessboard'; its play has no meaning beyond itself and it rests on nothing.[24] This is why I have replaced Cupitt's term 'sea' for my term, or rather Derrida's explicit term, 'abyss'. The metaphor 'abyss' features regularly in Derrida's work *The Truth in Painting*, while in his book *Signéponge* he 'plays' with the three words *abîme* (placement in decay), *abyme* (self-representation in heraldry) and *abîme* (placement in abyss).[25]

Chaos and confusion have become associated in the Western tradition with the story of Babel. For 'Babel' results in the narrative of Genesis 11 from two factors: first, as Bruce Vawter points out, it represents a

[20] Cupitt, *The Sea of Faith*, 269.

[21] Don Cupitt, *Only Human* (London: SCM, 1985), xii, 219, 221 (his italics).

[22] Don Cupitt, *Life Lines* (London: SCM, 1986), 116, 137, 159, 172–3, 193–7 (on Derrida); 192 (on Barthes); and 137, 142, 145, 172–6, and 183–5 (on Foucault).

[23] Don Cupitt, *The Long Legged Fly. A Theology of Language and Desire* (London: SCM, 1987), 5; cf. 5–12, 20–1, 145–9.

[24] Jacques Derrida, *Speech and Phenomena, and Other Essays on Husserl's Theory of Signs* (French, 1967) (Eng. Evanston: North Western University Press, 1973), 154.

[25] Jacques Derrida, *The Truth in Painting* (Eng. Chicago: University of Chicago Press, 1987), 16, 291–2.

religious symbol or source of powers which man *'prefers to carve out for himself'*; second, it results in the *loss of criteria to interpret* meaning other than within a sub-culture.[26]

Postmodern theories of signs and language cannot offer, and do not wish to offer, criteria for the 'right' meaning of a text. Indeed texts become 'textures' created out of which *readers* find a moving situatedness within a prior linguistic world. We *make* our meaning, just as we *make* our god. Cupitt endorses this Derridian view. In *Life Lines* (1986) he asserts: 'There is nothing outside the text.'[27] In *The Time Being* (1992) he tries to go even further, speaking of a 'post-Buddhism of the sign'.[28] Closure of meaning is 'the enemy of freedom . . . the sign moves on . . .'[29] It is time to ask how any theologian could arrive at such a position.

[26] Bruce Vawter, *On Genesis. A New Reading* (New York: Doubleday, 1970), 157–8; cf. 152–8.
[27] Cupitt, *Life Lines*, 193.
[28] Don Cupitt, *The Time Being* (London: SCM, 1992), 38.
[29] Ibid. 81.

14

Successive Stages in Cupitt's Interpretations of God

Don Cupitt was ordained to the Diocese of Manchester in 1959, and from 1966 until very recently has been Dean of Emmanuel College, Cambridge. In a succinct summary in a Foreword to Scott Cowdell's book *Atheist Priest?* Cupitt sums up his own development over the twenty years from around 1968 to 1988. The 1960s witnessed the publication of John A. T. Robinson's *Honest to God* (1963) in which his questioning of the imagery of God 'up there' seized the popular mind in Britain.[1] Although this did not influence Cupitt profoundly, nevertheless it formed the background against which he recalls of this period: 'I hoped to move from grossly inadequate to less inadequate images of God.'[2] This concern is expressed in his first major work *Christ and the Hiddenness of God* (1971).

In his teaching of the philosophy of religion at Cambridge no doubt Cupitt's wrestling with issues of religious language and especially the implications of Kant's *Critiques* made an increasing impact on his thought. His book *Crisis of Moral Authority* (1972) takes up the cudgels on behalf of 'freedom' against various forms of authority, repression and heteronomy. *The Leap of Reason* (1976) is arguably his best book. Pressing Kantian and Kierkegaardian perspectives to their limit, he recollects later: 'The trail of broken images would become an arrow pointing to the transcendent.'[3] Nevertheless, as we shall see, this book sits on a razor edge, and allows Cupitt to fall into the more problematic and questionable side with the appearance of *Taking Leave of God* (1980).

Cupitt's autobiographical reflections cohere with this diagnosis. He recalls: 'Then as objective truths began to fall away, and I decided that no dogmatic theology was possible, the arrow pointing up to heaven became, as one might say, internalized. It was an inner pathway of self-transcendence.'[4] Kant had pointed the way to a 'God' who was

---

[1] J. A. T. Robinson, *Honest to God* (London: SCM, 1963), *passim*.
[2] Don Cupitt, 'Foreword', in Scott Cowdell, *Atheist Priest? Don Cupitt and Christianity* (London: SCM, 1988), x.
[3] Cupitt, in Cowdell, loc. cit.
[4] Ibid.

simply *constitutive for* a moral imperative freely appropriated by the self, as *a priori* for moral selfhood.

In the 1980s however, even '*self*-transcendence' (his italics) became increasingly problematic for Cupitt. The 'personal' (up to around 1984) became combined with the 'variable' (from 1985 onwards). By 1985 he had begun to feel the pull of postmodern views of language. Hence in 1988 he writes: 'Finally, and most recently of all, the spiritual movement became the movement of meaning itself, endlessly spilling over sideways. "I" – the human self – became decentred.'[5]

In *What is a Story?* (1991) Cupitt looks in a very generalized way at story in literary theory. He has passing allusions to Roland Barthes and J.-F. Lyotard, but he does not engage with narrative theory at a serious level through such major seminal thinkers as Gérard Genette, Paul Ricoeur and Seymour Chatman.[6] His book *The Time Being* (1992) looks once again at 'the world of signs' as perceived by postmodern theorists as endlessly transient, shifting and on the move. Hence language about 'God' can never reach any conceptual 'closure'.

Finally, in *After All* (1994) Cupitt repeats the postmodern perception: 'language *is* transience. It slips by at such a rate that the object of our desire never fully arrives, and before it has come it is already disappearing'.[7] But he endeavours to couple this with the notion of a cycle of 'self-renewal'. Nietzsche's myth of eternal return, he argues, may perhaps allow some new reinterpreted interrelations between religious expression and scientific understandings of the world. A consideration of the universe as a torus together with notions of black holes may perhaps cohere with notions of ends-as-beginnings.[8] 'We have sided with Heraclitus . . . and Nietzsche.'[9]

Cupitt repeatedly asserts two things about his development. First, he began from orthodoxy; second, he is ever on the move. Cupitt produced twenty books (more than a book a year) over the period 1976 to 1994. We cannot help recalling that Friedrich Schelling matched this pace until Napoleon attacked the Prussian army at Schelling's home city of Jena in 1806. In his *Lectures on the Philosophy of Religion* Hegel lamented Schelling's rapid move towards subjectivism; his dissolution of 'God' into the self and nature; and his seduction by what Hegel termed 'Oriental Knowledge'.[10] Hegel tartly remarked: 'Schelling carried out his philosophical education in public. His series of writings

---

[5] Ibid.
[6] Don Cupitt, *What is a Story?* (London: SCM, 1991), 118–19 (Barthes) and 93–4 (Lyotard).
[7] Don Cupitt, *After All. Religion Without Alienation* (London: SCM, 1994), 57 (his italics).
[8] Ibid. 59.
[9] Ibid. 116.
[10] G. W. F. Hegel, *Lectures in the Philosophy of Religion* (Eng. 3 vols., London: Kegan Paul, Trench, Trubner, 1895), vol. 2, 53–4.

is at the same time the history of his philosophical education' (*zugleich Geschichte seiner philosophischen Bildung*).[11]

In an earlier draft of this section, I devoted very many pages to a careful critique of each of Cupitt's successive books. By the time I had reached the end of the whole study, it had become clear that I needed to reduce these twenty pages to about four. Hence I now offer only a brief digest of an earlier draft, selecting only those works which constitute decisive signposts for Cupitt's development.

In *Christ and the Hiddenness of God* (1971), three themes begin to emerge. First, Cupitt attacks 'objectifying theology'.[12] Negative statements about what God is *not* provide, at least in the realm of statement, 'the only safe way of speaking about God'.[13] As Tillich had forcefully argued,[14] God is not merely one 'object' among others. Since imagery risks anthropomorphism, 'the logic of God appears to be irreducibly "vague"'.[15] Second, Cupitt regards Kant as 'the principal-modern philosopher', and follows Kant's emphasis on will, as against reason, for interpreting 'God'.[16] Third, since history and faith do not intersect (other than in a very loose way) in the person of Christ, Cupitt cannot appeal to a theology of the history of Jesus for what Ian Ramsey had called in a different context 'an empirical placing' of theological language.[17]

Cupitt's essay 'One Jesus, Many Christs' (1972) develops the theme of 'hiddenness' in Christology, but not in the sense expounded by Luther or Bonhoeffer, where it is anchored in a rich theology of the cross, as decisive for the identity of God. On the contrary, as against Luther, Cupitt asserts that Jesus would not be 'troubled by being many Christs' to different interpreters.[18]

We do not have space to discuss Cupitt's book *Crisis of Moral Authority* (1972).[19] But two of its themes appear in later works: first, the notion of truth as human search rather than disclosure or discovery;

---

[11] G. W. F. Hegel, *Sämtliche Werke* (rp. Stuttgart: Frommann Verlag, 1965), vol. 19, 647. I am indebted to Colin Brown for locating the source of the German, which is more loosely translated in W. Kaufmann, *Hegel: Reinterpretation, Texts, and Commentary* (London: Wiedenfeld & Nicolson, 1966), 179.

[12] Don Cupitt, *Christ and the Hiddenness of God* (London: Lutterworth Press, 1971), 19.

[13] Ibid. 21.

[14] Ibid. 23; cf. Paul Tillich, *Systematic Theology* (3 vols., London: Nisbet, 1953–64), vol. 1, 227.

[15] Cupitt, *Christ and the Hiddenness of God*, 28.

[16] Ibid. 19; cf. 62–3, 99, 191–2.

[17] Ibid. 96–137, 154–67 (esp. 136, 162–5); cf. also 138–53.

[18] Don Cupitt, 'One Jesus, Many Christs', in S. W. Sykes and J. P. Clayton (eds.), *Christ Faith and History: Cambridge Studies in Christology* (Cambridge: Cambridge University Press, 1972), 143. Cf. Cupitt, *Christ and the Hiddenness of God*, 213.

[19] Don Cupitt, *Crisis of Moral Authority. The Dethronement of Christianity* (London: SCM, 1972, 2nd edn. 1985).

and second, a harsh polarization between 'repressive' tendencies in monotheism, and the emancipatory critiques of Kant and Hegel. The twin ghosts of generalization and polarization begin to haunt his rhetoric. We shall see in Part IV how disastrous is his neglect of God as Trinity, with all of its implications for non-authoritarian, non-manipulative, love which Moltmann in particular expounds with great force and relevance.

The Leap of Reason (1976) becomes a watershed in Cupitt's thought. It is more carefully written than most of his other works. He makes much of the notion of *interpretation*, and, had he grounded his work in rigorous hermeneutical theory, his conclusions might have been different. For Cupitt, interpretation entails 'social constructivism' or, in summary, the view that we bring with us and indeed *create* an *interpretative frame*. The difference between *creating* (Fichte) and *conditioning* (Kant) data becomes confused and blurred. It is a great pity that he utilizes the *earlier* work of T. S. Kuhn in the first edition of *The Structure of Scientific Revolutions* (1962), for already in the second edition of 1970 (available to Cupitt at the time) Kuhn began to modify his views about social construction in the sciences and was to modify them more radically still in his later work *The Essential Tension* (1977).[20]

At the heart of the book lies a parable. Cupitt modifies Plato's allegory of the cave.[21] Unlike Plato, for whom shadows play on the wall of the cave, Cupitt asks us to imagine a cave which has no opening. Inside the cave the 'world' within the cave represents a self-regulating system. There is no *reason* to think that any other 'world' exists outside it. Hence there is no logical grammar to speak of being 'inside' rather than 'outside' the cave. Yet a prisoner within the cave one day speculates that there *could* be an 'outside', or a 'beyond'. This constitutes a 'leap of reason': 'The act of by which the prisoner thinks "outside" might be represented as a passage from sleep to waking, from bondage to freedom, darkness to light.'[22] Yet this glimpse of new possibility has not entailed any fresh information. The prisoner is sure to have doubts. But discontent, aspiration, and hope have stirred: 'beyond' may be a fuller, wider, world. Cupitt comments: 'When I speak of spirituality, I mean the capacity in man for a "leap of reason" of the kind which figures in the parable.'[23]

Each system of interpretative framework, Cupitt continues, has its own internal criteria of meaning and truth.[24] We cannot make a sharp distinction between 'the sheerly given and the construction [*sic*] which

[20] Don Cupitt, *The Leap of Reason* (London: SCM, 1976, 2nd edn. 1985), 13; cf. 22–6.
[21] Ibid. 27–37.
[22] Ibid. 32.
[23] Ibid. 37.
[24] Ibid. 93.

we place upon it'.[25] Hermeneutical understanding amounts to 'a programme', namely 'a complex interpretative framework' by which we 'put a construction upon' our experience.[26] But each hermeneutic must be undermined: 'it would be spiritually yet another prison [i.e. like the cave] if it did not contain within itself an iconoclastic or autodestructive principle'.[27]

Three strengths characterize *The Leap of Reason*. First, Cupitt makes positive use of certain themes in Kierkegaard, although curiously alludes to Kierkegaard's notion of 'leap' in relatively minor works rather than in the context of Kierkegaard's major discussion.[28] He also takes up the role of irony, the comic, indirect communication, and 'stages' on life's way.[29] With Kierkegaard he stresses the 'how' of subjectivity rather than the 'what' of a detached objectivity.[30] Second, he rightly stresses the role of interpretation, as against purely deductive or inductive reasoning in matters of faith. Third, he develops the insight which we associate with Tillich, namely that Christ 'points away' beyond himself to the God who 'sent' him, just as the Spirit and the church point beyond themselves to Christ, or to God.

Nevertheless there are fundamental weaknesses. First, the notion, for example, that every 'interpretation' must be undermined or 'deconstructed' by another owes more to Nietzsche (who will shortly enter most of Cupitt's writings but seems to be absent here) than to Kierkegaard or to Kant. Indeed in a brilliant study based on a close knowledge of the original Danish of all of Kierkegaard's writings, my Nottingham colleague Roger Poole, Reader in Literary Theory, demonstrates that while the 'aesthetic' writings of Kierkegaard (mainly from 1843 to 1846) genuinely invite deconstruction without closure, it is otherwise with Kierkegaard's 'religious' writings.[31] Here, again, Cupitt is haunted by the ghost of generalization.

Second, Cupitt's parable of the cave remains, as he would admit, only one exploratory model among many other possible models. At the same time much of the argument depends on giving particular privilege to this model as one which describes by analogy issues of faith and unfaith. Third, Cupitt jumps too readily from a social and

---

[25] Ibid. 94.

[26] Ibid. 95.

[27] Ibid. 96.

[28] Ibid. mainly only 35–6, where Cupitt selects *The Sickness unto Death*, as against S. Kierkegaard, *Philosophical Fragments* (Kierkegaard's writings VII) (Eng. Princeton: Princeton University Press, 1985), 43, 138, 191; cf. further 324–5.

[29] S. Kierkegaard, *The Point of View in my Work as an Author* (Eng. Princeton and New York: Princeton University Press, 1941 rp. 1962), 22–43; and more fully in *Stages on Life's Way* (Eng. Princeton: Princeton University Press, 1945).

[30] S. Kierkegaard, *Concluding Unscientific Postscript to the Philosophical Fragments* (Eng. Princeton: Princeton University Press, 1941), 51, 181.

[31] Roger Poole, *Kierkegaard. The Indirect Communication* (Charlottesville and London: University Press of Virginia, 1993), esp. 26, 262–87, *et passim*.

empirical observation about pluralism to a hermeneutical claim that each frame of interpretation 'has its own *internal* criteria of meaning and truth'.[32] This leads on to the kind of contextual pragmatism advocated by Rorty which I have rejected in Part I of this study and subjected to rigorous criticism in *New Horizons in Hermeneutics*.[33]

Finally, J. Brown rightly observes that 'subjectivity' in Kierkegaard has little or nothing to do with what Cupitt will later call 'internalization', and Brown calls 'grubbing about in the depths of one's particular psyche'.[34] Kierkegaard does indeed stress active decision, but his notion of 'obedience' is far removed from 'autonomy'. In terms of our previous section, as against *Taking Leave of God* he is all too aware of relationality with an 'Other' who is infinitely beyond the human self, and invites worship.[35] Kierkegaard stands at an infinite distance from Cupitt's positive evaluation of Buddhism and its virtues for Christian spirituality.[36]

Cupitt develops the theme of the use of 'irony, humour, and stories to awaken perception' in his essays on Jesus in his *Explorations in Theology 6* (1979).[37] In his essay 'The Original Jesus' (1976) he prunes away later dogmatic portraits.[38] In 'Myth Understood' (1978) Cupitt observes concerning the term 'Son of God': Jesus 'did not utter oracles about himself, but used language as a tool for revealing the coming and the claims of one other than himself'.[39] Thus while Cupitt's view of will, subjectivity, and the hiddenness of God in *The Leap of Reason* prepares us for the possibility (although not the necessity) of *Taking Leave of God* (1980), the role of his Christology in this development is puzzling. For if God is to be 'internalized' in selfhood in what sense does Christ point 'beyond' a self which is the model of all human selfhood? To what does Christ point, if he points away from *himself*? All this, however, constitutes only an initial preview of factors which lie behind the fuller developments expounded over the next four chapters.

---

[32] Cupitt, *The Leap of Reason*, 93; cf. 22–3.

[33] Thiselton, *New Horizons in Hermeneutics*, 393–405, 439–52, 534–50.

[34] J. Brown, *Subject and Object in Modern Theology* (London: SCM, 1955), 46; cf. 34–82.

[35] S. Kierkegaard, *The Last Years: Journals 1853–55* (Eng. London: Collins, 1965), 336.

[36] Cupitt, *The Leap of Reason*, 27–9 and 61–2 on the virtues of Buddhism.

[37] Don Cupitt, *Explorations in Theology 6* (London: SCM, 1979), 68–9.

[38] Ibid. 68; cf. 65–9.

[39] Ibid. 73; cf. 70–8. See further Don Cupitt, *The Debate about Christ* (London: SCM, 1979), 18, and 25–6 for a critique of 'incarnational' approaches.

15

'Taking Leave of God' as Internalizing, De-objectifying and Autonomy

CUPITT'S *Taking Leave of God* (1980) adopts as its point of departure the rejection of any notion of 'dependency' in religion. Within a couple of pages we have already encountered references to 'spiritual autonomy' and a wistfully positive reference to 'Buddhism which has no trace of dependency' and therefore escapes the criticisms of the Judaeo-Christian tradition put forward by Freud.[1] This 'autonomy' may be achieved by re-examining 'the great theme of internalization'.[2] Once again, the key issue is one of hermeneutics, although Cupitt neither mentions the word nor engages with the traditions of seminal thinkers. The heart of his argument may be expressed thus: '*Religious meaning ... is to be sought within rather than from above us*' (my italics).[3]

Cupitt brings together three key themes: internalization, autonomy and an inner 'spirituality' generated from within rather than imposed from without.[4] This spirituality turns out to consist in 'internalized *a priori* principles'.[5] It is not surprising that Cupitt finds a very close affinity with Buddhism. God, in the early part of the 1980s, still remains a 'unifying symbol', but this symbol can be found within: 'On our account the gap between it (Buddhism) and theism is largely closed.'[6]

Where will this take us? Cupitt writes: 'Of the great world faiths Buddhism comes closest to what I have in mind.' The content, the spirituality and values are Christian; the form is Buddhist.[7] 'Non-realist faith locates "God" within, rather than in terms of the model of inter-personal encounter with another characteristic of "prophetic experience".'[8] In the end Cupitt works round to the Kantian notion that 'God' is a projection devised from the pre-Enlightenment

[1] Cupitt, *Taking Leave of God*, 2.
[2] Ibid. 3.
[3] Ibid.
[4] Ibid. 3–6 *et passim*.
[5] Ibid. 9.
[6] Ibid.
[7] Ibid. xii.
[8] Ibid. 85.

93

internalization of the experience of a moral imperative 'over against me'. But in authentic spirituality we choose this for ourselves; we do not surrender to it as 'the will of God' externally imposed.[9]

Cupitt concludes: 'For us God is no longer a distinct person over against us who authoritatively . . . imposes the religious demand . . . If he did so present himself, we should have to reject him.'[10] Cupitt would reject him partly on the ground that sheer omnipotence does not merit worship or obedience; partly because such a God would undermine human autonomy. But he does so most decisively because language about God is perceived to be radically symbolic, instrumental and metaphorical.

On what grounds does Cupitt argue all this? In a review of *Taking Leave of God* James Mark notes that it is essentially a *statement* of Cupitt's position: 'there is no question . . . of *reasoning* to a conclusion'.[11] Mark rightly asks how Cupitt can somehow perceive his view as any kind of 'requirement' if he is genuinely serious about everyone's 'autonomy'. There is more than a hint that, within a voluntarist frame of reference, Cupitt simply wishes to say 'Well, this is what we do'. He asserts: faith 'is a matter of the will rather than the intellect'; it 'uses myth, but it also transcends it into autonomy'.[12]

Cupitt begins his observation about religious language with a 'soft sell', reminding us of John Robinson's critique of 'images' of God in *Honest to God* (1963). Robinson selected strands from Tillich, Bultmann and Bonhoeffer which provided the theological substance of his argument. Yet Tillich does not evaporate 'God' into the structures of human autonomy. Admittedly, every statement concerning God remains to Tillich 'symbolic', with the single exception of the proposition that 'God is Being-itself'.[13] But for Tillich, God is 'beyond' the God of immature pietistic or atheistic imagery, as well as the Ground for the very possibility of Being. In Tillich's view, God transcends *both autonomy and heteronomy*.[14]

Tillich quite explicitly asserts that neither the 'autonomous means' of Hegel and Schelling nor the 'radical autonomous reactions' of the post-Hegelian thinkers were any more convincing or successful than the 'heteronomous reactions' of revivalism.[15] Like Ian Ramsey, he utilizes a varied range of symbols, which thereby avoids a largely reductive account of religious language. Thus God is *both* 'above', 'within' *and* 'beyond'; he is not simply 'within'. While God is not a

[9] Ibid. 94–5.
[10] Ibid. 85.
[11] James Mark, Review in *Theology* 84 (1981), 211–13.
[12] Cupitt, *Taking Leave of God*, 126, 167.
[13] Tillich, *Systematic Theology*, vol. 1, 265.
[14] Ibid. 92–9.
[15] Ibid. 95.

'person' in the anthropomorphic sense of the term, nevertheless Tillich insists that God is 'not less than a person'.[16]

Tillich may lead part of the way towards 'de-objectifying' God as an object of conceptual thought; but he does not go all the way exhaustively. Neither does Tillich's 'internalizing' of God preclude other qualifying or modifying symbols in Ian Ramsey's sense of 'models and qualifiers'.[17]

Cupitt's interpretation of Rudolf Bultmann's hermeneutics serves his own objectives more directly. He addresses Bultmann's programme of de-objectifying and demythologizing in chapters 3 and 4 of his book.[18] Cupitt's utilization of Bultmann weaves together three distinct strands. First, with an arguable plausibility he seeks to extend Bultmann's hermeneutics to include an expressive or instrumental interpretation of God-language. Second, he allies with this his notion of 'God' as human projection drawn from Kant, Feuerbach and Freud. Finally, he attempts to give a privileged position to notions of 'autonomy', of pluralistic contextualism, and of a 'Buddhist' mode of perception. To weld these three into one Cupitt has to merge hermeneutics (theories of understanding) or theories of knowledge with truth-claims about the nature of reality. It is no accident that Don Cupitt and Anthony Freeman import the *functionalism* which they enjoyed using in their earlier *scientific* pursuits into theories of *truth in the humanities and in theology.*

Just as he began with a 'soft sell' through Robinson, Cupitt initially places Schleiermacher in his shop window. Schleiermacher, as we have noted, viewed doctrine as derivative from experience. He declared: '*Doctrines are accounts of the Christian religious affections set forth in speech*' (his italics).[19] But this does not mean subjectivism. Virtually all contemporary Schleiermacher specialists have expressed reservations about the older translation of '*schlecthin abhängig*' as a human '*feeling of absolute dependence*' on God. Rather, they believe, Schleiermacher wanted to say that the heart of religious experience was in '*a sense of being utterly dependent*' on God.[20]

---

[16] Ibid. 271.

[17] We have discussed above Ian T. Ramsey, *Religious Language* (London: SCM, 1957); cf. also Jerry H. Gill, *Ian Ramsey: To Speak Responsibly of God* (London: Allen & Unwin, 1976), 87–105.

[18] Cupitt, *Taking Leave of God*, 34–55.

[19] F. D. E. Schleiermacher, *The Christian Faith* (Eng. Edinburgh: T&T Clark, rp. 1989 [from the 2nd German edition]), sect. 15, 76; cf. I.4, sects. 15–19, 76–93.

[20] Schleiermacher, *The Christian Faith*, 12 (sect. 4:1; cf. 5:1). Cf. among others, B. A. Gerrish, 'Friedrich Schleiermacher', in Ninian Smart, J. Clayton, P. Sherry and S. T. Katz (eds.), *Nineteenth Century Religious Thought in the West*, vol. 1 (Cambridge: Cambridge University Press, 1988 (1985)), 123–56; John Macquarrie, *Studies in Christian Existentialism* (London: 1965), 31–5; Richard Niebuhr, *Schleiermacher on Christ and Religion* (London: SCM, 1964), 128, 144–6. The older view is represented by H. R. Mackintosh and Rudolf Otto, while an ambivalent account occurs in Richard B. Brandt, *The Philosophy of Schleiermacher* (New York: Harper, 1941), 175–99, 258–98. Brandt finds 'equivocation' in *The Christian Faith* on this issue.

Here, however, is the very reverse of Cupitt's 'autonomy'. Schleiermacher presents an ontology of immediacy, but it remains a truth-claim about a relationship, not merely a psychological analysis of consciousness for which Christian doctrine serves as mere self-expression. The conscious shift from the less-guarded Romanticism of the *Speeches* (1799) to the more carefully formulated theology of *The Christian Faith* (1821) and his *Hermeneutics* (mainly 1809–10 and 1826–33) underlines this. Consciousness of self and consciousness of Other, as we have seen, remain bipolar (German, *Duplizität*). 'God' is more than the irreducible individuality (*Eigentümlichkeit*) of the self coming to expression. As B. A. Gerrish observes: 'All of our "self- activity" comes from somewhere else.'[21] Those sentences which appear to equate 'the deity' with what is 'immediately present in the feeling' come from the early *Speeches* of 1799, which Schleiermacher later consciously modified in a more 'orthodox' direction.

At first sight, Cupitt appears to move onto more sympathetic ground for his own purposes when he moves from Schleiermacher to Bultmann. Perhaps for the first time in his writings, he spends three pages explicitly on hermeneutics. This is not, however, because he wishes to disentangle hermeneutical modes of understanding from positivist ones. He tends to operate with a less subtle polarity between 'cognitive-objective' and 'expressive-subjective'. I have tried to show how disastrously inadequate this contrast is for many purposes in my discussion of feminist hermeneutics.[22] Cupitt appeals to the terms to distinguish 'descriptive' exegesis from 'modern appropriation' of biblical texts.

It appears that in 1980 Cupitt still has a fairly innocent view of value-neutral exegesis which he must implicitly reject in 1985–6 when he enters his postmodern period. However, his purpose here is to disengage a supposedly exegetical conclusion that the New Testament writers believed in supernatural providence and the interventions of angels and demons, from a view supposedly validated by hermeneutics that for modern readers such language functions without remainder existentially or expressively.[23]

Oddly, Cupitt thinks that Bultmann failed to perceive that this was a linguistic problem, not a problem about differing truth-claims. But Bultmann fully appreciates that language frustrates and impedes the true 'intention' of the New Testament writers. Both Cupitt and Bultmann, for example, view language about creation or about the last judgement not as language describing past or future events as 'facts', but as a call to an admission of human creatureliness, stewardship and

---

[21] Gerrish, loc. cit. 137.
[22] Thiselton, *New Horizons in Hermeneutics*, 450–1; cf. 430–70.
[23] Cupitt, *Taking Leave of God*, 43; cf. 43–5.

responsibility.[24] Hans Jonas had given Bultmann a decisive clue by suggesting that the bizarre cosmology of second-century gnosticism was not understood even by the gnostics as descriptive language about planets and planetary guardians, but as a language of salvation relating to present knowledge or action.[25]

Some of this (although not all of it) is constructive. It is indeed the case that 'the point' of much creation language is not primarily to satisfy historical curiosity about archetypal events. Much eschatology has more to do with a present call to responsibility and hope than with providing a celestial time-chart analogous with a map of the London underground system on which is stamped 'You are standing here'. But is the point *wholly and exclusively* this? Is it to be interpreted 'internally' or 'as subjective appropriation' *exhaustively and without remainder*?

---

[24] Rudolf Bultmann, 'Reply', in Charles W. Kegley (ed.), *The Theology of Rudolf Bultmann* (London: SCM, 1966), 263–8 (replies to Heinrich Ott and Paul S. Minear); and Cupitt, *Taking Leave of God*, 55.
[25] Argued carefully in James M. Robinson, 'The Pre-History of Demythologisation', in *Interpretation* 20 (1966), 65–77; and R. A. Johnson, *The Origins of Demythologising* (London: Brill, 1974), 116–23, 170–6, 240–54.

16

Rehearsing an Over-played Script: 'Facts', World-Views and Divine Agency

LINGUIST after linguist has lamented Karl Bühler's influence in polarizing and separating cognitive, emotive and volitional language as if each operated independently of the other, rather than multi-functionally.[1] Sometimes, furthermore, these categories sub-serve more basic or primitive distinctions between propositional *content* and illocutionary or perlocutionary *force*. Donald Evans' early applications of J. L. Austin's linguistic philosophy to language about creation in the biblical writings makes this abundantly clear. There are parallels with N. T. Wright's critique of certain 'functional' assumptions in more radical form criticism, and in my own work I have drawn on J. Searle and F. Recanati. For much behavioural, expressive, or performative language to *operate efficaciously, certain states of affairs* must be true.[2]

This renders utterly irrelevant Cupitt's logically questionable discussion about whether New Testament writers in a pre-scientific age were capable of recognizing facts conceptually as 'facts'. He does his best to press an impossible case by offering a definition of 'fact' so modern as to be almost excluded by definition. Cupitt writes: 'We use the word "fact" of descriptive propositions whose truth is testable in ways independent of local cultural beliefs, human wishes, and so on. Our concept of a fact is the concept of a truth which is religiously and morally neutral.'[3] By 1986 Cupitt will begin to doubt not simply

[1] Karl Bühler, *Sprachtheorie. Die Darstellungsfunkton der Sprache* (Jena: Fischer, 1934), cf. J. Habermas, *The Theory of Communicative Action* (Eng. 2 vols., Cambridge: Polity Press, 1984), vol. 1, 274–9.

[2] John L. Austin, *How to Do Things with Words* (Oxford: Clarendon Press, 1962, 2nd. edn. 1975), 45; Donald D. Evans, *The Logic of Self-Involvement* (London: SCM, 1963); John R. Searle, *Speech Acts. An Essay in the Philosophy of Language* (Cambridge: Cambridge University Press, 1969), and *Expression and Meaning. Studies in the Theory of Speech Acts* (Cambridge: Cambridge University Press, 1979); Thiselton, *New Horizons in Hermeneutics*, 272–312; and further, A. C. Thiselton, 'Christology in Luke. Speech-Act Theory, and the Problem of Dualism in Christology after Kant', in Joel B. Green and M. Turner (eds.), *Jesus of Nazareth. Lord and Christ* (Grand Rapids: Eerdmans, and Carlisle: Paternoster Press, 1994), 453–72. Cf. further, N. T. Wright, *The New Testament and the People of God* (Minneapolis: Fortress, 1992), esp. 418–35; cf. 435–43.

[3] Cupitt, *Taking Leave of God*, 44.

whether *the New Testament writers* could conceive of 'facts' in this way, but indeed whether *anyone* can. For postmodernists construct *all* language and truth-claims within a contextually relative language-world.

Let us suppose that he wishes to stay with his argument in 1980. Whether or not biblical writers are aware of what constitutes a 'fact', certain expressive or behavioural utterances *presuppose* 'facts' by their very force or logic. It is absurd to suggest that if I say (as an expressive utterance) 'I bid you welcome', this remains unconnected with any 'fact' about whether or not you have actually arrived. Whether I *conceive* of this *as* a 'fact' remains irrelevant to its *extra-linguistic* status as a fact.

Bultmann and Cupitt ignore this dimension in 'interpreting' language about (for example) the last judgement and the creation. Does such language call me to responsibility if I am told that it does not matter whether what *seems* to be said all turns out to be a bluff? Cupitt and Bultmann both speak repeatedly about coming to the end of self-assertion in experiencing the cross, and 'rising' to new beginnings. But J. Macquarrie asks: 'Does it . . . make sense to talk of "dying and rising with Christ" without an assurance that, in some sense, Christ actually died and rose . . . Can we be assured that the possibility is a genuine one unless we see it actually exemplified under the conditions of historical existence in the world?'[4]

Two other components loom large in Cupitt's attempt at a hermeneutics of de-objectification. One is his attempt to equate a 'modern world-view' with a conceptual frame of neo-positivism in which there is no room for any 'new' or providential event. Such 'events', Cupitt argues, spring only from the propensity of religious people to see ordinary events *as* events of this kind. In other words, we return to a Kantian schema in which the natural world remains a domain of 'laws' and 'natural facts', while 'values' are projected out into the noumenal world. Especially in his *Critique of Judgement* Kant regarded the mind itself as a pseudo-source for 'reading' such events as notions of divine providence 'into' a positivistic universe, while simultaneously arguing that belief must be based on 'facts'.[5]

In 1941 Bultmann could speak of the supposed incompatibility between notions of divine agency in the world and the use of aspirin or the radio, along neo-Kantian lines. He wrote: 'It is impossible to use electric light and the wireless and to avail ourselves of modern medical and surgical discoveries, and at the same time to believe in the New Testament world of spirits and

---

[4] J. Macquarrie, 'Philosophy and Theology in Bultmann's Thought', in Kegley (ed.), *The Theology of Rudolf Bultmann*, 141.

[5] Immanuel Kant, *Critique of Judgement* (Eng. London and New York: Collier MacMillan and Hafner Press, 1951), esp. Part II, sects. 88–91, 304–39.

miracles.'[6] Macquarrie felt able to comment in 1955: 'He is still obsessed with a pseudo-scientific view of a closed universe which was popular half a century ago.'[7]

We do not wish to labour Macquarrie's point, but Cupitt repeatedly follows Bultmann's world-view in this context. Yet numerous writers share Macquarrie's critique. A. Boyce Gibson considers the problem from the standpoint of a full-blooded empiricist critique such as that of David Hume. Under Hume's terms of approach, he notes, natural 'laws constitute *by definition* no more than "progress reports" if Hume is serious in basing all knowledge on experience alone'.[8] It becomes a very different matter if empiricism is transposed into naturalism or positivism as a philosophical *doctrine*. In this case, any 'new' event such as the resurrection or a miracle is excluded *a priori*. Nothing 'new' can happen for the first time (for example, the resurrection of Jesus Christ).[9] Hume remains faithful to the issue of probability not possibility.

Wolfhart Pannenberg takes up the theme of 'newness' in experience and in history. Christian eschatology, he holds, must leave room for novelty in life, as futurity and promise come to shape the present through God's agency. Ancient myth worked in cyclic principle within an effectively closed system. Indeed Cupitt appeals to Nietzsche's notion of 'eternal return', or 'eternal recurrence'.[10] But this is incompatible with a Christian theology of history, hope and promise. Pannenberg declares that a notion of divine agency in the world is 'fundamental to every religious understanding of the world . . . Neither belief in demons nor the "three storey" world of primitive Christianity is specifically mythical.'[11] 'What is historically unique is as far as anything possibly can be from myth which expresses what is archetypal.'[12]

In *A Gospel Without Myth? Bultmann's Challenge to the Preacher* (1960), David Cairns distinguishes carefully between mechanical and teleological causation, and demonstrates additionally that there is a strong link between Bultmann's historical scepticism about the gospels, his theological 'flight from history', and his theological dualism between law and nature on one side and freedom and

[6] R. Bultmann, 'New Testament and Mythology', in Hans-Werner Bartsch (ed.), *Kerygma and Myth*, vol. 1 (London: SPCK, 1964), 5.

[7] J. Macquarrie, *An Existentialist Theology* (London: SCM, 1955, 168) (rp. Harmondsworth: Penguin, 1965, 158).

[8] A. Boyce Gibson, *Theism and Empiricism* (London: SCM, 1970), 268.

[9] Ibid.

[10] F. Nietzsche, *Works*, vol. 16: *The Antichrist*, 237–58; cf. Cupitt, *After All*, 56–61.

[11] Pannenberg, *Basic Questions in Theology*, vol. 3, 14, 67, cf. 1–17; and also his *Theology and the Philosophy of Science* (Philadelphia: Westminster Press, 1976), 43–71 *et passim*.

[12] Pannenberg, *Basic Questions in Theology*, vol. 3, 71.

grace on the other.[13] In his judicious book *Bultmann* (1992), David Fergusson writes:

> The scientist does not make the assumption that God cannot intervene in the course of nature. The only assumption the scientist makes is that, in the search for the natural explanation of types of event, considerations of divine intervention are largely irrelevant. This resembles more a working assumption about the proper domain of natural science than a philosophical conviction about the impossibility of miracles.[14]

Fergusson helpfully adds: 'Bultmann's tendency to overlook this reflects his rather Kantian isolation of the self from the social and natural world.'[15] He rightly observes that in mainstream Christian theology God is perceived to act through observable events and that Bultmann's own account of the kerygma presupposes that 'the God who addresses and encounters us in Jesus of Nazareth must be capable of acting *upon* history rather than merely *within* it'.[16]

To be sure, certain writers propose counter-arguments which would support Bultmann. Schubert Ogden and Walter Schmithals are probably among the best known.[17] We could cite numerous authors who adopt the criticisms of Cairns, Macquarrie and Fergusson.[18] However, the issue at stake is Cupitt's apparent indifference to the whole detailed debate. He never troubles to take seriously either the literature in English or the huge detailed discussions in a multiplicity of essays in the six-volume German original *Kerygma und Mythos*.[19]

This absence becomes even more conspicuous when we turn to the second issue. Cupitt attempts to extend this programme of de-objectification not only to the events of salvation, or even to Christology, *but to God himself*. Yet once again, in the essays in *Kerygma und Mythos* this issue is widely debated. In particular Karl Jaspers, Fritz Buri and Herbert Braun become major contenders in this area. Buri, for example, writes at length in the German volumes under a title which may be translated 'Demythologizing or De-kerygmatizing Theology'. Buri suggests that Bultmann retains, in still talking of God as a personal Being, 'a remnant of illogically retained

---

[13] David Cairns, *A Gospel Without Myth? Bultmann's Challenge to the Preacher* (London: SCM, 1960), 123–4, cf. 112–35; 136–63, esp. 140.
[14] David Fergusson, *Bultmann* (London: Chapman, 1992), 122.
[15] Ibid.
[16] Ibid. 123.
[17] S. M. Ogden, *Christ Without Myth* (London: Collins, 1962), 38–50; W. Schmithals, *An Introduction to the Theology of Rudolf Bultmann* (Eng. London: SCM, 1968), 153–4.
[18] For example, A. Malet and L. Malevez; cf. Thiselton, *The Two Horizons*, esp. 252–92; cf. 205–51.
[19] H. W. Barstch (ed.), *Kerygma und Mythos. Ein Theologisches Gespräch* (6 vols. with supplements, Hamburg: Reich & Heidrich, 1948 onwards).

mythology'.[20] 'God' becomes only the 'discovery of a general human potentiality'.[21] Myths of deity are merely modes or devices of 'self-understanding' (*Selbstverständnis*).[22]

Herbert Braun maintains that truth concerning God becomes valid in so far as it becomes anthropology.[23] The New Testament message could be described without using the word 'God', in its de-objectifying form.[24] Braun aims to transcend both 'atheism' which appears to him to be 'trivial', and 'theism' which appears 'colourless'.[25] The New Testament, he claims, implies a 'non-objective God'.[26]

Helmut Gollwitzer criticizes Braun in terms which equally apply to Cupitt. But he is another writer in whom Cupitt appears to show no interest. Gollwitzer observes:

> Braun thinks in terms of the following alternatives: 'God as thinglike and given, and God as not thinglike and given', so that there corresponds the antithesis: on the one side sits 'the naive idea of God' that belongs to what is for us a 'vanished apocalyptic picture of the world' . . . and on the other side 'we today'.[27]

He continues: 'Another corresponding antithesis is: "theonomy as heteronomy" and "theonomy as autonomy".'[28] Gollwitzer wrote all this in 1964 (English, 1965) sixteen years before Cupitt's 'new' approach. Yet Cupitt never even addresses the well-worn debate, thereby failing to anticipate standard criticisms of what he proposes as 'radical'.

Gollwitzer rightly points out that Braun's argument turns on *hermeneutics*. We come to understand God *as God* not when we engage in abstract discussions *about* him ('theism') but when God addresses and encounters us in ways which *involve, challenge and transform* the self, or at very least when we use self-involving logic. As Luther and Calvin both stressed, first, knowledge of God and understanding ourselves remain bound up together; second, the word of God achieves its sharpest edge when it confronts us 'as our adversary', not as neutral enquirers.[29]

---

[20] Fritz Buri, 'Entmythologisierung oder Entkerygmatisierung der Theologie', in Barstch (ed.), *Kerygma und Mythos*, vol. 2 (1952), 92.
[21] Ibid. 96.
[22] Ibid. 92–6.
[23] Herbert Braun, *Gesammelte Studien zum Neuen Testament und seiner Umwelt* (Tübingen: Mohr, 1962), 298.
[24] Ibid. 297; see further Barstch (ed.), *Kerygma und Mythos*, vol. 3, 166–8.
[25] Braun, *Gesammelte Studien*, 298.
[26] Ibid. 340.
[27] Helmut Gollwitzer, *The Existence of God as Confessed by Faith* (Eng. London: SCM, 1965), 82–3.
[28] Ibid.; Gollwitzer alludes especially to Braun's lecture, 'The Problems of a Theology of the New Testament', in *Gesammelte Studien*, 324–41; here especially, 332–7.
[29] John Calvin, *Institutes of the Christian Religion* (Eng. Edinburgh: T&T Clark, 1937), vol. I: 1:iii (p. 39).

Yet Cupitt treats the issue as if a hermeneutic of self-involvement entails a 'non-realist' or 'non-objective' view of God. Here Don Cupitt and Herbert Braun again confuse a theory of knowledge with a theory of reality. To propose that we come to *understand* God through a reshaping of selfhood is utterly different from interpreting the *reality* of God as the *reality* of human selfhood *exhaustively and without remainder*. The project of 'de-objectification' constructively recovers 'the point' of much biblical and Christian language; but it does not offer a comprehensive account of the *whole* point.

The logic of such reductionism is pursued by Gollwitzer. 'There is no authoritative proclamation of the being and will of God', as Braun [and Cupitt] readily concede. 'God' becomes an 'expression' of what *we* find convincing or helpful.[30] What, Gollwitzer asks, now becomes of the logic of 'trust'? He writes: 'Trust in what? Not in a fixed point, not in anything that confronts me, but in the event from which I already live . . . Are not all doctrines, including "God" . . . merely "ciphers" which we use to promise these possibilities . . . to each other?'[31] 'When decoded, the Gospel means a specific human state – and nothing but that.'[32] On this basis no gospel remains.

[30] Gollwitzer, *The Existence of God*, 85.
[31] Ibid. 88.
[32] Ibid. 89.

17

'God's Second Death' in the Postmodern Self: An 'Internalized' God Now?

UP to 1984, with the publication of his book *The Sea of Faith*, Cupitt had stressed in his 'middle' period (*c.* 1976–84) the themes of the 'internalizing' of God and the autonomy of the active human self. Given the self of modernity, it is understandable, even if it is not convincing, to follow Kant and especially Feuerbach in claiming that the traditional faith of the Christian church somehow diminished the humanity of the heroic nineteenth-century self. With the success of the natural sciences and the supposed success of social sciences yet to come, one might conceive of the mature human self 'come of age', released from its bonds of immature dependency on the pre-modern God 'out there'.

After 1985–6, however, Don Cupitt began, as we have noted, to make increasing reference to Derrida and to Foucault, and to imbibe the climate of postmodernism. Already in *The World to Come* (1982) more serious accounts of Nietzsche begin to emerge. Cupitt concedes that 'Objectless awareness remains: the ego has lost internal structure . . . In this way passive nihilism leads to a condition of complete inner loss.'[1] By 1985 Lacan enters the picture, and we begin to wonder what room has now been left for 'autonomy'. It becomes even more difficult to find room for a God who has become identified with a self which, in postmodernism, is fast disappearing, to assume the role of a merely passive opacity within a system of signs. The phrase '*God's second death*' comes from Cupitt in *The Time Being* (1992) as well as from Nietzsche.[2]

Reinforced by Freudian psychoanalysis, postmodern understandings of selfhood perceive the self as largely a construct of the interaction between pre-conscious forces and social conventions. It is perceived as a 'de-centred' construct within the sign-system, in which signs, not selves, occupy a privileged status. 'Reality', if we may even use such a term, becomes only signs chasing signs. There is no 'self' which is of such a kind that we can speak any longer of 'internalizing' God. That proves itself to have been a blind alley, however much energy and

---

[1] Don Cupitt, *The World to Come* (London: SCM, 1982), 136–7.
[2] Cupitt, *The Time Being*, 10.

disruption was entailed in explaining it. In *The Time Being* (1992) Cupitt briefly (as so often) considers Lacan's view of the self as 'signs in motion'.[3] He writes: 'Today the self is an animal with cultural inscriptions [signs] written over its skin. Below it, there is only a *trembling of biological energies* and responses.' Cupitt comments: '*And that is what we are.*'[4]

We may recall that in the philosophy of mind and philosophy of religion, a massive debate still addresses Hume's attack on the notion of a stable continuity of selfhood. We examined Hume's approach in Part II, and considered responses which ranged from C. A. Campbell and H. Noonan to Paul Ricoeur. On grounds different from those of Hume's empiricism, postmodern writers share with Hume the rejection of any notion of a *stable* identity which determines any 'centre' of agency. *Fleeting* perceptions constitute a self entirely conditioned by temporal, social and biological processes. Thus Cupitt writes (1992): 'Religious thought has got to be not just secularized but temporalized, made . . . mobile . . . We urgently need a true religion for the fleeting moment and the stripping away of meaning.'[5]

If self has now become the postmodern self, where or how can 'God' be 'internalized', and can such a 'self' hope to share in any life beyond this world? Cupitt writes: 'Result? . . . The purging of residually-theological ways of thinking from the culture, *God's second death*'.[6]

'Eternity' now undergoes redefinition as against the more usual meaning in theology, philosophy and everyday life. The context of approach is that which Cupitt commends as 'a post-Buddhism of the sign'. This is an approach which combines the Buddhist negation of a stable differentiation between levels or between opposites with a postmodernist theory of signs as semiotic system. Cupitt sees all 'reality' as 'on the same level', and seeks to explain: 'We are developing a new style of thinking, temporal, pragmatic and horizontal.'[7] Some useful clues, he claims, come from Zen Buddhism.

'Eternity' is a *metaphor* for the Zen theme of a unity of subjectivity and objectivity in the instant of the present moment. Eternity here becomes 'a ripple . . . read as a sign . . . which can then activate other signs'.[8] Cupitt declares: 'And that's eternity. It's all eternity *can* be. An art-unity of mind and feeling in the present moment, with which one is content.'[9] The criticism that the postmodernism of the later Cupitt (1985–6 to 1994) undermines the 'modern' view of self-hood and Godhood in the 'middle' Cupitt (1976–84) seems so transparently valid as to invite the question: did Cupitt fail to perceive

[3] Ibid. 103.
[4] Ibid. (my italics).
[5] Ibid. 13, 15.
[6] Ibid. 10 (my italics).
[7] Ibid. On 'post-Buddhism of the sign', see 2, 8, 9.
[8] Ibid. 18.
[9] Ibid. 19.

this, or is he simply busily rushing on, leaving past writings to take care of themselves?

The seriousness of the question stems from the existence of the Sea of Faith Network. For while Cupitt has become muted now about 'autonomy', 'internalization', and even 'liberal integrity', many who have followed him with respect still try to hold together two incompatible sets of themes. It needs to be publicized widely that one cannot simultaneously wave the flag of 'modern' autonomy, as if the self were the heroic active agent of the late nineteenth century, *and* promote postmodern perspectives about the self as a passive product of language, history and society. *Either* one can join Kant, Feuerbach and Marx, and agree that 'theism' diminishes the heroic self; *or* one can join Foucault, Derrida and Lyotard, and call for the unmasking of truth-claims as transient power-claims. But one cannot logically be committed to both programmes simultaneously.

Cupitt sustains a questionable stance, with respect to another parallel issue. It is no accident that both Cupitt and Nietzsche see 'the end of theism' as making way for 'a new order', and that both offer a positive evaluation of Buddhism. The 'new order' theme appears in Cupitt especially in *The World to Come* (1982). In Nietzsche the declaration of the 'madman' that 'God is dead' comes, as is well known, in *The Gay Science* (1882 and 1887). But the theme is also explored in several works including *The Twilight of the Idols* (1889) and *The Antichrist* (written in 1888, but published in 1895).

When he proclaims 'the death of God', Nietzsche's 'madman' in *The Gay Science* draws two consequences: 'Must we not ourselves become gods?'; yet in view of the bewilderment of the crowd: 'I came too early.'[10] Cupitt interprets Jesus' critique of pharisaism as a critique of moralism and thereby a call to a new order. But such a construal not only conflicts with more recent 'post-Sanders' interpretations of pharisaism but also presupposes a 'modern' notion of selfhood. Cupitt's appeal to be 'free to create whatever moral reality is most fitting for it' uneasily combines, once again, the heroic modern self seeking 'autonomy' and the de-centred postmodern self.[11] For Cupitt continues in postmodern vein to claim that foundational beliefs are 'a fiction devised for the strong to justify their own self-affirmation'.[12]

Such an interpretation runs counter to the entire argument of the present study, both up to this point and in what still needs to be said. It vindicates the attention which we paid to Nietzsche and to postmodernism. Although Cupitt refers to the counter-arguments of Alasdair MacIntyre on virtue, and on a choice between Nietzsche and Aristotle, it does not seem to occur to him that appeals to 'freedom'

[10] Nietzsche, *Works*, vol. 10: *The Joyful Wisdom* [Penguin edn. *The Gay Science*], aphorism 125; and Cupitt, *The World to Come*, 42–4.

[11] Cupitt, *The World to Come*, 130.

[12] Ibid.

from theism may be no less manipulative and power-seeking than any other kind of approach in theology, religion or social theory. Indeed in his book *Radicals and the Future of the Church* (1989) Cupitt explicitly advocates that 'radicals' in the church use strategies of 'evasion' and 'deception' in order to have their way.[13]

A prominent figure in the Sea of Faith Network, David Hart, alludes to this statement 'without wishing to dissent from Cupitt's analysis'.[14] Yet the advocates of 'non-realist' religion constantly speak as if belief in God who stands in an inter-personal relationship of reciprocity with the world remains exclusively responsible for manipulative strategies which evade truth in the interests of power.

The broadcast talks later published under the title *The Sea of Faith* (1984) cannot escape the charge of using a manipulative *Tendenz* in its interpretations of some major thinkers. If one subtracts purely biographical material from the chapter on Wittgenstein, for example, Cupitt leaves less than six pages to discuss one of the most profound and complex of all thinkers. Yet whereas Wittgenstein himself resolutely refused to generalize, and consciously resisted compartmentalization, Cupitt describes him as subscribing to a number of '-isms', which he would almost certainly have disowned. The terms 'constructivist', 'voluntarist' and 'linguistic naturalism', for example, do not sit easily with this subtle thinker.[15] The assertion that 'Wittgenstein is still a non-realist in theology' implies a hermeneutic that addresses an agenda in which Wittgenstein has little concern, and only a few scattered aphorisms are cited to try to justify this claim.[16] We need only remember Wittgenstein's blistering comments about 'generality' to feel uneasy about such sweeping assertions about his views. He was emphatically less enthusiastic than Cupitt about 'the method of science'.[17] I have offered my own more detailed interpretations of Wittgenstein elsewhere.[18]

A further example from *The Sea of Faith* concerns Cupitt's exposition of Freud. Is it the case that Freud 'would show people that religion is human . . . and reveal how much of projection . . . there has been in religion'?[19] Hans Küng and Paul Ricoeur are careful to follow Freud's own admission that scientific *methods* do not necessarily amount to a scientific *world-view* on the basis of that same science.[20] As Küng acutely

[13] Don Cupitt, *Radicals and the Future of the Church* (London: SCM, 1989), 100.
[14] David Hart, *Faith in Doubt*, 76.
[15] Cupitt, *The Sea of Faith*, 222.
[16] Ibid. 224.
[17] L. Wittgenstein, *The Blue and Brown Books*, 18.
[18] Thiselton, *The Two Horizons*, 357–427, and *New Horizons in Hermeneutics*, 124–31, 323–6, 361–7, 383–8, 405–47, 584–92.
[19] Cupitt, *The Sea of Faith*, 71.
[20] Hans Küng, *Freud and the Problem of God* (New Haven: Yale University Press, 1979), esp. 15; and Paul Ricoeur, *Freud and Philosophy. An Essay on Interpretation* (Eng. New Haven, and London: Yale University Press, 1970). Ricoeur compares 'forces' in Freud's neurology (e.g. 93, 94) with 'explanation' (374) and 'world-view' (531, 543).

observes, on the basis of purely descriptive natural science, how can we say whether a theist's wish to 'project' a God who can help or affirm may more probably or necessarily constitute a manipulative wish-fulfilment than an anti-theists's vested interest in reducing 'God' to a human projection in order to escape God? Freud had little time either for his own father or for God. Does his work 'show' that religion is human? Or does it primarily confirm the biblical tradition that self-deception is at hand on all sides, including among 'the religious'? Küng insists that what the theist or anti-theist *wish* for does not itself speak either for or against whether the state of affairs which is desired is *true* to reality.

Brian Hebblethwaite rightly points out that Cupitt's 'use' of Kant, Pascal, Kierkegaard and Wittgenstein owes more to rhetoric than to fair-minded scholarship.[21] To cite a further example, we may question his evaluation of D. F. Strauss. Whether Cupitt is right is not the issue. The issue is that estimates and interpretations of Strauss diverge, and it is only fair to point this out if manipulative interpretation is to be avoided. As against Cupitt's 'assertion', my first-year undergraduates are regularly reminded how differently Strauss's thought has been assessed by F. C. Baur, J. C. O'Neill, J. Macquarrie and Karl Barth.[22]

It therefore causes disquiet when the assertion that 'God (and this is a definition) is the sum of our values' appears to be offered as a *conclusion to be drawn* from the historical survey.[23] Some might even regard this as a 'manipulative' strategy. Cupitt makes this view even more explicit in his book *Only Human* (1985). He asserts: 'We constructed all the world-views, we made all the theories . . . They depend on us, not we on them.'[24]

We have come, however, to the turning-point which we identified at the beginning of this section. All the labour of trying to demonstrate that 'God' and 'religion' are no more than a human construct had been designed in the late 1970s and early 1980s to provide – following Kant, Hegel, Feuerbach and Marx – an enhancement of human dignity and an emancipatory critique. Even for Nietzsche such a critique seemed to herald a 'new order' in which the self, in spite of its capacity for deception and petty mediocrity, could nevertheless assert an affirming 'yes' to life and to the will-to-power. But by 1985, and more especially from *Life Lines* (1986) onwards, the postmodern de-centred self begins to replace the active, heroic, self of modernity.

---

[21] Brian Hebblethwaite, *The Ocean of Truth. A Defence of Objective Theism* (Cambridge: Cambridge University Press, 1988), 43–52; cf. 58–61.
[22] Anthony C. Thiselton, 'New Testament Interpretation in Historical Perspective', in Joel B. Green (ed.), *Hearing the New Testament: Strategies for Interpretation* (Grand Rapids: Eerdmans, and Carlisle: Paternoster Press, 1995) 11–37, esp. 19–22; as against sheer assertion in Cupitt, *The Sea of Faith*, 96.
[23] Cupitt, *The Sea of Faith*, 269.
[24] Cupitt, *Only Human*, 9.

The work of the later Cupitt now undermines that of his middle period. Cupitt, to be sure, acknowledges that he changes his mind and 'moves on'. Our concern, however, is with the 'Network' of potential followers who do not seem to perceive how unstable and self-defeating his work has become, and that it cannot offer *criteria* to determine in what sense it succeeds or fails, and whether it coheres with, or contradicts, mainline Christian testimony and tradition, or even whether this matters. We need always to ask of someone who 'advocates' Cupitt's views: 'Of which Cupitt are you speaking?'

18

Pluralism or Propaganda?
The Forked Rhetoric of
Postmodern Interpretation

IN postmodernity the 'self' has now become de-privileged. The grand
narrative of the 'shift to the subject' from Descartes to Kant and
Kierkegaard has been swallowed up as a social construct of signs, which
serve only to 'clothe' biological, opaque and conflicting drives. But if
this is so, how can the story which Cupitt now tells as one self among
others deserve any more attention than anyone else's story?

In his incisive book *The Contest of Faculties* (1985), Christopher
Norris points out that postmodernist accounts of truth deconstruct any
'centre', 'foundation', 'frame', or claim to 'privilege'. For on their
own showing there is no meta-level on the basis of which truth-
claims about 'centres' or 'ranking' may be judged. That is why
Cupitt's apparently first reference to Derrida, in *Only Human* (1985),
as 'the most intellectually correct' of techniques is logically odd.[1]
'Correct' is not the kind of word Derrida uses; nor does he regard
deconstructionism as a mere 'technique'. The very word 'correct' lets
the cat out of the bag. Cupitt *is* about to give privileged status to the
'truth' of Derrida, even though 'foundations' tend to collapse – partly
in Derrida but decisively in Lyotard and Baudrillard – into
autobiographical narrative or into Baudrillard's 'simulacre' or 'self-
referring' virtual reality.

Christopher Norris puts his finger on the issue in his critique of
Richard Rorty: narrative philosophies can only claim to be 'just one
story among many'; otherwise they self-destruct. But in practice
they claim to be 'the last word ... Under cover of its liberal-
pluralist credentials, this narrative very neatly closes all exits except
the one marked "James and Dewey"'.[2] In Cupitt's case we need
only substitute the postmodern 'Derrida and Cupitt' for the pragmatist
'James and Dewey'. Norris rightly asserts that the rejection of the
meta-narrative (in Cupitt's terminology, single-level naturalism)
entails a refusal to entertain various alternative accounts: '*It is this
use of a liberal rhetoric to frame an authoritative message* which

[1] Cupitt, *Only Human*, xii.
[2] Christopher Norris, *The Contest of Faculties. Philosophy and Theory after
Deconstruction* (New York: Methuen, 1985), 159.

marks the real kinship between Rorty's pragmatism and nineteenth-century narrative forms'.[3]

Bernstein powerfully presses this critique, with Norris and Harries. How, he asks, can such writers as Rorty 'ridicule the very idea of "judicious critique", while giving privilege to their own?'[4] In correspondence, N. T. Wright has suggested an anology which is parallel to my criticism of the sign-theory of Barthes and Derrida which I proposed in *New Horizons in Hermeneutics*. The 'story' about dethroning stories is rather like A. J. Ayer's use of the principle of verification to rule out all discourse as 'emotive' or as 'non-sense' other than empirically testable or analytical propositions. But, *by sheer decision* he refused to regard the principle of verification as 'non-sense', even though it was neither empirical nor analytic.

Two or three works from the Sea of Faith Network, *and these only*, reflect a 'tolerant pluralism'. Scott Cowdell argues that *Only Human* and *Life Lines* reflect 'the apparent tolerance of a variety of religious positions'.[5] The characteristic method of Cupitt is well described in a very recent and judicious critique by Stephen Ross White. He writes concerning Cupitt's *methods*: 'First, then, he is guilty of one-sidedness in his methods of presenting arguments ... Cupitt's scornful dismissiveness is fair neither to the scriptural roots of Christianity nor to the more enlightened believers of every generation.'[6] Cupitt offers sweeping assertions, for example, about the impossibility of belief in providence, in which he unfairly loads the dice by making providence 'an "all or nothing" affair in which God either pulls every string ... or does so little as to be reducible to nothing'.[7] Given the option 'fundamentalist or deist', the reader feels obliged to follow Cupitt's way out of the problem.

Brian Hebblethwaite confirms this by making the identical claim about Cupitt's refusal to consider counter-arguments. Hebblethwaite urges that in addition to misinterpreting major thinkers, Cupitt ignores those interpreters who could have saved him from mistakes. Lonergan, Rahner, Küng, and many others are ignored (for example, on Kant and God), together with Moltmann, Pannenberg, Brümmer, Wolterstorff and many more.[8]

This is *precisely* the series of criticisms which (we noted above) Gollwitzer had already directed against Herbert Braun and F. Buri. Yet Cupitt never alludes to the established arguments, never offers a

[3] Ibid. (my italics).

[4] R. J. Bernstein, *The New Constellation* (Cambridge: Polity Press, 1991), 6; cf. R. Harries, *The Real God* (London: Mowbray, 1994), 30.

[5] Scott Cowdell, *Atheist Priest?*, 33.

[6] Stephen R. White, *Don Cupitt and the Future of Doctrine* (London: SCM, 1994), 122, 123.

[7] Ibid. 124–5.

[8] Hebblethwaite, *The Ocean of Truth*, 53–70.

scholarly account concerning balance of evidence and argument, seldom publicly consults primary literature which would undermine his case, but merely *asserts*. How can Cupitt claim that his writings represent a 'thought-experiment' when so often authoritative rhetoric replaces exploratory argument? White concludes: 'Cupitt is inclined to be carried away by his own persuasiveness to the detriment of his judgement.'[9] But 'judgement' sits ill with postmodernism. 'Rhetoric' is all that postmodernity can offer. *In theology its renunciation of a rational dialogue which can operate outside the immediate context of the speaker or writer gives birth to a new Fundamentalism.*

Cupitt perceives the 'pluralist' side in *Life Lines* (1986). He writes: 'The postmodern age is a silver-age . . . Reality becomes a beginningless, endless shimmering interplay of signs on a flat surface.'[10] All that is left is 'devised, ironical . . . the mockery of seriousness'. This may take various forms, 'teasing, malicious, ribald, boisterous, surreal, or black . . . ironical and fictional'.[11]

Life Lines is closer to the spirit of postmodernity in *method* than any of Cupitt's other works, although *The Time Being* well reflects the 'flux' of postmodern thought. He concedes that Marx, Darwin, Nietzsche and Freud 'were too keen to pass off their personal views as universal truths . . . No such legitimating myth has a privileged status.'[12] So Cupitt presents 'lines' rather than 'centres' or 'systems', and the 'bottom line' labelled 'Good Night' turns out to be Buddhism once again. This is not surprising, for in postmodernism (and now for Cupitt), *'there is no substantial individual self'*.[13] 'Postmodern theories of interpretation are decidedly [sic!] permissive.'[14]

By 1989, however, a double-forked rhetoric has emerged. One prong thrusts by *'moving on before you can catch me'*. This is the genuinely postmodern strategy. But the other prong continues to *assert* and to *accuse*. In 1989, David Edwards produced a book called *Tradition and Truth: The Challenge of the Church of England's Radical Theologians 1962–1989*. Edwards rightly attacks Cupitt's bypassing of major works of theology, philosophy and social history which offer a very different interpretation of God from his own. Cupitt is invited to reply to his critique. In part Cupitt displays the rhetorical strategy of paid-up postmodernists. He cannot engage with counter-arguments because: 'By the time they have come in, I have moved on.'[15]

[9] Stephen R. White, *Don Cupitt and the Future of Doctrine*, 127.
[10] Cupitt, *Life Lines*, 1–2.
[11] Ibid.
[12] Ibid. 10.
[13] Ibid. 198 (my italics); cf. 197–201.
[14] Ibid. 127.
[15] David Edwards, *Tradition and Truth: the Challenge of the Church of England's Radical Theologians 1962–1989* (London: Hodder & Stoughton, 1989), 83.

At the same time a questionable desire to have it both ways also emerges. Cupitt tells a 'privileged narrative'. He asserts not only that 'Non-realism *is not* an aberration'. He adds: 'The values that David Edwards still seems to cherish are to me anti-Christian and even *demonic*.' 'I *want* root-and-branch reform.'[16] But within a postmodern frame, what counts as 'aberration' or 'non-aberration' when identity of tradition has been explicitly dissolved as meta-narrative, and 'eternity' is only being content with the present moment? 'Want' is the only applicable word. To accuse another writer of a 'demonic' approach is to undermine everything in *Life Lines* (1986) and *The Time Being* (1992), at a point in time precisely mid-way between the two books. The most charitable characterization of such writing is *unstable*; but this is what postmodernists concede is unavoidable. Whether it coheres with Christian theology, with its stress on *faithfulness*, is another matter.

The problem remains, however, that Cupitt as well as other Sea of Faith writers, who include Anthony Freeman, take up *aggressively propagandist stances*. This becomes most transparent in Cupitt's book *Radicals and the Future of the Church* (1989) and to some extent in Freeman's *God in Us* (1993). Part of the agenda in *Radicals and the Future of the Church* is to attack [sic] 'liberalism' as an insipid and fuzzy half-way house which never reaches 'radicalization' as it should [sic]. 'We [i.e. radicals] see clearly that the liberal ideology is mythical and has collapsed.'[17] Cupitt asserts the generalized *doctrine*: 'The more realistic your God, the more punitive your morality.'[18]

The forked or double-pronged rhetoric of *Radicals and the Future of the Church* becomes transparent. It would be consistent with the admissions of Rorty and Fish to concede that no 'external' criteria outside communities of given interests can give rise to 'reform' in a social or moral sense. Nevertheless Cupitt calls for 'major changes'. But what look like calls for reform turn out to be power-bids. They are those which allow radicals to be 'at ease' within the church. Whichever 'side' Cupitt wishes to press, the claims of Georgia Warnke and Cornel West that social pragmatism or postmodern politics can offer *no basis or criteria for social reform* hold out only despair for others and we shall trace these social 'consequences' further in the first half of Part IV.[19] Meanwhile, this emphasis undermines the very motivation of the work from 1980 to 1984 which seemed to seek those social values which had allegedly been obscured by 'theism'.

---

[16] Ibid. 283–5 (my italics).
[17] Cupitt, *Radicals and the Future of the Church*, 167.
[18] Ibid. 168.
[19] With S. Fish, *Doing What Comes Naturally* (Oxford: Clarendon Press, 1989), 27; cf. Cornel West, 'Afterword', in J. Rajchman and C. West (eds.), *Post-Analytic Philosophy* (New York: Columba University Press, 1985), esp. 267 and *Prophetic Fragments* (Grand Rapids: Eerdmans, 1988); and Georgia Warnke, *Gadamer. Hermeneutics, Tradition and Reason* (Cambridge, Polity Press, 1987), esp. 146, 154. Significantly Warnke is a translator of Karl-Otto Apel who makes parallel points.

The clearest acknowledgement of the duality, perhaps even duplicity, of this double or forked rhetoric comes in the frank admission: 'Recent literary theory has shown that *absolute integrity . . . is a myth.*'[20] Quite apart from lumping together the theories of Derrida, Lacan, and others as 'recent literary theory-in-general', Cupitt openly utilizes this principle for a double purpose. He uses it on one side to advise radicals that 'deception', 'evasion' and other such manipulative strategies may enable them to disguise their stance as 'playing the game' in the eyes of the orthodox.[21] On the other side he universalizes the recommendation that 'the religious teacher *must* [his italics] use language manipulatively, rhetorically and deceitfully'.[22] He continues: 'We are anarchists . . . We love . . . mobility. We don't want creeds.'[23]

This stress on manipulative rhetoric as against rational argument coheres with the postmodern view held in *Life Lines* that reality is no more than 'a shimmering interplay of signs'.[24] Echoing Derrida, Cupitt urges in *The Time Being* that meaning 'slips away' as 'shifting, elusive' and incapable of 'closure'.[25] In *What is a Story?* (1991) the quest for the transcendent constitutes 'a life-enhancing mistake that we need to keep on making'.[26]

Each of the twin prongs of the forked rhetoric of postmodernity, however, renders the other less credible. We noted that in 1985 Cupitt described Derrida's theory of language as the most 'correct'.[27] In 1992 Cupitt 'knows' that humans need religion without God: 'We need – don't we know it by now – a religion without God?'[28] By 1994, after what bears all the signs of a rather hurried reading of Lacan, Cupitt not only disposes of the mind/matter problem which has occupied the best philosophical minds for centuries, but actually entitles a major and lengthy chapter 'How It Is'.[29] He can even assume a stable meaning for such a metaphysical question as whether the nature of reality is cyclical.[30] Especially in the light of all the 'shoulds' and 'musts' of *Taking Leave of God* and *Radicals and the Future of the Church*, the reader is left wondering how seriously Cupitt wishes him or her to take his developing claims.

Cupitt's relation with the Sea of Faith Network, however, leaves us in no doubt that he intends his theological radicalism to change lives and to change the church *from within*. We may consider

[20] Ibid. 106–7.
[21] Ibid. 106–16.
[22] Ibid. 111.
[23] Ibid. 112.
[24] Cupitt, *Life Lines*, 2.
[25] Cupitt, *The Time Being*, 15, 38.
[26] Cupitt, *What is a Story?*, 139.
[27] Cupitt, *Only Human*, xii.
[28] Cupitt, *The Time Being*, 81.
[29] Cupitt, *After All*, 36–92; cf. 47.
[30] Ibid. 59.

some parallel claims in the work of Anthony Freeman and David Hart.

Hart defines his own 'non-realist faith' as belief 'that language about God is really about the self'.[31] Hart and Freeman both describe this belief as 'liberating'.[32] Hart rightly perceives that such a view cannot be integrated logically within a traditional conceptual frame of theism. Radicalism cannot operate with the scissors-and-paste principle of accommodation which characterizes theological liberalism. We may refer readers to a phenomenological discussion of this issue by George Lindbeck, in a broader context.[33]

Anthony Freeman more explicitly operates with a double rhetoric. First, like Cupitt, he *asserts* rather than argues, seldom if ever engaging seriously with competing views. Yet he simultaneously and disingenuously appeals to '*pluralist' tolerance* within the church. Second, he follows postmodern fashion in *dissolving criteria of continuity* in the sea of language while at the same time insisting that his *entirely new* theology actually *accords with church tradition as its authentic heir.*

The first point needs little illustration. Freeman *asserts*: 'By developing the doctrine of the trinity the church has managed to retain its distant [sic] father-god away in heaven.'[34] He *asserts*: 'The idea of the Holy Spirit as a supernatural force . . . and the idea of God the father as a supernatural person . . . have got to go.'[35] He makes assertions about Jesus and Paul, about God as 'dictator', and numerous truth-claims which would at very least be thrown into question by the major works of Moltmann, Brümmer, Ward, Van den Brink and many others. His criterion of truth comes from his undergraduate days in natural science: 'the most *useful* theory was the one adopted'.[36] He wishes to remain a clergyman because 'I *need* the community'.[37]

Astonishingly, Freeman adds that he sees his work as 'the legitimate heir to the tradition, even on its own terms'.[38] It is quite remarkable that Freeman defends his own view that as he looks at Christian theism he feels like the little boy 'who called out that the emperor had no clothes on' by observing that this should not be regarded as discontinuous with the tradition since truth must change 'for each generation'.[39] If he cannot say in what continuity might consist, how can he say this? Moreover if part of his work seeks to argue that heirship

---

[31] David Hart, *Faith in Doubt*, 14.
[32] Ibid. 8, 46; Freeman, *God in Us*, 12, 76.
[33] George Lindbeck, *The Nature of Doctrine. Religion and Theology in a Postliberal Age* (London: SPCK, 1984).
[34] Freeman, *God in Us*, 47.
[35] Ibid. 48.
[36] Ibid. 75.
[37] Ibid. 78 (my italics).
[38] Ibid. 79.
[39] Ibid. 58, 77.

does not matter, why return to it when the area of discussion moves to that of continuity in church office? Harries comments: 'Freeman himself is open to deconstruction.'[40]

Postmodern views of language throw into question what may be thought to *count* as a *criterion* of continuity of identity. Indeed this brings us back to the substance of the second main part of our argument, especially to Paul Ricoeur's masterly book *Oneself as Another*. Ricoeur, we saw, established that mere 'sameness' and 'otherness' alone could not provide this kind of criterion. Yet Cupitt, Freeman, and others try to side-step the complexities which Ricoeur's hermeneutics of the self exposed. Once again, the arguments of each of our four main parts prove themselves to be all of a piece. We commence Part IV by reconsidering the problem that postmodernist approaches not only offer no criteria for a social programme, but even give rise to conflict, potential violence, and despair in society. The postmodern self, I shall argue, has greater realism than the illusory optimism of the self of modernity about human nature and society; but it can find hope only in the context of a theology of promise.

Yet postmodernism without promise or vision of a 'beyond' offers only what the sociologist John O'Neill calls social poverty and religious betrayal. In a recent work (1995) he declares:

> It is a conceit of postmodernists that they are charged with survival on behalf of a humanity whose gods they alone have declared dead . . . What is degenerate about much postmodern celebration is that it lacks any religious sense of space and time . . . In practice, the footings of postmodernism are sunk in fast food, information desks . . . and indifferent elevators that marry time and money to the second. The postmodern celebrants of the irreal, of the screen and its simulcra, ought to be understood as religious maniacs, or as iconoclasts breaking the gods, and not at all as sophisticates of modern science and art.[41]

---

[40] Harries, *The Real God*, 30.
[41] John O'Neill, *The Poverty of Postmodernism* (London and New York: Routledge, 1995), 197.

PART IV

POSTMODERN SELF
AND SOCIETY:
TOWARDS A THEOLOGY
OF PROMISE

19

The Collapse of the Hope of the 'Modern' Self: From Active Agency to Passive Situatedness

THE most prolific theological writer on hope, Jürgen Moltmann, has compared theologies of hope with theologies of faith and of love. Generally speaking, he writes, 'theologies of the Middle Ages were all theologies of love' while 'theologies of the Reformers . . . were decidedly theologies of faith'. But the fundamental issue of modern times 'is the question of the future' which invites theologies of hope.[1] For Moltmann this entails a critique of the present which brings about its transformation.

'Modernity', in contrast to the self-perceptions of the postmodern self, tends to be optimistic. It draws confidence from the mood of the Enlightenment when scientific method appeared to open up new possibilities for the self as active agent to carve out and to control its own destiny. Leaving behind the constraints of authority and medieval hierarchy, the self of modernity becomes, with Descartes, the starting-point for knowledge. With Kant it becomes the locus of autonomy and free decision. This mood of optimism in which the human self seems to be situated at the centre continues from the Enlightenment until perhaps around the end of the 1960s or the early 1970s.

By contrast the self of postmodernity has become *de-centred*. It no longer regards itself as active agent carving out any possibility with the aid of natural and social sciences, but as an opaque product of variable roles and performances which have been imposed upon it by the constraints of society and by its own inner drives or conflicts. Even if the sciences hypothetically make almost anything possible, no global strategy can ensure that appropriate scientific activity receives either adequate funding or more especially adequate moral or strategic guidance concerning its constructive and beneficial application. The sciences unleash vast forces, but how these are ordered now appears to depend on scientific guilds and their capacity to invite necessary economic funding.

Ranking orders of societal needs or agendas for the human self are now also more likely to be set by localized guilds, management theorists,

---

[1] J. Moltmann, *Theology Today* (Eng. London: SCM, 1988), 23.

economists, or 'Quasi-Autonomous Non-Governmental Organizations' than by the more conscious choices of the human self as agent of decision concerning its own destiny. It has become caught up in a prior agenda as a performer of pre-determined roles. The subjectivity of the self as agent in Descartes, Kant and Kierkegaard has collapsed into an imposed functionalism within a social system and a sign-system. The social situation appears to reflect the literary theory implied in the post-structuralism of Derrida. The self appears to be constituted not by consciousness and moral agency but by Heidegger's 'situatedness' (*Befindlichkeit*), 'historicality' (*Geschichtlichkeit*), or 'being-there' (*Dasein*).[2]

Can a theology of hope, or more precisely a Christian theology of promise, address the postmodern condition? The collapse of the self-hood of modernity, I propose to argue, opens the way for, and invites, such a theology. For the arguments of Feuerbach that theism positively reduces the humanness of humanity remains arguably credible only as long as the self is perceived as a primary source of moral worth, which controls its destiny. Practical atheism may remain cheerful, provided that the self is free to make its own choices, and influence its future.

In ancient Greece Epicurus could base his materialist philosophy of life on the supposed ultimacy of present experiences of pleasure or pain on the ground that the intelligence (*phronēsis*) directs choice. Practical wisdom measures pleasure against pain, choosing pains only if they lead to greater pleasures. The virtues of courage, justice and moderation ensure that while the body lives in and for the present moment, the mind projects forward possibilities as hopes, which then constitute a basis for stable patterns of meaning and action. But what happens when the self of 'the virtues' has become de-centred as a product of social and psycho-linguistic forces? Alasdair MacIntyre's well-chosen titles of his influential works from 1981 to 1990 make the point. His *After Virtue* (1981, 1985) leads on to *Whose Justice? Which Rationality?* (1988), and to *Three Rival Versions of Moral Enquiry* (1990).[3] In technical philosophical terms we face the problem of *incommensurability*, and the disastrous consequences of contextual pragmatism. What rational criteria or norms, if any, can command agreement as common measurements (*commensurable* ones) which can arbitrate between the competing truth-claims of rival social groups, or are the respective claims of each simply 'untranslatable' as what *counts* as rational or 'normal' within a competing group?

[2] M. Heidegger, *Being and Time* (Eng. Oxford: Blackwell, 1962 [1973], esp. sects. 29–31, 179–88.
[3] Alasdair MacIntyre, *After Virtue. A Study in Moral Theory* (London: Duckworth, 1981, 2nd edn. 1985); *Whose Justice? Which Rationality?* (London: Duckworth, and Notre Dame: University Press, 1988); and *Three Rival Versions of Moral Enquiry* (London: Duckworth, 1990).

Atheism, in such a situation, can no longer offer the apparent cheerfulness which marked the 'practical' or 'virtual' atheism of pre-moderns such as Epicurus, or the 'avowed atheism' (as David Berman calls it, by contrast) of Feuerbach, Marx, and other thinkers from after around the 1770s.[4] Berman follows Schopenhauer in perceiving the influence of Kant's third Critique as decisively providing a basis for 'avowed' atheism.[5] For Kant's *Critique of Judgement* ascribed order, purpose and evidence of design not to nature or to the world as it is, but to patterns read into it by the mind. Hence it no longer seemed necessary to presuppose some intelligent ground for this sense of intelligible order beyond the 'modern' self. Whereas previously it seemed irrational to ascribe order to mere chance, Kant now diagnosed 'the formal purposiveness of nature as a transcendental principle of judgement'.[6]

Within the context of Enlightenment modernity, it followed that, if this supposition were valid, an atheistic philosophy such as several 'left wing' Hegelians proposed could be more effectively 'emancipatory' or liberating for the self than even Hegel's attempt to offer an 'emancipatory' philosophy. Hegel's historical and logical dialectic presupposed that 'order' was compatible with freedom; indeed that it was necessary for freedom. His philosophy of historical reason served to underpin an explicit politics of order and structure in society, and his political philosophy carried weight in defending constitutional monarchy.[7] By contrast, many of the 'left wing' Hegelians offered very different 'emancipating' philosophies. Ludwig Feuerbach (1804–72) wished explicitly to liberate the self of modernity from 'its double bondage *to heavenly and earthly monarchy* . . . into *free, self-confident* citizens of the world' (my italics).[8]

Feuerbach anticipated Nietzsche in regarding the notion of 'God', other than in the form of a recognized human construct, as diminishing humanity, and as repressing the creativity of the self. In his Epigrams he equates Christianity with servile obedience to authority and convention. He writes: 'Christianity is now the pass into the land of the Philistines, where one can securely eat one's bread in obedience to authority.' 'What distinguishes the Christian from other honourable people? At most a pious face and parted hair.'[9] But the self of modernity need not be constrained in this fashion: 'God . . . is only smoke left

[4] David Berman, *A History of Atheism in Britain from Hobbes to Russell* (London and New York: Routledge, 1988 and 1990), 1–43, 153–89.
[5] Ibid. 27–8; cf. Schopenhauer's Appendix to his *World as Will* (1819).
[6] Immanuel Kant, *Critique of Judgement* (Eng. London and New York: Collier Macmillan and Haffner Press, 1951), 17; cf. also Part I, sect. 10, 54–72.
[7] G. W. F. Hegel, *The Philosophy of Right* (German, 1821, 2nd edn. 1833) (Eng. Oxford: Oxford University Press, 1942); on 'lordship and bondage' cf. further his *Phenomenology of Mind* (German, 1807) (Eng. London: Allen & Unwin, 1931).
[8] L. Feuerbach, *Gesammelte Werke*, vol. 6 (Berlin: Akademie Verlag, 1967), 31.
[9] L. Feuerbach, 'Epigrams', in *Thoughts on Death and Immortality* (Eng. Berkeley and London: University of California Press, 1980), 214, 205.

when these gentlemen (theologians) have exploded all their powder.'[10]

Can Feuerbach's optimistic atheism survive, however, in a post-modern era in which many (rightly or wrongly) perceive *all* instantiations of postmodern self-hood as victims of imposed role-performances and social norms constructed by a variety of social groups, whether theist or anti-theist, male or female, professional or artisan, black or white? Every counter-culture or protest takes on its own internal norms of truth, value, acceptability, and selfhood. It has become fully evident that Feuerbach was mistaken in imagining that simply to jettison belief in a personal God would guarantee the new 'Bethlehem' of freedom which he imagined that Hegel had made possible, once his system had been purged of 'absolute spirit' or 'God'. Even Kant's 'autonomy' has a hollow ring in the light of the immense gap which has opened between Kant's self of the categorical moral imperative and the postmodern self.

Karl Marx (1818–83) and (as we have seen) Friedrich Nietzsche (1844–1900) shared Feuerbach's view concerning the damaging effects of theism, as well as its illusory basis. In one respect, however, Marx anticipated a perspective of postmodern selfhood. He diagnosed its powerlessness as due to structural forces which dominate and oppress the self in the interests of the powerful. Vested interests depersonalize the self into a mere unit of production, valued only as a unit of exchange-value in the market of labour. Here indeed emerges the postmodern self.

Nevertheless Marxism remains 'modern', not postmodern, because it also adopts a global universalized philosophy or 'meta-narrative' in accordance with which history-as-a-whole moves towards a universal goal. The conflict in which the isolated self would be a powerless victim becomes transposed into a collective, structural, class struggle. As a collectivity it has an active part in a grand design. Just as capitalism subsumed and overcame feudalism and property became diversified into the hands of a middle-class bourgeoisie, even so capitalism will *inevitably* become subsumed within, and overcome by, the rise of the proletariat and the *parousia* of universal public ownership. Eventually even state socialism will wither away, and the need for coercion be replaced by the eschaton of voluntary communism. Even if Engels retained reservations about historical inevitability, Marx proclaimed in principle an unstoppable gospel of the final emancipation of the self.[11]

In such a context, theism merely appeared to slow down the process. It did so by pacifying the proletariat with language about order, providence and authority. But whereas Christian faith appeared merely to slow down the process, the collapse of Marxism as an efficient socio-

---

[10] Ibid. 198.

[11] Karl Marx, *Capital* (Eng. 3 vols., New York: International Publishers, 1967); cf. *The Writings of the Young Marx on Philosophy and Society* (Garden City, NY: Doubleday, 1967).

economic system has more fundamentally undermined it over the last few years than any theory about religion. Even if the Republic of China, at the time of writing, still clings to a 'modern' centrally-structured monolithic system, elsewhere in formerly Marxist societies, for the most part, even nation-states threaten to break up into diverse, more 'tribal', entities, while economic productivity has entered a potentially chaotic period of transition into fragmented interest-groups which struggle for economic power. It is arguable that Marxist theory transparently failed to take account of human nature with the realism of Christian theology. Feuerbach's epigram 'If you wish to be delivered from sin . . . become a pagan; sin came into the world with Christianity' appears, in the light of current civil wars at the time of writing, to be naïve, if not infantile.[12]

Moreover, the warnings of non-theist postmodern writers, especially those of Michel Foucault, confirm that the Marxist faith in bureaucrats to hold the ring against potentially competing power-groups was also naïve. Foucault has little difficulty in showing that the power of bureaucrats to define 'norms' and 'acceptable' procedures, together with the escalating of power which they gain through 'surveillance' and the possession of files and databanks makes it impossible for them to fail to exercise power-play.[13] At very least they build their own empires. At worst they load norms and agendas to try to ensure that their position of control becomes unassailable. They have become the new élite. The history of the Eastern Bloc has amply vindicated this analysis, while the West flounders in its attempts to balance centripetal and centrifugal forces.

Nietzsche's self-confidence, we have already noted, was as great as Feuerbach's in his misplaced trust in the 'freedom' and 'affirmation of life' which would result from heeding the message that 'God is dead'. Nietzsche's 'madman' proclaims the death of God in *The Gay Science* of 1882.[14] In his later work, The *AntiChrist*, he speaks of 'God', especially in Christianity, as a 'contradiction of life', which denies 'the eternal *Yes*' of humanity. Belief in God, he says, is 'a declaration of hostility towards life, nature, the will to life . . . [It is] the will to nothingness sanctified'.[15]

In the late nineteenth century, before the First World War, 'Yes' seemed to affirm progress, science, autonomy and human dignity. Moreover, while secular culture appeared to offer grounds for optimism,

---

[12] Feuerbach, 'Epigrams', 224.

[13] Michel Foucault, *Discipline and Punish* (French, *Surveiller et punir*, 1975) (Eng. New York: Pantheon, 1977), and other works cited below.

[14] Nietzsche, *Works*, vol. 10: *The Joyful Wisdom / The Gay Science*, aphorisms 108 and 343 (also in W. Kaufman (ed.), *The Portable Nietzsche* (New York: Viking Press, 1968 (1954)), 447.

[15] Nietzsche, *Works*, vol. 16: *The AntiChrist*, 146, aphorism 18; cf. 142–50, aphorisms 16–21.

much Christian theology was at the same time trapped within an idealist philosophical frame which lent support to a dualist or 'hellenized' version of the Christian gospel. Nietzsche and Heidegger perceived it as 'Platonism for the people'. The physical realm appeared to reflect something inferior to the supposed realm of 'the soul'.

Moltmann rightly protests against such a distortion of biblical faith. He comments: 'In this gnostic form the Christian hope no longer gazes forward to a future when everything will be created anew. It looks upwards, to the soul's escape from the body and from this earth, into the heaven of blessed spirits.'[16] Moltmann rightly laments the effects of this 'dualism of body and soul', and will have none of it. Hence, almost as if he were explicitly addressing Nietzsche, Moltmann affirms: 'True spirituality will be the restoration of the love for life . . . The full and unreserved "yes" to life . . . the "well of life".'[17] With this theme Moltmann links 'vitality' and 'liberty'. But Moltmann's liberty is not the 'autonomy' of Cupitt or Feuerbach, or of the lone Kantian thinker. It is grounded in social bonds which it shares with *the Other* and with *Others* in love. It is *social in its very nature*.

---

[16] Moltmann, *The Spirit of Life*, 90.
[17] Ibid. 97.

20

More Social Consequences of Postmodern Selfhood: Despair, Conflict and Manipulation

THE work of Sigmund Freud (1856–1940), like that of Nietzsche, contributes to perceptions of the self which characterize the self of postmodernism. In contrast to the notion of the modern self in control of its own choices, values and goals, Freud portrays the self, first, as an amalgam of neurological, quasi-physical, or psychic 'forces' which serve to define and to shape it; second, as a victim of its own manipulative deceptions.

Freud explicitly stated that psychoanalysis derives 'all mental processes . . . from *the interplay of forces* which assist or inhibit one another'.[1] Whereas Hume, as a sceptic but also a sceptic of modernity, spoke of the self as a bundle of 'perceptions', Freud interprets selfhood in terms of force-flows of psychic energies. His models are physical, neurological, mechanical, or even drawn from economics. Thus, for example, *cathexis* and *countercathexis* represent inputs and outputs of energy-forces which become 'invested' in another person or in some object. Ricoeur and Küng, two of the most astute commentators on Freud who write from within a non-reductionist anti-positivist frame, expose the far-reaching consequences of Freud's reliance on largely mechanistic models. Küng observes: 'A method of investigation was turned into a world view; people "believed" in it.'[2]

On the second issue, namely that of self-deception, we have already discussed Freud's work on the interpretation of dreams, and noted Ricoeur's constructive use of Freud's claims in this area for a hermeneutic of suspicion (Part II, Chapter 11). While he rightly rejects Freud's account of the self primarily, if not exclusively, in terms of drives, forces and causal processes, Ricoeur fully accepts, also rightly, Freud's perceptive analysis of the capacity of the self to fall victim to its own deceptive, self-protective and manipulative devices. The interpreter, on this basis, seeks to understand 'another text . . . beneath

---

[1] S. Freud, *The Standard Edition of the Complete Psychological Works of Sigmund Freud*, 24 vols. (London: Hogarth Press, 1953 onwards), vol. 20 (1959), 265.
[2] Hans Küng, *Freud and the Problem of God* (New Haven: Yale University Press, 1979), 15; cf. P. Ricoeur, *Freud and Philosophy: an Essay on Interpretation* (Eng. New Haven and London: Yale University Press, 1970).

the text of consciousness'.[3] Deception disguises one or more sets of opposing interests. For example, the self may mask battles between the pressures of social, moral, or moralistic constraints (cf. the *superego*) and drives towards self-satisfaction or self-gratification (cf. Freud's *id*).

As we argued more fully above in Part I, we need not dispute whether *in some or in many cases* a neurosis which emerges from the pressures of inner conflicts may give rise to religious projections. This may lie behind certain religious myths, or trigger infantile regressions into a strong need for religious affirmation or religious dependency. No doubt even within the selfhood of those who may hold valid religious beliefs, elements of religious manipulation and self-deception may co-exist with other motivations and responses.

This coheres entirely with the perspective in Paul, in Hebrews, and in the Johannine writings that believers remain fallible and fully capable of continuing self-deception (1 John 1:8; cf. 1 Cor. 3:18; Heb. 3:13). As Cullman memorably asserts, Christians still sin and still die, since the transforming processes of the work of the Holy Spirit are experienced as the 'first fruits' of a future yet to be actualized fully.[4] Nevertheless, if we follow Freud in speaking either metaphorically or literally of 'forces', in the context of Christian theology other 'forces' which elude a positivist approach also become operative, as part of a wider picture. In the theology of Paul, for example, the renewed self does not remain entirely victim to the social, moral, or cause-effect forces which determine its historical situatedness. In theological terms, bondage to a cause-effect process of sin, law, and death does not have the final word (Rom. 6–8). Although forces from the past still operate, the Holy Spirit also brings about a process of transformation 'from ahead' which loosens and eventually breaks the ties which bind the self to its pre-given situatedness. The goal of promise now becomes transformation from a failed or distorted 'image' of humanness into the 'image' of Jesus Christ (1 Cor. 15:49; 2 Cor. 3:18). In Cullman's words: 'the Holy Spirit is nothing else than that anticipation of the end in the present'.[5]

Karl Rahner rightly related this 'openness to the future' to 'interior truthfulness'. Those who become open in this way have 'the courage to accept themselves as they are . . . because one whom God has accepted . . . can accept himself'.[6] 'The need no longer remains to hide behind devices of deceit and manipulation. There is no need for interior

[3] Freud, *Standard Edition*, vols. 4–5: *The Interpretation of Dreams* (1953), and Ricoeur, *Freud and Philosophy*, 392. For a further exposition and critique, cf. Anthony C. Thiselton, *New Horizons in Hermeneutics. The Theory and Practice of Transforming Biblical Reading* (London: HarperCollins, and Grand Rapids: Zondervan, 1992), 344–50.

[4] O. Cullman, *Christ and Time* (Eng. London: SCM, 1951), 155.

[5] Ibid. 72.

[6] Karl Rahner, 'On Truthfulness', in *Theological Investigations*, vol. 7 (Eng. London: Darton, Longman, & Todd, 1971), 239; cf. 229–59.

deceitfulness with one's self, dishonesty, "putting up a façade" . . . affectation and other forms in which a man tries to avoid facing up to his own nature.'[7] The biblical writings allude to this dimension of self-deception and concealed depths within the self under the terminology of 'the heart'. The 'heart' thus becomes the sphere for the 'pouring out' of the Holy Spirit. The heart may be 'slippery' or 'deceitful' (Jer. 17:9); and the 'depths' of the heart may conceal hidden things (1 Cor. 4:5). But, Paul declares, 'God's love has been poured into our hearts through the Holy Spirit' (Rom. 5:5). Where conflict within the self has hitherto been provoked by a series of forces which Paul describes in Romans 6–8 as corporate or individual self-interests (sin, Rom. 6), as inescapable cause-effect processes (law, Rom. 7), and as self-defeating, stultifying projects (death, Rom. 8), these chapters hold out the corresponding promises of liberation from self-interest, the future-orientated work of the Spirit rather than past entanglements with the law, and creative transformation rather than the collapse of present projects into decay.

Three theologians corroborate these themes in different ways. As against the illusory optimism of 'modernity', which lacks any adequate notion of the self's vulnerability and bondage in the grip of stronger forces, Emil Brunner declares: 'Belief in progress as hope resting upon self-confidence is the opposite of Christian hope, which is founded upon trust in God.'[8] In the same vein, Anders Nygren sees the experience of self-worth in the creative, transforming, power of divine love. The self, he comments: 'acquires worth just by becoming the object of God's love . . . *Agapē is a value-creating principle . . . a creative work of divine power*'.[9] Moltmann sees in these processes the restoration of a genuinely reciprocal openness to others and to the Other which defines the very nature of personhood as it is intended to be: 'Personhood is always being-in-relationship.'[10] Only within a context of love can the self eventually come to discard its self-deceptions (for in this context it has no need for self-protection or to disguise 'interests'): 'Love never ends . . . the partial will come to an end . . . Now we see in a mirror dimly, but then we shall see face to face. Now I know only in part; then I will know fully, even as I have been fully known' (1 Cor. 13:8, 10, 12). Liberation becomes a possibility, and the promise of redemption in due course becomes substantiated (Rom. 5:5).

Freud's emphasis on self-deception, then, entirely coheres with Christian theology. As Ricoeur comments, this necessitates a hermeneutics of the self as 'text' for the human subject, which, contrary to Descartes and to secular modernity, 'is never the subject one thinks

---

[7] Ibid. 235.
[8] Emil Brunner, *Eternal Hope* (Eng. London: Lutterworth Press, 1954), 10.
[9] Anders Nygren, *Agapē and Eros* (Eng. London: SPCK, 1953), 78, 80 (his italics).
[10] Moltmann, *The Spirit of Life*, 11.

it is'.[11] Christian theology also coheres with Freud's analysis of the self as falling victim to forces which it does not fully understand and which certainly it cannot fully control. The postmodern self at this point stands closer to biblical realism than to the innocent confidence of modernity. Yet even if, to re-apply J. L. Austin's phrase, this is indeed the first word, it is nevertheless not the last word. For where experiences of bondage, constraint, or domination at the hands of external forces or groups nourish despair, conflict and anger, the Christian *kerygma* holds out the possibility or even promise of 'God's love . . . poured into our hearts through the Holy Spirit' (Rom. 5:5), against the background axiom that 'love builds' (1 Cor. 8:1).

The phrase 'poured out' in all probability alludes to the tradition of Pentecost, in which the 'pouring out' of the Holy Spirit (Acts 2:17) looks, in turn, to the promise of a corporate or social 'pouring' of the Spirit on all varieties of people (Joel 2:28, 29). Here Pentecost becomes a reversal of Babel. Where manipulative interest resulted in destruction, dispersal, and fragmentation by centrifugal forces, to receive the Holy Spirit as mediator of God's love in Christ draws together the fragmented peoples into one, as joint-shareholders or common participants in the 'social commonality' (*koinōnia*) of the Holy Spirit. J. Hainz has explored over some three hundred pages the links between 'the fellowship of the Holy Spirit' (2 Cor. 13:13) and community or worldwide 'commonality' as Paul sees this.[12]

To return to Moltmann, Paul speaks of 'supra-personal forces which enslave people, destroy their world, and make the whole creation . . . "groan"'.[13] But the renewed self of God's promised future involves 'the personal experience of sociality . . . To call God Lord, promises freedom'.[14] But, as we have recently noted, such freedom, in Moltmann's view, has little or nothing to do with the illusory 'autonomy' of Kant (or, we might add, of Cupitt). Moltmann observes: 'Through faith the hitherto unexplored creative powers of God are thrown open in men and women. So faith means becoming creative with God . . . Faith leads to a creative life which is life-giving through love.'[15]

However, without this promise, the transition from the selfhood of optimistic modernity to the postmodern self has deeply destructive social consequences. First, a loss of stability, loss of stable identity, and loss of confidence in global norms or goals breed deep uncertainty, insecurity and anxiety. To recall the incisive analysis offered by David Harvey, the postmodern self lives daily with fragmentation, indeterminacy, and intense distrust of all universal or 'totalizing' discourses. Insecurity, in turn, invites a defensiveness, a letting down of shutters, and an

---

[11] Ricoeur, *Freud and Philosophy*, 420.
[12] J. Hainz, *Koinonia. Kirche als Gemeinschaft bei Paulus* (Regensburg: Pustet, 1982).
[13] Moltmann, *The Spirit of Life*, 88.
[14] Ibid. 94, 101.
[15] Ibid. 115.

increasing preoccupation with self-protection, self-interest, and desire for power and the recovery of control. *The postmodern self is thus predisposed to assume a stance of readiness for conflict.*

Second, in the case of the self of modernity, misfortune or loss of privilege may be construed at best as a challenge to courageous action, in the belief that such action can make a difference; or at worst, as bad luck arising from random forces or from some inevitable by-product of an otherwise stable strategy for society as a whole. But if the modern self is content to say, *'That's life'*, the postmodern self assumes the discourse of *accusation and conflict*: *'It's Them'*. For the loss of power, loss of privilege, or loss of well-being is now ascribed *to the manipulative power-interests of competing persons or competing groups*. Misfortune seems to be neither random nor unavoidable, but a by-product of the success of some other group. This group may take the form of some professional guild, especially lawyers, doctors, clergy, or managers, or of some different social class, gender, or ethnic profile. At all events, *blame*, *accusation* and *hostility* come to absorb the concerns of the postmodern self. A breakdown of trust in virtually all governments, whether democratically elected or not, has become a hallmark of the mid 1990s.

It is not difficult to identify the initial emergence of this trend with the rise of postmodern perspectives towards the end of the 1960s. In Britain it became noticeable that whereas in the 1950s it was broadly conventional to speak of 'the' British Government, by the late 1960s the phrase had widely become 'this' government, implicitly subordinating 'national' to 'party' hopes, fears, or interests. But this phenomenon did not arise from purely social or political factors. More deeply, the impact of *literary and political postmodern philosophies* lay behind everyday events and attitudes especially in the main writers to whom we have already called attention, namely Jacques Lacan (1901–81), Roland Barthes (1915–80), Michel Foucault (1926–84), and Jacques Derrida (b. 1930). If we were required to extend this major four to eight, we might well add, for example, Jean Baudrillard, Jean-François Lyotard, Gianni Vattimo, and perhaps Julia Kristeva. There would be little point in extending the list, but numerous works and anthologies address postmodern issues, including those by Kevin Hart, Seyla Benhabib, L. J. Nicholson and others.[16]

In his recent book *Postmodernity* (1994) David Lyon has shown clearly how the social and philosophical, as well as the literary and

---

[16] Kevin Hart, *The Trespass of the Sign* (Cambridge: Cambridge University Press, 1989); S. Benhabib, *Situating the Self* (Cambridge: Polity Press, 1992); L. J. Nicholson (ed.), *Feminism/Postmodernism* (New York and London: Routledge, 1990); cf. from another angle, R. J. Bernstein, *The New Constellation* (Cambridge: Polity Press, 1991); and P. Berry and A. Wernick (eds.), *Shadow of Spirit. Postmodernism and Religion* (New York and London: Routledge, 1992).

political, became inextricably woven together.[17] He introduces postmodernity with reference to a recent film or movie, namely *Bladerunner*, set in a Los Angeles of AD 2019. The story revolves around a group of bio-engineered 'replicants' who are neither robots nor human in the normal sense of the term. They object to their four-year life-span and seek full human status. The 'blade runner' has the task of 'eliminating' escaped replicant. As Lyon rightly observes, here social and philosophical aspects of postmodernity interact. The search for identity raises issues about personal or corporate history as against the transient; the social environment is one of urban decay in which one featureless shopping mall with its peeling walls and uncollected rubbish leads on to another; and, above all, it is unclear what constitutes 'reality'.

Lyon observes: 'Here is one way of seeing the postmodern: it is a debate about reality. Is the world of solid scientific facts and purposive history, bequeathed to us by the European Enlightenment, mere wishful thinking? Or worse, the product of some scheming manipulation by the powerful? . . . What are we left with? A quicksand of ambiguity . . . artificial images, flickering from the TV screen, or joyful liberation from imposed definitions of reality?'[18] Remnants of 'modernity' survive in *Bladerunner* in streets and buildings, but these are in decay. The 'new' reality seems to be the 'virtual' reality of electronic or simulated constructs. But what, in these circumstances, is the difference between 'display', or 'sign', and 'reality'? Indeed what would count as a 'real' thing? Is a self-constructed photofit an identity or a self? Is anything still 'solid'? In *The Archaeology of Knowledge* Foucault rejects any notion of 'objects prior to discourse'.[19]

We alluded to Roland Barthes's fundamental distinction between the contrived and the supposedly 'natural' or allegedly value-neutral which emerges powerfully in his *Mythologies* and more technically in his attempt to utilize Saussure in his *Elements of Semiology*. We noted, similarly, that especially in his 'White Mythology' Derrida followed Nietzsche in viewing metaphor largely as concealing values and power-bids under the guise of promoting truth-claims. The meanings of texts never achieve a stable 'closure', for successive shifts of 'codes' generate successive shifts of 'performances' of meaning.[20] We alluded finally to Foucault's work on the social construction of norms and criteria of meaning in his earlier works *A History of Madness* (French, 1961) translated as *Madness and Civilization* (1965).

[17] David Lyon, *Postmodernity* (Buckingham: Open University Press, 1994).
[18] Ibid. 2.
[19] M. Foucault, *The Archaeology of Knowledge* (Eng. New York: Pantheon, 1972), 47.
[20] The detailed theories of Barthes and Derrida are expounded and criticized in my *New Horizons in Hermeneutics*, 80–141; cf. also 393–405, 495–507, 534–50.

Norms or criteria shift as history moves on. In the classical period, Foucault observes, 'madness' is perceived primarily as *unreason*. Hence in a minority of instances, mad people may have been revered as 'inspired'; but more often they assumed the virtual status of animals without reason; to be fed and watered, but confined. By the nineteenth century a concept of madness as *mental illness* had emerged. 'Asylums' became, at least in theory, places of sanctuary, where the illness could be treated away from the stresses of everyday life.[21] Since 'illness' for most people today has become what madness *is*, perhaps here we may speak with Peter Berger and Thomas Luckmann of the *Social Construction of Reality*.[22]

A moment's reflection on issues about 'madness' in the Eastern Bloc of the cold war years will remind us of how closely socio-political views of what counts as 'normal' are related to issues of power and control. How often is mere deviation of outlook characterized as madness? A deviant or idiosyncratic university teacher in the West may be described as 'eccentric' with tolerance or even affection. Among ordinary working people or, among schoolchildren, however, such deviancy is more likely to invite suspicion or even ostracism. 'Eccentricity' becomes 'oddity'. In some political regimes, the consequences may be severe, sometimes leading to deprivation or confinement.

Foucault turns his attention more explicitly to institutions and to language in his book translated under the title *The Order of Things* (English, 1970; French, *Les mots et les choses*, 1966). Institutions, or how society and traditions are 'ordered', rest on arbitrary factors of social history and power. Moreover, as against the 'modern' innocence of Descartes, 'I think' already operates from a pre-given social situatedness within an order; namely in the system of all its own possibilities.[23] Whatever 'thought' touches, it 'causes to move'; thus self and society cannot be perceived as 'given', but 'shimmer' as ever-changing norms, structures and language move on.[24] Certain language cannot 'represent'.[25]

In the middle period of *The Archaeology of Knowledge* (French, 1969; English, 1972) and *Discipline and Punish* (French, *Surveiller et punir*, 1975; English, 1977) Foucault turns in more detail to social power especially in relation to the penal service. 'Surveillance' provides the tools for correction and control. Data are organized into files, data-banks and documented sources. In such institutions as prisons, hospitals,

---

[21] M. Foucault, *Madness and Civilization. A History of Insanity in the Age of Reason* (Eng. New York: Pantheon, 1965).
[22] Peter Berger and Thomas Luckmann, *The Social Construction of Reality* (Harmondsworth: Penguin, 1971 (1966)).
[23] M. Foucault, *The Order of Things* (Eng. New York: Random House, 1970), 324; cf. 357.
[24] Ibid. 325, 327, 339.
[25] Ibid. 354; cf. 324.

the armed services and schools these effectively become mechanisms for control and manipulation.[26] Further, 'accepted' knowledge which is documented in the 'right' sources can become a vehicle through which 'education' can now serve power-interests. Bureaucrats build empires on the basis of 'privileged' information. Even if feudal and high-modern structures were paternalistic, at least kings, leaders, heads, or fathers could in many cases invite and repay trust. But in the bureaucratic world of the late twentieth century the database has now become the depersonalized instrument of power for those anonymous bureaucrats or managers who have gained access to these resources.[27]

Structures which depend on 'accepted' knowledge maintain their power by 'regimes'. Independently of regimes, Foucault argues, 'truth' cannot *amount* to anything. Knowledge is not the same as power. But 'epistemic fields' or recognized areas of what 'counts' as knowledge provide for what Foucault calls 'strategic alignments' of power. The self as an individual falls victim to a regime. Not only is the self unable to evade its control, but little or no room has now been left for negotiation *through rational dialogue and argument*. Where truth has largely become absorbed into structures and spheres of power, argument and reason *collapse into a rhetoric of force*, using persuasion or pressure.

The devaluation of the currency of rational dialogue into that of rhetoric, I suggest, brings about *one of the most socially sinister and destructive consequences for the postmodern self*. For let us return to my earlier point about the contrast between a courageous or accepting 'That's life', and an accusatory 'It's Them'. How can the human self respond to the power-interests of 'them'? There is nothing new about the problem of competing power-interests. From the politics of the city-states of ancient Greece to the democratic parliaments or congress of early twentieth-century Britain and America, rational debate in the public domain supposedly held the ring between these competing interests. As Alasdair MacIntyre, among others, reminds us, as long as there remains a sufficient consensus concerning *what counts as reasoned, rational, or moral*, reasoned debate in the public domain remains an effective arbiter within that frame or common tradition. But if each competing group, class, ethnic tradition, gender, guild, or party produces its own *internal* criteria of supposed rationality in order to serve its own power-interests, rational debate collapses *not only into mere rhetoric*, but soon also into *accusation, blame, corporate self-righteousness and conflict*.

The social consequences now become severely damaging. For where reasoning and appeal to decency fails, resort to *pressure* takes its place. In place of reasoned letters to the press, people try to force the hand of

---

[26] Foucault, *Discipline and Punish*, 190 (on 'medical discipline') and 143 (on 'knowing, mastering, using').

[27] Ibid. 176–7, on 'anonymous' power.

elected governments by 'demonstrations', by 'pressure groups', and by a rhetoric of force. This inevitably invites a response in kind from the competing group. What can the 'weaker' party do when they believe that their cause is rational or just, against opposing power-interests? Inevitably, *the pressure of rhetoric escalates into the pressure of violence.* Violence, in turn may further escalate from the limited physical aggression of an angry demonstration to the violence of weapons and armed forces in a full-scale civil war. Similarly, where confidence in reason or justice has been lost, and deprivation is ascribed to opposing power-interests, what begins in petty vandalism against the owners of houses or vehicles readily escalates into the violence of assault on persons, and in turn into major, organized crime. At the time of writing many economically and socially secure people speak of this as 'loss of the feel-good factor'. But for underprivileged others, the prospect of the postmodern self seems to be simply hopeless.

In our conclusion to Part III we spoke of the forked rhetoric of postmodernity. This turns hopelessness to despair. On one side it has de-centred the self, de-centred ethics, and de-centred society; on the other side it claims simply to leave everything as it is. But how can it be 'emancipatory' if it leaves everything as it is? It rightly unmasks instances of manipulative power which disguise themselves as claims to truth. But *does this lost innocence entail the universal doctrinal cynicism* that *all* truth-claims are bids for power? Does it invite contextual pragmatism which views *all* truth-claims as relative only to the internal norms of given communities?

This is the point at which to turn to the writings of an unduly neglected theologian in this context. Reinhold Niebuhr was fully aware of self-deception in corporate structures for the purposes of power. But side by side with a realism about the human condition, he held firmly to the truth-claims of Christian theology, and to the reality of promise from 'beyond' the horizons of the present.

21

Corporate Power and Corporate Self-Deception

REINHOLD NIEBUHR (1892–1971) has been described by Richard Harries, currently Bishop of Oxford, as 'in the realm of public affairs ... the most influential theologian of our century'.[1] Although he became most widely known for his two-volume work *The Nature and Destiny of Man* (1941 and 1943), he regarded his book *Moral Man and Immoral Society* (1932, but first published in Britain only 1963) as his 'first major work'.[2] In this study he offered an incisive and at times brilliant analysis of the connection between social power-interests and the capacity of the human self to deceive itself and to manipulate values and actions in the name of supposed 'morality' or 'truth'. His social analysis is masterly; yet he draws on authentic traditions about grace, sin, and the human predicament from Paul through Luther to the present. The author of his standard biography, Richard Fox, observes that 'he saw society as a realm of power blocs to be adjusted ... America was culturally pluralistic, devoid ... of moral consensus ... Society was "in a perpetual state of war"'.[3] Fox suggests that the major importance of *Moral Man and Immoral Society* is to subvert the liberal optimism that dominated American thought from 1930 to 1980. Clearly there are affinities with postmodern perceptions of selfhood, but these find their place within a firmly theological frame.

Niebuhr argues that human persons allow themselves to be seduced into operating manipulative power-interests by deceiving themselves into interpreting their own acts as altruistic concerns for the sake of the corporate structures to which they belong. In the name of some corporate or social entity they devise programmes and implement policies of which, on a purely individual level, they would be ashamed. 'National interest' as concern for the nation offers a key example. Niebuhr writes: 'The selfishness of nations is proverbial ... There is

---

[1] Richard Harries (ed.), *Reinhold Niebuhr and the Issues of our Time* (London and Oxford: Mowbray, 1986), 1.
[2] Kenneth Durkin, *Reinhold Niebuhr* (London: Chapman, 1989), 41.
[3] Richard W. Fox, *Reinhold Niebuhr. A Biography* (New York: Pantheon, 1985), 140.

an alloy of projected self-interest in patriotic altruism.'[4] Individuals will support the structural, corporate, aggressive self-interest of their own nation in trade, economics, treaty, or in war, on the grounds of loyalty to their fellows, and the desire for the well-being of their neighbours.

The presentation of essential national cultural values offers a more subtle pretext for corporate self-interest. German soldiers fought British and American troops in the name of the heritage of Beethoven and Goethe; British trade agreements were made in the name of stability of the British Empire. Western nations still give 'aid' which entails trade agreements that may then widen the gap between rich and poor nations.[5] In situations which call for 'patriotism', Niebuhr writes, often 'the rational understanding of political issues remains such a minimum force that national unity for action can be achieved only ... by popular emotions and hysterias which from time to time run through a nation'.[6] 'Loyalty to the nation' appears in the dress of 'a high form of altruism when compared with lesser loyalties ... Altruistic passion is sluiced into the reservoir of nationalism with great ease.'[7]

The welfare of the group therefore invites what Niebuhr calls 'that self-deception and hypocrisy [which] is an unvarying element in the moral life of all human beings'.[8] Political speeches are often addressed to a different audience from the one in the presence of the politician, and may even decisively determine the agenda and claims of the speaker. 'The dishonesty of nations "becomes" a political necessity.'[9]

Class-interests, Niebuhr continues, invite the same element of corporate self-deception and manipulation. Professional guilds may 'load' procedures and performance-criteria in their own favour. Anticipating a postmodern analysis, Niebuhr identifies a tendency to elevate a social power-interest into 'general interests and universal values'.[10] A dominant group may succeed in defining norms for the whole of society, but only to ensure its own continued dominance. Yet, although his main criticisms fall on the socially privileged, Niebuhr equally exposes the 'cynicism' of a Marxism that reduces *all human value* to the power-interests of labour, production or class-struggle.[11] He comments: 'The exaltation of class loyalty as the highest form of altruism is a national concomitant of the destruction of national loyalty.'[12] A fighting proletariat absolutizes class-interests as an ultimate,

[4] Reinhold Niebuhr, *Moral Man and Immoral Society* (London: SCM, 1963 (1932)), 84, 93.
[5] Ibid. 89–90.
[6] Ibid. 88.
[7] Ibid. 91.
[8] Ibid. 95.
[9] Ibid.
[10] Ibid. 117.
[11] Ibid. 142–51.
[12] Ibid. 152.

but Marxist theorists seem to be too involved in moral cynicism to notice this.[13]

Religious group-interests undergo the same incisive critique. Churches and theological traditions may become manipulative and self-serving. Individuals may even be deceived into doing something otherwise shameful 'for the sake of the family', or to sustain a religious tradition. Nevertheless, in principle, Niebuhr insists, Christian theology has made persons *conscious of the sinfulness of their pre-occupation with the self. There is nothing that modern psychologists have discovered about the persistence of egocentricity in man which has not first been anticipated in the insights of the great mysteries of the classical periods of religion.*[14] 'At the heart of the Christian gospel lies the words of Jesus, "*Whoso seeketh to find his life shall lose it, and he that loseth his life for my sake shall find it*"(Matt. 10:39).'[15] *Love* binds together into one and remains the highest virtue. Yet theological realism 'would *distinguish between what we expect of individuals and of groups*'.[16] In the case of the latter, the drive to self-interest is deeply hidden and disguised, but nonetheless powerful.

In two respects Niebuhr's analysis of society and of hope was influenced by Luther. First, he shared Luther's view that 'order' must be preserved in defence of justice for the weak, and of peace for the work of the kingdom by the civil law supported by duly appointed powers of state. He endorses Luther's injunction 'to place the gospel in heaven and the law on the earth . . . In civil policy obedience to law must be severely required.'[17] He shares with Luther too much realism about human nature to propose that the Christian believer should guard the lambs of the flock by laying down his or her weapons and inviting in the oppressor. In Luther's words: 'If anyone attempted to rule the world by the gospel, and to abolish all temporal law and the secular sword . . . he would be loosing the ropes and chains of the savage wild beasts and letting them bite and mangle everyone.'[18] Second, like Luther, Niebuhr accepted that much of the promised transformation of the church and society lay in the future, not in the present. He endorsed Luther's belief that 'the pretension of finality and perfection in the Church was the root of spiritual pride and self-righteousness'.[19] Against what he termed 'ecclesiasticism', Niebuhr stressed divine promise and divine agency.

[13] Ibid. 161.
[14] Ibid. 54 (my italics).
[15] Ibid. 56.
[16] Ibid. 271 (my italics).
[17] Niebuhr, *The Nature and Destiny of Man*, 2 vols. (London: Nisbet, 1941 and 1943), vol. 2, 199.
[18] Martin Luther, 'Temporal Authority' (1523), in *Luther's Works*, vol. 45: *The Christian Society II* (Philadelphia: Mülhenberg Press, 1962), 91.
[19] Niebuhr, *The Nature and Destiny of Man*, vol. 2, 192.

Although similarities may be perceived between the respective approaches to 'power' by Niebuhr and by Foucault, this first point about a kingdom of 'order' stands in tension with attitudes towards the state and 'authorities' in Foucault. For Foucault, power-structures and institutions are in principle 'arbitrary' products of particular areas in social history: the tribal chief, the king, the feudal lord, the modern manager, and his most focused target, 'those in which power wears a white coat and a professional smile'.[20] Foucault's approach stands in tension, for example, with Emil Brunner's view in theology that, together with commitments of marriage, the restraining and stabilizing authority of the state constitutes one of two 'natural' ordinances of God. The state, Brunner insists, has an ordained 'order' to restrain evil and to conserve justice. Indeed, Brunner perceives five beneficial 'orders' which cannot shift because they stem from the structures of divine creation: male-female relations and family; achievement in work and exchange structures; state and law; cultures; and communities of worship.[21] The German title behind the less happy English *The Divine Imperative* (1934) alludes explicitly to Brunner's positive evaluation of orders *Das Gebot und die Ordnungen* (1932).

Admittedly this issue remains controversial in Christian theology. Recently Elizabeth Castelli and Stephen Moore have both appealed to the approach of Foucault to provide a critique not only of institutional power within the New Testament writings and especially in Paul, but also of the 'pastoral power' instantiated in such Pauline injunctions as that of 'imitating' his own style of discipleship and obedience.[22] 'Imitation' (*mimesis*), E. A. Castelli argues, becomes part of Paul's strategy of power and social control. She writes: 'By promoting the value of sameness he [Paul] is also shaping relations of power', although she adds, 'Whether Paul *meant* or *intended* that his discourse be understood in the way I have argued is not a question that I have answered . . . My reading is not the only possible or plausible one.'[23] Nevertheless in effect Paul, she claims, utilizes for his purpose the approach which we have just noted in Brunner: 'orders' or a 'regime' promote stability and unity as if they were 'natural' and pre-ordained. Castelli appeals in particular to a specific interpretation of such passages as 'be imitators of me, as I am of Christ' (1 Cor. 11:1) and 'become imitators of us and of the Lord' (1 Thess. 1:6), as moving 'only in one

---

[20] The memorable phrase occurs in Stephen D. Moore, *Poststructuralism and the New Testament. Derrida and Foucault at the Foot of the Cross* (Minneapolis: Fortress, 1994), 112.

[21] Emil Brunner, *The Divine Imperative* (Philadelphia: Westminster, 1947). Cf. further, *Natural Theology* (Eng. London: Bles, 1946) for his debate with Barth on the issue.

[22] Elizabeth A. Castelli, *Imitating Paul: A Discourse of Power* (Louisville: Westminster and John Knox, 1991), 21–58, and Moore, *Poststructuralism and the New Testament*, 83–112.

[23] Castelli, *Imitating Paul*, 119, 120, 121; cf. esp. 35–58.

direction . . . the hierarchical view of imitation . . . power relations; an issue of "group identity" . . . exclusivity . . . sameness'.[24] She also discusses 1 Thess. 2:14; Phil. 3:17; 1 Cor. 4:16; and Gal. 4:12.

Following Foucault's particular interest in such areas as medicine, penal correction and gender, Castelli argues that Paul shows a special concern to impose power and to eliminate deviancy in matters relating to the physical dimensions of life, such as food practices and sexual conduct (1 Cor. 5:1–5; 7:10–11; 10:14–22; 11:3; 11:27–32). Paul 'punishes' his own body (9:27). She suggests that to appeal to one's own submission in order to obtain the submission of others constitutes a manipulative device, which serves purposes of power and social control in the interests of pre-determined norms which exclude 'deviancy' (1 Cor. 5:5).

Stephen Moore expounds this approach more broadly, with reference to Foucault's works. He writes: 'Christian discipline is also bound up with power: "The kingdom of God does not consist in talk but in power" (1 Cor. 4:20) . . . Discipline has only one purpose, according to Foucault: the production of "docile bodies".'[25] Hence Paul initiates the practice of using the threat of divine judgement (Rom. 2:16, 29; 1 Cor. 4:5) to extract admissions, acknowledgements, agreements and 'confessions'.

Following Foucault, Moore sees 'confession' as a fundamental tool in the process of manipulative power-play. He quotes Foucault with approval: 'One confesses – or is forced to confess. When it is not spontaneous or dictated by some internal imperative, the confession is wrung from a person by violence or threat.'[26] Whether we think of the medieval church or in very many instances the modern state, power-techniques, whether open or 'pastoral', regulate 'the individual's inner existence'.[27] As a former monk who finally experienced emancipation from the 'regime' of the monastery with 'great exhilaration and deep sadness', Moore recalls that the image of the tortured Jesus on the cross was repeatedly used in his earlier years to enact what Foucault calls 'the quiet game of the well behaved'.[28]

If Castelli and Moore were correct, Paul's appeal on behalf of unity and well-being of the whole community might be said to have arisen from a combination of self-deception (of the kind diagnosed by Niebuhr) and manipulation (of the kind noted in the claims of Graham Shaw to whom Castelli alludes). But can such interpretations of Paul genuinely

---

[24] Ibid. 113, 114; cf. 89–117.
[25] Moore, *Poststructuralism and the New Testament,* 109.
[26] Ibid. 111; M. Foucault, *The History of Sexuality* (Eng. 3 vols., New York: Pantheon, 1978–86), vol. 1, 58–9.
[27] Ibid.
[28] Moore, *Poststructuralism and the New Testament,* 114. But see also Jean Baudrillard, *Forget Foucault* (New York: Colombia University Semiotext(e), 1987) for a critique of Foucault, partly on his own ground.

command acceptance? Do they do justice to his theology and to his writings as a whole?

We are not permitted space to enter into the degree of detail that would make an adequate response possible. If we restrict our attention, however, to one or two very relevant works, we may note, first of all, that Robert Jewett's book *Christian Tolerance* (1982) presents the very opposite claim about Paul, namely that he showed a strong concern for tolerance and for the acceptance of a measure of diversity and pluralism within the church.[29] Second, Andrew D. Clark's recent work *Secular and Christian Leadership in Corinth* (1993) offers a social and historical analysis which demonstrates precisely the difference between three models of power: between Graeco-Roman modes of leadership based on power; Corinthian attitudes towards leadership based largely on expediency or on borrowed notions about claims to 'wisdom'; and Paul's own redefinition of leadership in relation to Christ and the cross.[30] But this appeal to 'Christ crucified' has nothing to do with Moore's notion of pointing to an image of a tortured man to promote moral blackmail. Quite the reverse: it springs from the freedom of love to which we alluded in Part I in our discussion of Bonhoeffer's understanding of discipleship, and in Parts I and IV in our comments on Moltmann's theology of love and freedom.

Third, as against the account of conformity and deviancy put forward by Foucault, Castelli and Moore, numerous recent specialist studies on Pauline rhetoric propose an entirely different evaluation of what is at issue for Paul. From a large literature we may cite only S. M. Pogoloff's *Logos and Sophia. The Rhetorical Situation of I Corinthians* (1992), P. Marshall's *Enmity at Corinth: Social Conventions in Paul's Relations with the Corinthians* (1987), Margaret M. Mitchell's *Paul and the Rhetoric of Reconciliation* (1991), and W. L. Willis's *Idol Meat at Corinth* (1985).[31] Pogoloff does not question that issues of social status and of rhetoric come to the fore. But Paul's call to the community to imitate a pattern of humility and servanthood is not for the purpose of 'conformity' or 'control'. It is precisely to protect those who might otherwise be despised or considered socially inferior; in other words, precisely to *protect* the 'social deviants' for whom Foucault shows concern.

---

[29] Robert Jewett, *Christian Tolerance. Paul: Message to the Modern Church* (Philadelphia: Westminster, 1982).

[30] Andrew D. Clarke, *Secular Christian Leadership in Corinth. A Socio-Historical and Exegetical Study of I Corinthians 1 – 6* (Leiden: Brill, 1993).

[31] S. M. Pogoloff, *Logos and Sophia. The Rhetorical Situation of I Corinthians* (Atlanta: Scholars Press, 1992); P. Marshall, *Enmity at Corinth: Social Conventions in Paul's Relations with the Corinthians* (Tübingen: Mohr, 1987); M. M. Mitchell, *Paul and the Rhetoric of Reconciliation. An Exegetical Investigation of the Language and Composition of I Corinthians* (Tübingen, Mohr, 1991); Wendell L. Willis, *Idol Meat at Corinth. The Pauline Argument in I Corinthians 8 and 10* (Chico: Scholars Press, 1985).

Similarly the motivation behind all the rhetoric and argument about 'idol meat' is not at all 'conformity', but the reverse: 'The idea of "building up" combines the motif of love with ecclesiology. Love is the hallmark of the church.'[32] Likewise Marshall also agrees that the rejection and humiliation of Jesus 'provides the intellectual and practical basis for Paul's expression of apostleship', but not as a device of manipulation; rather, to attack 'discrimination of social standing' on behalf of those whom the privileged regarded as 'weak' or of low esteem at Corinth.[33] These researches turn the proposals of Castelli and Moore on their head, while allowing that 'power' is part of the issue.

We may go further. Paul's social analysis of the plight of the social world of Gentile 'pluralism' in Rom. 1:18–31 substantiates precisely the kind of analysis proposed by Niebuhr. Moreover in Rom. 13:1–7 his stress on 'duly appointed authorities' as providing an 'order' necessary for peace, relative justice, and a measure of stability corroborates the aspect of Niebuhr's approach which finds less cautious expression in Brunner. They are to protect the weak; not to impose uniformity within a pluralist Empire.

In Rom. 1:18–39 Paul is not grinding some personal axe. Drawing on standard material regularly used in hellenistic-Jewish synagogue sermons about the folly of abandoning belief in the one universal God and his laws, Paul traces the escalating consequences of surrendering universal rational and ethical norms for those of sub-cultural constructs, or the corporately-sanctioned idols, of Gentile pluralism. 'Order' which restrains and conserves collapses ('God gave them up . . .' 1:24). 'The glory of the immortal God' is exchanged for a diversity of 'images resembling a mortal human, beasts, or animals' (1:23). Their consequent focus on the context-specific as 'ultimate' results in a loss of rationality and ethics: people 'became futile in their thinking and their senseless minds were darkened' (1:21).

The subsequent heaping up of a long list of 'vices' admittedly follows a rhetorical pattern used in the Book of Wisdom (Wis. Sol. 14:25–26) and in Philo (e.g. De Sacrificiis Abelis 32). But it does more than this. In common with some hellenistic-Jewish preachers, Paul calls attention to unfettered *escalation* of the social consequences which we described in the previous section. Where confidence in rationality has been lost, despair breeds envy, deception, manipulation, conflict, initially controlled violence, and in due course all-out violence. In Paul's language, the uncontrolled situatedness of the corporate plight breeds 'evil, covetedness, malice, envy, murder, strife, deceit, craftiness, gossip, slander, insolence, haughtiness, self-congratulation, new forms of evil, conflict with parents, folly, faithlessness to commitments, heartlessness,

[32] Willis, *Idol Meat at Corinth*, 295.
[33] Marshall, *Enmity at Corinth*, 402, 403.

ruthlessness' (Rom. 1:29–31, with one or two glosses on the Greek). These 'vices', Dunn confirms, constitute 'the consequence of God's "handing over"'.[34] The 'order' which equally constrains and conserves has been rejected and has dissolved into instability.

The reverse situation emerges in Rom. 13:1–7. Although conflict and violence cannot be avoided where people live by a variety of incommensurable value-systems, these phenomena may be held in check to a relative degree if 'due authorities' retain some restraining and conserving role, even if only in selective areas of civil life. Admittedly the exegesis of the passage is controversial. Fitzmyer includes up to around 150 monographs and research articles which relate directly to these verses.[35] The main upshot of his detailed and careful discussion, however, is that 'living at peace' (Rom. 12:18) stems not from the notion of 'docility' (as Nietzsche, Foucault, Castelli and Moore imply) but from a oneness of relationality grounded in 'what Christ does . . . to span the chasm between Jew and Gentile'.[36] It is implausible to suggest that manipulation on behalf of apostolic power could be at issue here. Paul does not appeal to 'order' in the state to impose 'order' in the church. He is not trying to impose 'agreement' or 'docility'. Rather, in recognition that the weak need the protection of civil authorities, even with all the blemishes of Roman imperial administration, he endorses 'the sword' (Rom. 13:4) 'legitimately possessed . . . to coerce recalcitrant citizens . . . for the common good'.[37]

This example calls into question a postmodern tendency to doubt the integrity of *all* 'order' as irredeemably linked with individual or corporate power-interests on behalf of some specific group. No doubt Graham Shaw and others would interpret support for the civil order of Imperial Rome as a triumphalist legitimation of the powerful and privileged. But we might wonder whether the otherwise unprotected would perceive Roman 'order' in this way. As Gadamer stresses, the basis of Roman law lay in a strong sense of the *sensus communis*. Sweeping generalizations which attack all 'order' merely instantiate the difficulty of a formed rhetoric among those postmodern writers who wish simultaneously to reject all 'isms' or 'meta-narratives' while making *general* claims about power and order. Baudrillard and Lyotard perhaps more consciously seek consistency here than Foucault and some of his theological imitators. Wherever there is civil war, virtual anarchy, and 'might is right' the oppressed long for 'order'. Baudrillard accuses Foucault's work of mirroring 'the power it describes . . . Foucault's discourse is no truer than any other'.[38]

---

[34] J. D. G. Dunn, *Romans 1–8* (Dallas: Word, 1988), 67; cf. 51–76.
[35] J. A. Fitzmyer, *Romans* (New York: Doubleday (Anchor Bible) 1993), 670–6.
[36] Ibid. 664.
[37] Ibid. 668.
[38] Baudrillard, *Forget Foucault*, 10.

22

Present and Future:
The Pluriform Grammar of Hope
and the God of Promise

As Moltmann rightly urges, following many specialists on Old Testament studies and apocalyptic, hope and promise come to occupy a central place in theology when the present situation is perceived to 'stand in contradiction' with what God has promised.[1] In these circumstances, Moltmann adds: 'the language of promise will then be an essential key to the unlocking of Christian truth'.[2] There is even a convincingly and appropriate postmodern ring to Moltmann's approach to promise. 'Theism', he concedes, runs the risk of appearing to give 'a *fixed form* to reality', whereas hope and promise constantly expand the horizons of the present in future orientation.[3]

Nevertheless we must not confuse their theology of promise with Cupitt's notion of eternity as a 'fleeting moment' in which everything is invested in the present. The reverse is the case: the present acquires understanding, significance and interpretation in the light of the relation between its 'situatedness' in terms of the past and its transformation and destiny in the future. It relates to creative processes (not fixed states) of transformation into the ever-maturing, ever-developing 'image' of Christ who alone bears the 'image' of true humanness, the capacity to give and to receive in the mutuality of love.

Moltmann judiciously observes that theological concepts 'do not limp after reality, and gaze on it with the night eyes of Minerva's owl, but they illuminate reality by displaying its future. Their knowledge is *grounded not in the will to dominate, but in love* to the future of things ... engaged in a process of movement [they] *call forth practical movement and change*'.[4] He writes in the same volume: 'They do not seek to make a mental picture of existing reality, but to lead existing reality towards the promised and hoped-for transformation.'[5]

---

[1] Moltmann, *Theology of Hope*, 103.
[2] Ibid. 41.
[3] Ibid. 36 (my italics).
[4] Ibid. (my italics).
[5] Ibid. 18.

This comment is important in at least three respects. First, whereas flat propositions in theology often simply describe what is the case, the logic of promise (like that of directives) is to bring about some transformation. If something is promised by an agent who is both faithful and capable of implementing the promise, some *change* in the situation of the present will occur. The Bible and Marx offer in different ways not simply 'interpretations' of the world, but also that which is to 'change' it.[6] Second, the transcendent is often more appropriately expressed in temporal terms as 'ahead' of us, rather than in exclusively spatial imagery as 'above' us. This opens up the possibility of incorporating the present moment within a larger narrative or temporal plot, which establishes its significance without resort to more problematic notions of a so-called two-storey world-view.[7] More important, along the lines indicated by Ian Ramsey (as discussed above) the co-operation of temporal and spatial imagery provide major 'qualifying' dimensions which cancel out unwanted resonances otherwise set up by each piece of imagery alone. Third, without this temporal dimension, Christian theology plays into the hands of the criticisms of Nietzsche and Heidegger that Christianity becomes a world-denying 'Platonism for the people'.

Moltmann takes up the powerful temporal imagery of the experience of the transcendent in the New Testament as dawn or daybreak. The 'beyond' enters our present horizons, he writes, as 'the divine quickening power of the new creation . . . It places the whole earthly and bodily person in the daybreak colours of the new earth . . . the raising from death to eternal life'.[8]

This temporal contrast between present and future entails in some cases temporal narrative, but probably in all cases promise. This appears in the Old Testament, the first three Gospels, Acts, Hebrews and Paul. Arguably recent literary and narrative-theory approaches to John also identify this aspect of temporal plot in the Fourth Gospel.[9] Without doubt, the 'formerly' of predicament and bondage and the 'now' or 'then' of promised freedom for a new future find paradigmatic expression in the Old Testament, especially in Exodus. Thus J. Severino Croatto sees the exodus events as a model of renewed selfhood for liberation theology.[10] The importance of this theological twentieth-century context and example is that it firmly gives the lie

---

[6] Marx's eleventh thesis in his *Theses on Feuerbach* reads: 'The philosophers have only *interpreted* the world . . . the point is, to *change* it' (*Writings of the Young Marx on Philosophy and Society*, New York: Doubleday, 1967, 402).

[7] Moltmann, *The Spirit of Life*, 90.

[8] Ibid. 95.

[9] E.g. R. A. Culpepper, *Anatomy of the Fourth Gospel* (Philadelphia: Fortress, 1983) and Mark Stibbe (ed.), *The Gospel of John as Literature* (Leiden: Brill, 1993).

[10] J. Severino Croatto, *Exodus. A Hermeneutics of Freedom* (Eng. New York: Orbis, 1981).

to any suggestion on the part of Nietzsche, Foucault, or others, that Christian theology *causes 'docility'*. It is beyond contradiction that liberation theology encourages *the throwing off of 'docility'*. Parallels with deliverance from a servile life-style in Egypt to a life of risk and venture intensify this rejection of claims about Christianity and 'docility'.

In the first three Gospels it has become virtually a convention to teach every generation of theological students that in the message of Jesus 'the Kingdom of God has come' (Matt. 12:28; Luke 11:20); 'the Kingdom of God has yet to come' (Matt. 6:10). The well-worn history of the interpretations of Weiss and Schweitzer, of C. H. Dodd and of J. Jeremias are regularly rehearsed and documented.[11] But the theological significance of these issues seems often to be left hanging in the air. These formulations may leave us with the notion that the fundamental message of Jesus either took the form of a temporal paradox, or, more positively, declared that while he has begun to inaugurate the reign of God, this remains hidden. But this does not seem radically to advance from the temporal situation of Israel in the Old Testament, for whom God also 'reigned', other than to say that the time of 'coming' is nearer than before (Mark 1:15).

My former Sheffield colleague Bruce D. Chilton draws on parallels with the Targum of Isaiah to indicate that the issue turns on modes of God's self-revelation. It sets up a contrast between a hidden but effective presence of God in Jesus and a future disclosure of God 'in strength'.[12] This no longer appears to offer only paradoxical estimates about present and future time, or 'imminence' as such, but something further when we translate it into the language of divine *immanence* and *transcendence*. Divine action and presence through 'weakness', humiliation and renunciation of 'power' in the incarnation and the cross reflect the dimension of immanence. It is a model of the rejection of manipulative power. But divine transcendence is disclosed more openly in a promised series of future events which culminate in the public disclosure of the end-time. Language about the kingdom attains its most effective currency when we perceive that divine transcendence finds expression in temporal imagery, alongside other modes of language. Thereby it places promise at the forefront of the agenda.

In Acts the theme of an ever-onward call ahead appears strongly in Stephen's speech (Acts 7:2–53). Fixed institutions, such as the temple, remain ambivalent, for they lose the ever-onward symbolism of the mobile tabernacle. David's request to build a temple was refused, since,

---

[11] The point is too well known to require documentation. A summary of classic approaches can be found in N. Perrin, *The Kingdom of God in the Teaching of Jesus* (London: SCM, 1963).

[12] B. D. Chilton, *God in Strength. Jesus' Announcement of the Kingdom* (Freistadt: Plöchl, 1979).

'the Most High does not dwell in houses made with hands' (7:46–48). The call of Abraham carried with it no advance information about his eventual destination (7:3). Moreover, 'possession' of the promised land lay beyond his own temporal horizon, except *as promised* (7:5).

Acts 7 has close affinities with the theology of the Epistle to the Hebrews, as most agree. We have already noted Cullmann's proposal that when faith is defined as 'the assurance of things hoped for' and the substance of 'things not seen' (Heb. 11:1), the parallelism may most convincingly be explained as 'not seen' because they have not yet taken place. This coheres with the series of examples of faith throughout this chapter.[13] Noah, for instance, built an ark to save his family from drowning when as yet any evidence of an impending flood was simply 'not seen' (11:7). The exodus and the entry into Canaan proceeded on the basis of promise alone, and thereby is described as taking place 'by faith' (11:29–31). Again, this has nothing to do with 'docility' or passive conformism. It invites venture and courage. It entails neither the 'presumption' of modernity that everything can be known and controlled, nor the 'despair' of postmodernity that no strategy, no purpose, no order, no future, can beckon from 'beyond' the horizons of the self in its present situatedness, to borrow Moltmann's terms. He comments: 'Both forms of hopelessness . . . cancel the wayfaring character of hope.'[14] Divine promise 'points beyond'.[15]

We have noted already the promissory orientation of the Pauline writings in passages about the Holy Spirit as the 'first fruits' of a yet fuller harvest still to come (Rom. 8:23; 2 Cor. 1:22). Paul resonates with a specific postmodern theme, however, in his emphasis on the *pluriform grammar of hope*. Hope can be born out of diverse situations. Sometimes, as in Rom. 4:18 it consists in 'hoping against hope' when the sheer emptiness of the present shifts our focus to the word of promise. As Moltmann declares in *The Crucified God*, '*unless it apprehends the pain of the negative, Christian hope cannot be realistic and liberating as hope*'.[16] In Paul's words, who 'hopes' for what they see? (Rom. 8:24). On the other hand, hope also functions with a different grammar. In other situations it is the prior experience of the faithfulness of God to perform his promise that engenders and nurtures a hope which is founded on more than a sheer act of venture. 'The One who calls you is faithful, and he will do this' (1 Thess. 5:24). There is nothing monolithic or globally 'fixed' about the grammar of hope in Paul and in other biblical writings.

[13] On Hebrews 11, cf. especially Paul Ellingworth, *Commentary on Hebrews*, New International Greek Testament (Grand Rapids: Eerdmans, and Carlisle: Paternoster, 1993), 558–633.

[14] Moltmann, *Theology of Hope*, 23.

[15] Ibid. 201.

[16] Moltmann, *The Crucified God*, 5 (my italics).

We do not have space to trace this pluriform grammar of hope elsewhere. But this is hardly necessary, since most can recall such Psalms as that which begins 'Out of the depths have I cried to Thee' (Ps. 130:1) and can compare such examples with expressions of confident hope based on successive experiences (whether corporately or individually) of promises already faithfully performed.

If we consider briefly one or two specific examples from the history of Christian thought, it emerges that a theology of the word of God in Luther and in Tyndale remains closely related to a theology of promise. Luther attacks 'presumption' (to use Moltmann's phrase) in the 'realized eschatology' of Carlstadt, Müntzer, and the radical 'enthusiasts' or 'spiritual fanatics'. They act as if all promise had already been performed and transposed into triumphalist statement. They abandon a *theologia crucis* for an illusory and manipulative *theologia gloriae*. But, Luther writes, God: 'rules through the Word, and not in a visible and public manner. It is like beholding the sun through a cloud . . . But after the clouds have passed, both light and sun rule . . . It is dark and hidden at present, or concealed and covered, comprehended entirely in faith and in the Word.'[17]

This theme of 'hiddenness' appears especially in the *Heidelberg Disputation* of 1518, where Luther speaks of 'the hinder parts of God'. God is not to be found 'except in sufferings and in the cross'.[18] But it would contradict all that Luther says elsewhere about faith or joyful boldness based on promise if we were to interpret this, with Nietzsche, as 'world-denying'. The issue is quite different and more profound. Faith is not some psychological 'inner state', but a bold appropriation of divine promise, upon which a person acts.

Among the English Reformers, William Tyndale stands nearest to Luther in his recognition of the close relation between the biblical writings and promise. Again, space prohibits a detailed comment. But 'promise' becomes Tyndale's most favoured term for the effective 'performance' of reading biblical texts. In his *A Pathway into the Holy Scripture* he defines the New Testament as 'a book wherein are contained the promises of God; and the deeds of them which believe them, or believe them not'.[19] 'Gospel' is the 'joyful tidings' which enact a series of what we nowadays call speech-acts: naming, appointing,

---

[17] Martin Luther, *Luther's Works*, vol. 28 (Saint Louis: Concordia, 1973), 124.
[18] Martin Luther, in *Luther: Early Theological Works*, ed. J. Atkinson (London: SCM, 1962), 291. The theme is developed in A. C. Thiselton, 'Luther and Barth on 1 Corinthians 15', in W. P. Stephens (ed.), *The Bible, the Church and the Reformation: Studies in Honour of James Atkinson on his Eightieth Birthday* (Sheffield: Sheffield Academic Press, 1995), 258–89.
[19] William Tyndale, 'A Pathway into the Holy Scripture', in *Doctrinal Treatises and Introductions to Different Portions of the Holy Scriptures* (Cambridge: Cambridge University Press (Parker Society edn.) 1848), 1–29. See further P. Satterthwaite and D. F. Wright (eds.), *Pathway into the Holy Scripture* (Grand Rapids: Eerdmans, 1994), esp. essays by Carl R. Trueman and A. C. Thiselton.

declaring, condemning, forgiving, justifying; but most repeatedly in these pages, promising.[20]

In the twentieth century Karl Barth has most characteristically related word and promise in the context of a contrast between the present and the future. God's word, he asserts, is God's very act and his very presence. Yet because of the temporal situation, 'I understand myself as confronted with promise . . . I see myself in the specific light that falls upon my existence from this'.[21] God's promise, however, is not empty, but 'is the transposing of man into a wholly new state of one who has accepted and appropriated the promise'.[22] A series of liberating and empowering speech-acts, namely 'election, revelation . . . calling . . . all denote a promise'.[23] These are not simply timeless statements about states of affairs as they now exist: 'the Word of God is itself the act of God'.[24]

For Barth, all this is fundamental for any possibility of interpreting or understanding God *as God*. God discloses his identity in acts of promise by which he 'gives himself', in that he freely chooses to bind himself to perform what he has pledged. Here we encounter two features which hardly appear in the perceptions of the postmodern self. First, *gift*, which *depends on nothing in return*, constitutes the *rejection of manipulative power or self-interest*. Second, gift comes *from beyond the horizons of the situatedness of the self*. That is why an 'expected' gift may lose something of its character of 'gift'. Gift ideally includes the delight of surprise. Part of Barth's peculiar stature lies in his interpreting God as self-imparting Trinity whose nature is to give in sovereign, unconstrained love. His gift of himself includes his pledge to give 'His time' in that his commitment of himself to act in love is bound up with a created sequence of 'a time of promise' and a contrast between 'what is and what is not yet'.[25] As we shall see, this decisively fits 'a logic of promise, in which God pledges himself to act. In this time of 'not yet', what the non-theist may construe as the *absence* of God in practice represents only a pregnant period of *hiddenness* in readiness to act.

Wolfhart Pannenberg (b. 1928) unfolds a pluriform grammar of hope and promise with impressive weight. At one level trust in God's promise arises on the basis of an ongoing tradition of experiences of hope and fulfilment in the public history of Israel and the New Testament communities. As successive hopes find fulfilment, a tradition of 'effective history', or 'history of effects' (*Wirkungsgeschichte*) emerges in which horizons of promise become enlarged and filled with new

[20] Tyndale, loc. cit., 8–14.
[21] Barth, *Church Dogmatics*, I/1, sect. 6, 218.
[22] Ibid. sect. 5, 152.
[23] Ibid. 149–50.
[24] Ibid. 143.
[25] Barth, *Church Dogmatics*, II/2, sects. 14 and 15.

content.[26] The new coheres with emerging, stable, patterns, but genuine newness leaves room for surprise. The content of hope becomes ever richer, fuller, and more capable of provisional definition.

Yet at a different level, the unsatisfactory absences or limitations of the present remain without meaning *until these receive meaning in the light of a promised future. Only within a larger temporal frame do the possibilities and constraints of the present moment find meaning and significance.*[27] Hence, primarily through biblical and systematic theology, but also partly through Hegel, Pannenberg arrives at a fundamental insight about an enlarged temporal context of meaning. We have noted close parallels in Ricoeur's hermeneutics of the self as finding meaning within the enlarged horizon of temporal narrative and temporal plot. In Part II we considered the value of this approach, in contrast to the problematic claims in Part III from Cupitt about 'instantaneousness' as a privileged vantage point. Such a narrow account, we observed, leaves insoluble problems about meaning, identity, self and God.

Pannenberg expounds with great rigour and sophistication a perspective which entirely matches the everyday experiences of ordinary people. In a play or in a story (and similarly in life), 'who a person is' emerges in that person's interaction with others within an unfolding temporal sequence. But our interpretation remains provisional until the last scene or the last chapter. Even so, in the case of Christian people *'who we are' emerges in terms of God's larger purposes and promises for the world, for society, for the church and for us.* This purposive anticipation of the future finds expression in our sense of *being called by God to a task within that frame.* We find our identity and meaning when we discover our *vocation.* This does not exclude a multiplicity of compatible vocations. For example, one may be called to work at a certain job, to be a good husband or wife, to give support to some community or person, and so forth. But this purposive 'beyond' makes the matter quite different from the imposed role-performances of the postmodern self which form *part* of his or her pre-given situatedness in life.

On the same basis we may discover what it means to interpret God *as God.* Pannenberg begins with Israel's experience of promise. He writes: 'On the basis of promise and beyond all historically experienced fulfilments, Israel expected further fulfilment.'[28] 'Effective history' provides a continuity within which Israel discovered a stability of meaning in the acts of the faithful God, while this also allowed for an 'open' future which points to an unfulfilled hitherto 'not yet'. Horizons of hope begin to assume stable directions or reference points, but these

[26] Pannenberg, *Basic Questions in Theology*, vol. 1, 15–80, 96–136, and in other writings.
[27] Ibid. vol. 3, 192–210.
[28] Ibid. vol. 1, 23.

do not foreclose new surprising events or experiences which nevertheless cohere with God's self-imparting 'character' hitherto disclosed. Regularities approximate to what Wittgenstein (in another context) called 'rules' of sufficient stability to provide markers for meaning, but also of sufficient flexibility to allow for the new creation in unpredicted ways. Continuity and stable markers, in Pannenberg's terms, arise from 'the one history which binds together the eschatological community of Jesus Christ and ancient Israel . . . Jesus Christ is the revelation of God only in the light of the Old Testament promises . . . Jesus . . . is understood in the framework of the history of God with Israel . . .'[29] Even the events of the ministry of Jesus point beyond themselves to the resurrection; and his resurrection and the event of Pentecost point, in turn, to yet future modes of promise and fulfilment. As Pannenberg, (following Gadamer) expresses it: 'A new horizon is formed.'[30]

[29] Ibid. 25, 26.
[30] Ibid. 117.

23

Further Issues on 'Interpreting God': Christology and Trinity

THE vistas opened up by this framework of promise should not mislead us into taking less than adequate account of the 'finality' of Christ in the New Testament as God's definitive representation of his identity to the world. This aspect cannot detract from our promissory perspective. For among all the writings of the New Testament, that which perhaps most strongly stresses promise and futurity, namely the Epistle to the Hebrews, is also precisely where we find the most explicit statements about the identity of Christ as 'the exact imprint (Greek, *charaktèr*) of his [God's] very being' (Heb. 1:3; cf. Col. 1:15). Whereas the disclosures of God through the prophets were varied, partial, or piecemeal, a definitive disclosure took place in Christ, who reflects God's glory (Heb. 1:1–3).

Nevertheless the *understanding* of that glory and 'imprint' may expand, as our horizons of corporate experience perceive and interpret its successive effects in what Gadamer and Pannenberg call the 'effective history' or 'history of effects' which constitutes an ongoing, but also stable, tradition (*Wirkungsgeschichte*).[1] Even as definitive word, 'the image of Christ' assumes a fundamental role in relation to *future* promise. To be transformed into 'the image of Christ' and to become 'like him' constitutes the heart of the divine promise which lifts the self out of its pre-defined situatedness and beckons from 'beyond' to a new future (Rom. 8:29; 1 Cor. 15:49; 2 Cor. 3:18; 1 John 3:2). Nevertheless this new future is by no means itself pre-packaged by fixed horizons fully determined in advance. The writer of 1 John concedes that 'What we will be has not yet been revealed. What we do know is this: when he is revealed, we shall be like him, for we shall see him as he is' (1 John 3:2).

How or *in what ways* that image will be reflected in a particular self's future transformation has not yet been specified. For the Hebrew people and the biblical writers to be 'living' was to be 'on the move'. Hence, since the God of promise is the 'living' God (who is ever on the move) even the post-resurrection mode of existence, the nature of which

---

[1] Gadamer, *Truth and Method* (revised edn.), 300–7.

is determined by the Spirit of life (1 Cor. 15:44) and bears the image of Christ (15:49), cannot be conceived of as a static existence. It is not like a final 'frozen' shot of a movie or film. Can we imagine that after the consummation of this world-order, God will do nothing further new? Will he set no further purposive tasks? Will he allow the renewed self to become as much a victim to a heavenly but now also routinized 'situatedness' which the postmodern self perceives as frustration? The reversal of decay and frustration promised in 1 Cor. 15:43–44 suggests otherwise.

This process of creative transformation through the Holy Spirit, however, begins in the present, even if as partial 'first fruits' only. Again, Moltmann gives profound expression to the main point: 'Through faith the *hitherto unexplored creative powers of God are thrown open* in men and women. So faith means *becoming creative with God and his Spirit*. Faith leads to a creative life which is life-giving *through love*, in places where death rules and people resign themselves and surrender to it. Faith *awakens trust* in the still unrealized possibilities in human beings – in oneself and in other people.'[2] Moltmann has earlier made it clear that such 'possibilities' depend not on *human* 'spirituality' in the sense of cultivating the so-called 'inner' human spirit; but in the biblical sense of 'that which pertains to the Holy Spirit of God'.[3] (This also decisively determines our understanding of 'spiritual body' [RSV] in 1 Cor. 15:44.)

Yet this 'creativity', which transforms and reverses the passive situatedness of the postmodern self, becomes possible through the Holy Spirit because the Spirit transposes self-interest, conflict, and bids-for-power into *love for others* (for individuals and groups) *and for the Other* (for God and for whatever is not-self). Hence the co-operative effects of the Holy Spirit and the cross of Christ together actualize God's self-giving *as God*. Thus E. Jüngel writes: '*The crucified is, as it were, the material definition of what is meant by "God"*.'[4] If God is interpreted *as God* because we understand him as self-imparting *love*, then the paradigmatic expression of his identity is his *cruciform action and being*. Here Jüngel broadly follows Luther and Barth. But more remains to be considered. If the cross constitutes the paradigm of God's gift of himself *to others*, not only suffering, pain and cost come to view, but also its *inter-personal, interactive relation to others*.

Here we perceive the relation between the interactive, inter-personal nature of the act of God in the cross of Christ, and God as holy Trinity. We may note almost in passing, however, that an account of the cross which interprets it only as an act of moral self-sacrifice which operated through 'moral influence' cannot address the predicament of humanity

[2] Moltmann, *The Spirit of Life*, 115 (my italics).
[3] Ibid. 8–10.
[4] E. Jüngel, *God as the Mystery of the World* (Eng. Edinburgh: T&T Clark, and Grand Rapids: Eerdmans, 1983), 13 (my italics).

as this is perceived by the postmodern self.[5] The more innocent self of modernity with its optimistic confidence in human consciousness to be in control and to determine its own destiny may more readily interpret redemption as relating to mental and moral states. But the postmodern self knows what it is to be trapped by its own past decisions and placed in bondage to a situatedness which is not of its choice. It knows the need to be released from external forces beyond its control, and to be delivered from the tyranny of corporate self-interests and competing power-interests. Hence the biblical language about 'redemption' may be heard in a more objective sense (Rom. 3:24; 1 Cor. 1:30, 6:20; Col. 1:14; Heb. 9:15). Redemption 'from the curse of the law' (Gal. 3:13) may plausibly be interpreted as more than freedom from legalism or moralism. It promises deliverance from all the cause-effect chains of forces which hold the self to its past, through the work of Christ and the agency of the Holy Spirit who opens new possibilities of futurity 'from beyond' the situatedness of the self.

The Holy Spirit, however, acts as more than a 'new force'. Woven into the logic of the work of Christ and the Spirit is the *inter-personal, interactive character of love*. Love is given and received by two or more persons *in relationship*. The cross *restores* this. Vincent Brümmer among others, expounds the inter-personal and creative character of this love, drawing on Nygren as well as his own conceptual analysis of personal language.[6] Brümmer points out that whereas Nygren saw *agapē* as creative, and *eros* as self-centred, Nietzsche regarded *agapē* as promoting a 'slave morality' which keeps humanity weak and inferior' as over against a 'superior' God, while eros reflected a will-to-power.[7] Brümmer himself offers a different conceptual analysis: 'In a relation of fellowship or love I identify with you by *serving your interests as being my own*. This devotion to your good is unconditional . . . I do not serve your interests on condition that you serve mine in return.'[8]

This at once invites a discussion of the *basis* of this self-giving, interactive, inter-personal love *as characterizing the very nature of God himself as Trinity. A solitary being cannot 'give' or 'love'* unless 'another' enters the scene *to receive and to be loved*. Yet if God's nature *as love* cannot find expression unless or until he creates a created order, must we not conclude that his identity *as God* depends on his creation?

[5] The so-called moral influence theory of the atonement is associated in historical theology with Peter Abelard, and developed more carefully by Schleiermacher. In England Hastings Rashdall, and with more caution G. W. Lampe, have been associated with this approach. 'Moral influence' undeniably forms *part* of the New Testament understanding of the cross. The controversial question is whether it offers a *complete* or *adequate* account of the varied New Testament imagery.

[6] Vincent Brümmer, *The Model of Love. A Study in Philosophical Theology* (Cambridge: Cambridge University Press, 1993), esp. 127–245.

[7] Ibid. 139–40.

[8] Ibid. 239 (my italics).

The consequences of interpreting God as Trinity for inter-personal understandings of love, respect, mutuality and more broadly human society, have been explored recently by Wolfhart Pannenberg and especially by Moltmann, as well as by such theologians as W. Kasper, Leonardo Boff and Colin E. Gunton. If God's identity (to follow Barth) consists in his self-imparting love as Trinity, divine personhood, independently of his creation, embodies the capacity for interactive reciprocity. At the same time, God's 'oneness' represents neither solitariness nor self-love of the like-minded, but that which *could be no other* if love is pure, non-manipulative love 'serving the interests of the Other as one's own' (to paraphrase Brümmer). This understanding of 'oneness' saturates the Fourth Gospel: 'The Father and I are one' (John 10:30; cf. 17:22). 'Whoever has seen me has seen the Father . . . I am in the Father and the Father is in me' (John 14:9, 10). This divine 'oneness' becomes a model and pattern for a community's oneness of love and mutual regard in John 17:10–24. We shall argue that it is over-hasty and unhermeneutical to write off this approach as mere 'social Trinity'.

In this kind of context Pannenberg works out a Trinitarian theology in which love constitutes the ground of selfhood. Pannenberg writes:

> In the mutual love of the Trinitarian persons, love does not simply denote activities in their mutual relations . . . *Their selfhood . . . manifests itself through the reciprocal relation of those who are bound together in love.* Each receives his or her self afresh from the other, and since the self-giving is mutual there is no one-sided dependence in the sense of belonging to one another. *The personality of each I is constituted by the relation to the Thou*, but the basis of its being thus constituted is not the Thou as such, as another I . . . It is the mystery that holds sway between the I and the Thou. *This mystery is the power of love.*[9]

Pannenberg alludes to the Johannine theme that 'God is love' and its instantiation in the mission of the Son (1 John 4:8 and 4:16).

Moltmann also argues that a Trinitarian understanding of God provides not only a basis for interpreting what it is to speak of God as personal, but also a foundation for respecting persons as persons in relations of love and mutuality in human society. He offers a constructive hermeneutic of historical theology, in as much as he refuses *to abstract* talk about 'the economic Trinity', 'the monarchic Trinity', 'the social Trinity', 'modal Trinity', or other construals from their *hermeneutical 'point'* in theological discourse. It is unhelpful simply to dismiss the approaches of Moltmann, Pannenberg, Boff, Kasper, Gunton or others simply on the grounds that one may have reservations about a so-called social model of Trinity. This is not to abandon caution in another direction, however. If our theological understanding of Trinity

---

[9] W. Pannenberg, *Systematic Theology*, vol. 1 (Eng. Edinburgh: T&T Clark, and Grand Rapids: Eerdmans, 1991), 426–7 (my italics).

calls into question our social assumptions, this is as it should be. If, however, we are tempted to opt for a 'social' Trinity in order to legitimate an egalitarian view of society, this becomes manipulation in the service of power-interests and ceases to be a quest for theological truth.

Moltmann stresses the utter mutuality and reciprocity of communion between Father, Son and Holy Spirit in an interactive intimacy for which he uses the Patristic term *perichoresis*. He seeks to integrate the different 'linear' abstractions which appear to imply a gradation of 'Father, Son and Spirit', or 'Son, Father and Spirit', or 'Father, Spirit and Son', in favour of 'the self-circling . . . movement of *perichoresis*' which 'puts an end to his [the Spirit's] position as "third Person" in the Trinity'.[10] He wishes to restore 'the Trinitarian Personhood of the Spirit' as entailing a subjectivity that is 'constituted by his inter-subjectivity'.[11] 'The personhood of God the Holy Spirit is the loving, self-communicating, out-fanning and out-pouring presence of the eternal divine life of the triune God.'[12] At the beginning of *The Spirit of Life* Moltmann observes: 'Personhood is always being-in-relationship.'[13] He concludes that it therefore misses the point to ransack biblical passages simply for examples of 'personal' activities on the part of the Spirit. The personhood of the Holy Spirit is perceived *as personhood* within the context of the mutuality of the Trinity.

Pannenberg follows a different method at this point, but space prohibits more detailed explorations. We may note, however, that from within a different ecclesial tradition Walter Kasper uses language very close to that of Moltmann's 'being-in-relationship' and Pannenberg's constitutive 'relation to the Thou'. In contrast to a more static, self-contained interpretation of God, Kasper interprets God-as-Trinity as 'being-from-another and being-for-another'.[14]

Leonardo Boff and Colin E. Gunton, like Moltmann in his earlier book *The Trinity and the Kingdom of God*, draw on notions of *perichoresis* and reciprocity in their interpretations of God as Trinity to draw implications not only for Christian theology but also for society. Boff's argument has now become widely known, especially as a reflection of the distinctive concerns of Latin American liberation theology. He concedes that there were historical reasons for an emphasis on the 'monarchichal' model among the Greek Fathers and perhaps for a certain tendency towards modalism in many Latin Fathers. Nevertheless, he urges, only a restoration of the *perichoresis* model of interpenetration, mutuality, co-sharing and loving reciprocity will provide an adequate basis for a less authoritarian and more 'equal'

[10] Moltmann, *The Spirit of Life*, 304; cf. 289–309.
[11] Ibid. 289.
[12] Ibid.
[13] Ibid. 11.
[14] W. Kasper, *The God of Jesus Christ* (Eng. New York: Crossroad, 1986), 288.

society.[15] Gunton shares with these four writers the view that person-hood, unlike mere individuality, is true 'personhood' not in solitariness but only in relation to other persons. This is instantiated not only in the personhood of God as Trinity, but also in the need for mutual respect, each for the other *as other* in society.[16]

If we had more space, we might have explored 'social' or more accurately *perichoretic* approaches to the Trinity in the work of my former Durham colleague David Brown, or in C. Plantinga, J. Zizioulas and others.[17] For the present we may note that the above approach accords precisely with our endorsement in Parts I and II of Betti's plea for hermeneutics as nurturing 'respect for the Other' and our work on the hermeneutics of the self in Dilthey and especially in Ricoeur. By contrast, it diverges from caricatures of traditional Christian views of God as a lone being consumed with his own power-interests noted in our discussion of Cupitt and the Sea of Faith Network. Might we wonder whether some of their critiques would have been less strident, less narrow, and more relevant if they had engaged explicitly in their writings with the Trinitarian interpretations of God proposed by Moltmann, Pannenberg, Gunton and others? In all probability their tendency to think of an outdated 'God' as the solitary being seldom found in contemporary systematic theology stems from their tendency to subsume Christian theology within philosophy of religion. Our conclusions in Part II, however, showed that even an interpretation of human selfhood which underrates the importance of 'relationality' to the other is doomed to fail.

---

[15] L. Boff, *Trinity and Society* (Eng. New York: Orbis, 1988).

[16] Colin E. Gunton, *The Promise of Trinitarian Theology* (Edinburgh: T&T Clark, 1991).

[17] David Brown, 'Trinity and Personhood' and C. Plantinga, 'Social Trinity' appear in R. J. Feenstra and C. Plantinga (eds.), *Trinity, Incarnation and Atonement* (Notre Dame: University of Notre Dame Press, 1989), 49–78 and 21–47 respectively; cf. J. Zizioulas, *Being as Communion* (New York: St Vladimir's Seminary, 1985); and a very recent critical survey by T. H. Speidell, 'A Trinitarian Ontology of Persons in Society', *Scottish Journal of Theology* 47 (1994), 283–300. Cf. also A. Thatcher, *Truly a Person, Truly a God* (London: SPCK, 1990), 122–33.

24

Will-to-Power De-centred,
Transformed and Re-centred in
Promise and Love

WE may now gather together strands from other parts of this study
as well as the earlier sections of this fourth part. We have noted
(above, p. 130) David Harvey's analysis of the postmodern self as
characterized by fragmentation, indeterminacy, and an intense distrust
of all claims to universal truth, or of claims to offer universal strategies
for arbitration or for progress. The postmodern self lives within a
labyrinth of diversified networks, and suspects 'order' and ordered
structures as disguising power-interests on behalf of the privileged.
Its multi-media linguistic world bombards the postmodern self with
images, myths and signs; but these carry sub-texts and multi-layered
meanings which never reach 'closure'. Signs point only to other signs,
ad infinitum.

The postmodern self, as Lyon reminded us, has a 'constructed'
identity. We considered this in terms of the social theory discussed by
Richard Harvey Brown and others. With Norman Denzin we noted
the anger, alienation and conflict which marks the situatedness of the
postmodern self. Loss of hope, we saw, sprang at least in part from the
collapse of any norm or truth which might otherwise be independent
of someone else's power-interest, into sexism, racism, or socio-economic
competition. Even the bureaucrats and politicians whose reason for
existence was to arbitrate between competing groups have become
drawn into the same empire-building power-interests as, at a more
modest level, the postmodern self seeks for its own security and self-
protection.

Worst of all, if, with Lyotard, no meta-narrative or 'larger picture'
can be trusted as constituting more than the disguised power-interests
of some tradition or sub-culture, what is the 'point' of trying ceaselessly
to become or to remain a 'winner'? In pragmatic power-play there are
only winners and losers; we cannot ask about 'the point' of seeking to
win, other than to secure the self-protection which keeps us from losing.
But is this all that human life consists in? Is every utterance to be 'erased'
before its sound has died away, every written word 'to move on' before
the ink is dry? Is every act of sacrifice for the company, for the family,
for the profession, for the nation, merely a competitive power-bid at

the expense of other families, other businesses, other nations, or the public?

Is everything only instantaneous and ethnocentric? Dilthey, Ricoeur and Pannenberg from quite different viewpoints have urged that 'the point' can emerge only within some larger frame or 'temporal narrative'. But how can the postmodern self, which has become habituated to suspect and to distrust, know whether such an extended narrative is anything but a wish-fulfilment deceptively projected by the self, or, still worse, a manipulative construct which serves the power-interests of those who suggest it?

We can only entertain a hypothesis to question this distrust. Let us suppose that all that Christian traditions claim about love, and about God as self-imparting Trinity, might be true. If love, to refer again to Brümmer, serves your interests as being my own (not my own as yours), what reason could there be for one who loves like that to use manipulation, or for the other to suspect it? A love in which a self genuinely *gives* itself to the Other *in the interests of the Other* dissolves the acids of suspicion and deception. For, as Rahner so powerfully argues, why should there be any need for the deception which serves to protect the self if the self is loved, welcomed, accepted, and reconciled-as-one with the Other? Yet is this not the meaning of Christology, the cross, and perichoretic Trinity as these relate to the plight and predicament of the postmodern self?

If this hypothesis is considered with sufficient seriousness to constitute a *working hypothesis*, then, as the author of the Epistle to the Hebrews, and Luther, among others, point out, acting in the present on the basis of that which is yet to be proven or 'seen' constitutes a faith that has world-transforming and self-transforming effects. It transforms the self because, like the experience of resurrection, it *'reconstitutes'* self-identity as no longer the passive victim of forces of the past which 'situated' it within a network of pre-given roles and performances, but opens out a new future in which new purpose brings a 'point' to its life. The self perceives its call and its value as one-who-is-loved within the larger narrative plot of God's loving purposes for the world, for society, and for the self.

Yet the suspicion may persist: is it not mere wishful thinking to act on the basis of a hypothesis which may prove to be without foundation? Three comments may be offered. First, we noted Küng's rejoinder to the claims of Freud that the mere wish for something to be the case makes *neither its truth nor its falsity more probable*. Fears about what might or might not be the case invite the same comment. Second, an *initial* venture on the basis of a hypothesis coheres closely with what is termed 'preliminary' or 'provisional' understanding ('pre-under-standing') in hermeneutics. It awaits subsequent confirmation, dis-confirmation, or modification and correction in the light of further advances in the process. We explored this principle in Part II. Third, in

Pannenberg's view initial or provisional acts of trust may lead to a discovery of patterns of promise and fulfilment which seldom exhaustively match expectations, but instantiate both continuity and room for novelty. It is injudicious to foreclose the possibility of discovering 'the new' beyond one's prior horizons. Neither the creative action of God nor new human experience remains entirely predictable on the basis of the past alone.

This initial and provisional exploration may lead to an experience of 'reconstituted' identity. We may begin to ask ourselves whether either the self of modernity or the postmodern self need be the only possible selfhood.

Perhaps the self of modernity had been right to hope, but wrong about the basis on which it built its hope. Perhaps the postmodern self had been right to despair if will-to-power exhausted the content of all reality, but wrong in its assumption that this exhausted all that might be called 'real'.

Indeed, it becomes arguable that a life based wholly on a hermeneutic of suspicion and iconoclasm has about it more than an element of self-contradiction. Granted that *many* bureaucrats live only to build empires, that *many* professional people put the interests of their guild before those of the public, or that *many* religious people treat religion and 'God' as a means of self-affirmation or for purposes of power, by what *doctrine* (when the postmodern self rejects doctrine) can we say that *all* bureaucrats, professionals, or religious people live in this way? We began with this question in Part I, when we considered Nietzsche.

Moreover, a theology of the cross underlines that the strategy of seeking *to gain goals by power or for power* is a *self-defeating strategy*. The will-to-power merely provokes conflict which escalates and can never be finally resolved in that those who gain it are trapped into ever-more-complex manipulative strategies to retain it. By contrast, *giving the self to the Other in love and serving the Other's interests as one's own remains ever fresh and creative, in that it builds*. It does not have to struggle ceaselessly with some other external force. It builds its own self-identity as lover-in-relation-to-the-loved, or as loved-in-relation-to-lover. In theological terms the transformation of will-to-power into will-to-love means being transformed into the image of Christ. As such, the self finds itself beloved and cherished by the Father and the Spirit, and, bearing the likeness of Christ discovers the joy of finding its life in losing it, of receiving in giving, of experiencing resurrection through the cross.

It now becomes apparent why in the early Christian communities of the first century it became fundamental that Jewish Christians and Gentile Christians were 'to accept and welcome one another' (Rom. 15:7). If the postmodern self survives by clinging to the internal values and criteria of specific sub-groups, this in the end leads to conflict between competing groups. But this stands in contradiction to the gospel not only because it is self-defeating, but because it is not the way of love, which dissolves conflict. Love not only 'builds' (1 Cor. 8:1); it reflects the character of Christ. 'Christ is our peace; in his flesh he has made both groups into one, and has broken down the dividing wall' (Eph. 2:14).

The New Testament applies this breaking down of barriers between cultures in ethnic traditions equally to gender (Gal. 3:28, 29). It is understandable why Simone de Beauvoir insisted in her work *The Second Sex* (1949) that the 'identities' of women should not be 'defined' in terms of their relation to some 'other' who is usually male, as 'the wife of X', but as 'themselves'.[1] But our discussion of inter-personal selfhood and the Trinity might suggest that her point could be strenghthened, but also purged of conflict, by expressing the issue the other way round: *all* persons, not only women, enhance their 'identity' in relationality with others and with the Other. This encourages reciprocity and equality without a potential for competition or conflict on behalf of one group as against another.

One of my current doctoral candidates, Mark L. Y. Chan of Singapore, has expressed the principle more broadly in a sensitive published essay on corporate spirituality. He writes: 'Self does not exist except in relation to others. There is no "I" without the "Thou" of others . . . though not in a way that gobbles up a person's individuality . . . In the kingdom of Mammon, people are commodities to be traded and objects to be manipulated.'[2] He points out that while the works of the flesh [in this context, the self in pursuit of its own ends] are divisive: 'strife, jealousy, anger, quarrels, dissensions, factions, envy' (Gal. 5:20, 21) the fruit of the Holy Spirit brings oneness and love: 'love, joy, peace, patience, kindness, generosity, fruitfulness, gentleness and self-control' (5:22).

The Holy Spirit comes to be experienced in the present, however, as we have seen, only as the 'first fruits' or first sample sheaf, of a fuller harvest yet to come. The 'fruit' may as yet not be fully ripe. No human person may yet be innocent of all manipulation or self-interest. Yet just as in the present the active agency of the Holy Spirit begins to reshape the self and to reshape the world, so the divine Trinitarian promise of love to complete this transformation will, in turn, reshape every horizon and every interest. For whereas the logic of descriptive statements can do no more than describe what is, the logic of promise shapes the world. As long as a speaker will faithfully stand by the word of promise and has the capacity to perform it, the

---

[1] Simone de Beauvoir, *The Second Sex*: 'Introduction' rp. in E. Marks and I. de Courtivron (eds.), *New French Feminism* (Sussex: Harvester, 1981), 144; cf. 41–56.

[2] Mark Chan, 'Corporate Spirituality', in Mark L. Y. Chan (ed.), *Mercy, Community and Ministry* (Singapore: Catalyst Books/Eagle Communications, 1993), 108, 109, 112; cf. 107–24.

one who speaks will change states of affairs until these finally match the word of promise.

Promise beckons 'from ahead' to invite the postmodern self to discover a reconstituted identity. But through its portrayal of Jesus as controlling model for interpreting both God and human selfhood, the Epistle to the Hebrews accepts the diagnosis offered by many postmodern writers about the vulnerability of the self as a victim to competing power-interests. Jesus chose to accept exposure to hostile forces and manipulation (Heb. 2:8b–17; 12:3). 'Like his brother and sisters in every respect' (2:17), Jesus accepted a role that required even 'trust' (2:13), and prayed 'with loud cries and tears' (5:17). Betrayal, arrest, torture and crucifixion carried this role of self-as-victim to the ultimate. But while this resonates with postmodern perceptions of selfhood, it is not the whole story. Being 'on the receiving end' of hostile power-interests (12:3), constituted for Jesus an *episode within the larger narrative* which only in its wholeness defined his selfhood. As perfect hearer of the image of God (Heb. 1:3) and therefore a definitive interpretation of true humanness as it was meant to be, Jesus recapitulated human experience in order that human selfhood may approach God and find 'grace' (4:16; cf. 2:10; 6:20; 12:2). 'Grace' means love 'without strings'. It signals the end of manipulation; God does not 'compete'.

This epistle now brings two themes together. First, everything rests on divine promise (Heb. 6:13–18; cf. 9:15–22). This constitutes 'a sure and steadfast anchor' (6:19) which *re-centres* the self. It bestows on the self an *identity of worth* and provides *purposive meaning* for the present. Second, the work of Christ gives substance to the promise of a restored 'family likeness', in which the human self, like Christ, once again comes to bear fully the image of God in Christ (Heb. 1:3; Gen. 1:26) as a self defined by giving and receiving, by loving and being loved unconditionally. In the present, self-interest still tarnishes selfhood; manipulation still occurs. But as future promise begins to dawn, interpreting God and human selfhood will come to display ever-closer affinities, even if God will always be God, and a human self, a human self.

Select Bibliography

Apel, Karl-Otto, *Towards a Transformation of Philosophy*, Eng. London: Routledge & Kegan Paul, 1980.

——, *Understanding and Explanation. A Transcendental–Pragmatic Perspective*, Cambridge, Mass: MIT Press, 1984.

Appignanesi, Richard, and Garratt, Chris, *Postmodernism for Beginners*, Cambridge: Icon Books, 1995.

Austin, John L., *How to Do Things with Words*, Oxford: Clarendon Press, 1962, 2nd edn. 1975.

Barrett, Cyril, *Wittgenstein on Ethics and Religious Belief*, Oxford: Blackwell, 1991.

Barstch, H. W. (ed.), *Kerygma und Mythos. Ein Theologisches Gespräch*, 6 vols. with supplements, Hamburg: Reich & Heidrich, 1948 onwards.

Barth, Karl, *Church Dogmatics,* Eng., 14 vols., Edinburgh: T&T Clark, 1957–75.

Barthes, Roland, *Elements of Semiology*, Eng. London: Cape, 1967.

——, *Mythologies*, Eng. London: Cape, 1972.

——, 'From Work to Text', in J. V. Harari (ed.), *Textual Strategies*, Ithaca: Cornell University Press, 1979, 73–81.

Baudrillard, Jean, *Forget Foucault*, Eng. New York: Columbia University Semiotext(e), 1987.

Bauman, Zygmunt, *Hermeneutics and Social Science. Approaches to Understanding*, London: Hutchinson, 1978.

——, *Intimations of Postmodernity*, London and New York: Routledge, 1992.

——, *Postmodern Ethics*, Oxford: Blackwell, 1993.

Benhabib, S., *Situating the Self*, Cambridge: Polity Press, 1992.

Bernstein, Richard J., *Beyond Objectivism and Relativism. Science, Hermeneutics, and Praxis*, Philadelphia: University of Pennsylvania Press, 1991 (1983).

—— (ed.), *Habermas and Modernity*, Cambridge: Polity Press, 1985.

——, *The New Constellation. The Ethical–Political Horizons of Modernity/Postmodernity*, Cambridge: Polity Press, 1991.

Berry, P. and A. Wernick (eds.), *Shadow of Spirit. Postmodernism and Religion*, New York and London: Routledge, 1992.

Betti, Emilio, *Die Hermeneutik als allgemeine Methodik der Geisteswissenschaften*, 2nd edn. Tübingen: Mohr, 1992 (1962).

Bloom, Harold, et al., *Deconstruction and Criticism*, London: Routledge, 1979.

Bonhoeffer, Dietrich, *Gesammelte Schriften,* 5 vols., Munich: Kaiser, 1958–66.
——, *The Cost of Discipleship,* Eng. (unabridged edn.) London: SCM, 1959.
——, *Letters and Papers from Prison,* Eng. (enlarged edn.) London: SCM, 1971.
Braun, Herbert, *Gesammelte Studien zum Neuen Testament und seiner Umwelt,* Tübingen: Mohr, 1962.
Breazeale, Daniel (ed.), *Philosophy and Truth. Selections from Nietzsche's Notebooks of the Early 1870s,* New Jersey: Humanities Press and Sussex: Harvester Press, 1979.
Brill, Susan B., *Wittgenstein and Critical Theory: Beyond Post-modernism and Toward Descriptive Investigations,* Athens: Ohio University Press, 1995.
Brown, David, *The Divine Trinity,* London: Duckworth, 1985.
Brown, R. H., *Society as Text. Essays on Rhetoric, Reason and Reality,* Chicago and London: University of Chicago Press, 1987.
Browning, Don S. and Francis Schüssler Fiorenza (eds.), *Habermas, Modernity and Public Theology,* New York: Crossroad, 1992.
Brueggemann, Walter, *The Bible and Postmodern Imagination. Texts under Negotiation,* London: SCM, 1993.
Brümmer, Vincent, *What are We Doing When We Pray? A Philosophical Inquiry,* London: SCM, 1984.
——, *Speaking of a Personal God,* Cambridge: Cambridge University Press, 1992.
——, *The Model of Love: A Study in Philosophical Theology,* Cambridge: Cambridge University Press, 1993.
Bultmann, Rudolf, *Glauben und Verstehen. Gesammelte Aufsätze,* 4 vols., Tübingen: Mohr, 1964–5.
Campbell, C. A., *On Selfhood and Godhood,* London: Allen & Unwin and New York: Macmillan, 1957.
Capps, Donald, *Pastoral Care and Hermeneutics,* Philadelphia: Fortress, 1984.
Caputo, John D., *Radical Hermeneutics,* Bloomington: Indiana University Press, 1989.
Castelli, Elizabeth A., *Imitating Paul: A Discourse of Power,* Louisville: Westminster and John Knox, 1991.
Connor, Steven, *Postmodernist Culture,* Oxford: Blackwell, 1989.
Cowdell, Scott, *Atheist Priest? Don Cupitt and Christianity,* London: SCM, 1988.
Cullmann, Oscar, *Christ and Time,* Eng. London: SCM, 1951.
Cupitt, Don, *The Leap of Reason,* London: SCM, 1976, 2nd edn. 1985.
——, *Taking Leave of God,* New York: Crossroad, and London: SCM, 1980.
——, *The Sea of Faith,* London: BBC, 1984, 2nd edn. 1994.
——, *Only Human,* London: SCM, 1985.
——, *Life Lines,* London: SCM, 1986.
——, *The Long Legged Fly. A Theology of Language and Desire,* London: SCM, 1987.
——, *Radicals and the Future of the Church,* London: SCM, 1989.
——, *What is a Story?,* London: SCM, 1991.
——, *The Time Being,* London: SCM, 1992.

Cupitt, Don, *After All. Religion Without Alienation*, London: SCM, 1994.
Davaney, Sheila G. (ed.), *Theology at the End of Modernity*, Philadelphia: Trinity Press International, 1991.
Denzin, Norman K., *Images of Postmodern Society. Social Theory and Contemporary Cinema*, London: Sage Publications, 1991.
Derrida, Jacques, *Speech and Phenomena and Other Essays on Husserl's Theory of Signs*, Eng. Evanston: North Western University Press, 1973.
——, *Of Grammatology*, Eng. Baltimore: Johns Hopkins University Press, 1976.
——, *Writing and Difference*, Eng. London: Routledge & Kegan Paul, 1978.
——, 'White Mythology: Metaphor in the Text of Philosophy' in his *Margins of Philosophy*, Eng. New York and London: Harvester Wheatsheaf, 1982.
——, 'No Apocalypse, Not Now (Full speed ahead, seven missiles, seven missives)' *Diacritics* 14, 1984, 20–31.
Dilthey, Wilhelm, *Gesammelte Schriften*, 12 vols., Leipzig and Berlin: Teubner, 1962.
Evans, Donald D., *The Logic of Self-Involvement*, London: SCM, 1963.
Fairlamb, Horace L., *Critical Conditions: Postmodernity and the Question of Foundations*, Cambridge: Cambridge University Press, 1994.
Feenstra, R. J. and C. Plantinga (eds.), *Trinity, Incarnation and Atonement*, Notre Dame: University of Notre Dame Press, 1989.
Feuerbach, Ludwig, *Gesammelte Werke*, vol. 6, Berlin: Akademie Verlag, 1967.
——, *Thoughts on Death and Immortality*, Eng. Berkeley and London: University of California Press, 1980.
Fish, Stanley, *Doing What Comes Naturally*, Oxford: Clarendon Press, 1989.
Flew, Antony, *Thinking about Social Thinking. Escaping Deception, Resisting Self-deception*, London: Fontana Press, 1985, 2nd edn. 1991.
Foster, Hal, *Postmodern Culture*, London: Pluto Press, 1985.
Foucault, Michel, *Madness and Civilization. A History of Insanity in the Age of Reason*, Eng. New York: Pantheon, 1965.
——, *The Order of Things*, Eng. New York: Random House, 1970.
——, *The Archaeology of Knowledge*, Eng. New York: Pantheon, 1972.
——, *Discipline and Punish*, Eng. New York: Pantheon, 1977.
——, *The History of Sexuality*, Eng., 3 vols., New York: Pantheon, 1978–86.
Freeman, Anthony, *God in Us. A Case for Christian Humanism*, London: SCM, 1993.
Freeman, Mark, *Rewriting the Self. History, Memory, Narrative*, London: Routledge, 1993.
Freud, Sigmund, *The Interpretation of Dreams* in *The Standard Edition of the Complete Psychological Works of Sigmund Freud*, 24 vols., London: Hogarth Press, 1953 onwards, vols. 4–5 published separately in 1955.
Gadamer, Hans-Georg, *Truth and Method* (2nd Eng. edn. from 5th German edn.), London: Sheed & Ward, 1993.
Geffré, Claude and Jean-Pierre Jossua (eds.), *The Debate on Modernity*, London: SCM, 1992 (*Concilium* series).
Gerkin, Charles V., *The Living Human Document. Re-visioning Pastoral Counseling in a Hermeneutical Mode*, Nashville: Abingdon Press, 1984, rp. 1991.

Gunton, Colin E., *The Promise of Trinitarian Theology*, Edinburgh: T&T Clark, 1991.

Haber, Honi F., *Beyond Postmodern Politics*, London: Routledge, 1994.

Habermas, Jürgen, *The Theory of Communicative Action*, Eng., 2 vols., Cambridge: Polity Press, 1984.

——, *The Philosophical Discourse of Modernity*, Eng. New York: Political Press, 1988.

Harries, Richard, *The Real God. A Response to Anthony Freeman's 'God in Us'*, London: Mowbray, 1994.

Hart, David A., *Faith in Doubt: Non-realism and Christian Belief*, London: Mowbray, 1993.

Hart, Kevin, *The Trespass of the Sign*, Cambridge: Cambridge University Press, 1989.

Harvey, David, *The Condition of Postmodernity. An Enquiry into the Origins of Cultural Change*, Oxford: Blackwell, 2nd edn. 1989.

Heal, Jane, 'Pragmatism and Choosing to Believe', in Alan R. Malachowski (ed.), *Reading Rorty: Critical Responses to 'Philosophy and the Mirror of Nature' and Beyond*, Oxford: Blackwell, 1990.

Hebblethwaite, Brian, *The Ocean of Truth. A Defence of Objective Theism*, Cambridge: Cambridge University Press, 1988.

Hegel, Georg W. F., *Lectures in the Philosophy of Religion*, Eng., 3 vols., London: Kegan Paul, Trench, Trubner, 1895.

Heidegger, Martin, *Being and Time*, Eng. Oxford: Blackwell, 1962 (1973).

High, Dallas M., *Language, Persons and Belief*, New York: Oxford University Press, 1967.

Hobbes, Thomas, *Leviathan*, Oxford: Blackwell, 1960.

Hume, David, *Treatise on Human Nature*, Oxford: Clarendon Press, 1897.

Jameson, Fredric, *Postmodernism, or, the Cultural Logic of Late Capitalism*, London and New York: Verso, 1991.

Johnston, Paul, *Wittgenstein: Rethinking the Inner*, London: Routledge, 1993.

Jüngel, Eberhard, *God as the Mystery of the World,* Eng. Edinburgh: T&T Clark, 1983.

Kant, Immanuel, *Religion Within the Limits of Reason Alone*, Eng. New York: Harper & Row, 1960.

Kierkegaard, Søren, *Philosophical Fragments*, Eng. Princeton: Princeton University Press, 1985.

Klemm, David (ed.), *Hermeneutical Inquiry*, 2 vols., Atlanta: Scholars Press, 1986.

Küng, Hans, *Freud and the Problem of God*, New Haven: Yale University Press, 1979.

——, *Eternal Life?* Eng. London: Collins, 1984.

Locke, John, *An Essay Concerning Human Understanding*, London: Collins, 1964.

Lundin, Roger, *The Culture of Interpretation. Christian Faith and the Postmodern World*, Grand Rapids: Eerdmans, 1993.

Luther, Martin, *Luther's Works* esp. vols. 35 and 51, Philadelphia: Fortress, 1959 and 1960.

Lyon, David, *Postmodernity*, Buckingham: Open University Press, 1994.

Lyotard, J.-F., *The Postmodern Explained to Children. Correspondence 1982–1985*, Eng. London: Turnaround, 1992.

——, *The Postmodern Condition: A Report on Knowledge*, Manchester, Manchester University Press, 1992.

MacIntyre, Alasdair, *After Virtue. A Study in Moral Theory*, London: Duckworth, 1981, 2nd edn. 1985.

——, *Whose Justice? Which Rationality?* London: Duckworth, 1988.

——, *Three Rival Versions of Moral Enquiry*, London: Duckworth, 1990.

Malachowski, Alan (ed.), *Reading Rorty*, Oxford: Blackwell, 1990.

Marx, Karl, *The Writings of the Young Marx on Philosophy and Society*, Garden City, NY: Doubleday, 1967.

McFadyen, Alistair I., *The Call to Personhood: A Christian Theory of the Individual in Social Relationships*, Cambridge: Cambridge University Press, 1990.

Merquior, J. G., *Foucault*, London: Fontana, 2nd edn. 1991.

Milbank, John, 'The End of the Enlightenment: Post-Modern or Post-Secular?', in Claude Geffré and Jean-Pierre Jossua (eds.), *The Debate on Modernity*, London: SCM, 1992.

Milbank, John, *Theology and Social Theory. Beyond Secular Reason*, Oxford: Blackwell, 1993.

Moltmann, Jürgen, *Theology of Hope*, Eng. London: SCM, 1967.

——, *The Crucified God. The Cross of Christ as the Foundation and Criticism of Christian Theology*, Eng. London: SCM, 1974.

——, *The Trinity and the Kingdom of God. The Doctrine of God*, Eng. London: SCM, 1981.

——, *The Way of Jesus Christ. Christology in Messianic Dimensions*, Eng. London: SCM, 1990.

——, *History and the Triune God*, Eng. London: SCM, 1991.

——, *The Spirit of Life. A Universal Affirmation*, Eng. London: SCM, 1992.

Moore, Stephen D., *Poststructuralism and the New Testament. Derrida and Foucault at the Foot of the Cross*, Minneapolis: Fortress, 1994.

Neufeld, Dietmar, *Reconceiving Texts as Speech Acts. An Analysis of 1 John*, Leiden: Brill, 1994.

Nicholson, L. J. (ed.), *Feminism/Postmodernism*, New York and London: Routledge, 1990.

Niebuhr, Reinhold, *Moral Man and Immoral Society*, London: SCM, 1963 (1932).

——, *The Nature and Destiny of Man*, 2 vols., London: Nisbet, 1941 and 1943.

Nietzsche, Friedrich, *The Complete Works of Friedrich Nietzsche*, 18 vols., ed. O. Levy, Eng. London: Allen & Unwin, 1909–13. (This translation is uneven. German edn. and later English editions also consulted.)

Noonan, Harold, *Personal Identity*, London and New York: Routledge, 1989 (1991).

Norris, Christopher, *The Contest of Faculties. Philosophy and Theory after Deconstruction*, New York: Methuen, 1985.

——, *The Truth about Postmodernism*, Oxford: Blackwell, 1993.

O'Neill, John, *The Poverty of Postmodernism*, London: Routledge, 1994.

Pannenberg, Wolfhart, *Basic Questions in Theology*, Eng., 3 vols., London: SCM, 1970–3, esp. 'What is Truth', vol. 2, 1–27.
——, *Faith and Reality*, Eng. London: Search Press, and Philadelphia: Westminster, 1977.
——, *Systematic Theology*, Eng., 2 vols., Edinburgh: T&T Clark, 1991 and 1995.
Pippin, Robert B., *Modernism as a Philosophical Problem*, Oxford: Blackwell, 1991.
Poole, Roger, *Kierkegaard. The Indirect Communication*, Charlottesville and London: University Press of Virginia, 1993.
Rahner, Karl, 'On Truthfulness', in *Theological Investigations*, vol. 7, Eng. London: Darton, Longman & Todd, 1971, 229–59.
Rajchman, J. and C. West (eds.), *Post-Analytic Philosophy*, New York: Columbia University Press, 1985.
Ramsey, Ian T., *Religious Language. An Empirical Placing of Theological Phrases*, London: SCM, 1957.
——, *Christian Discourse. Some Logical Explorations*, Oxford: Oxford University Press, 1965.
Rickman, H. P. (ed.), *W. Dilthey: Selected Writings*, Cambridge: Cambridge University Press, 1976.
Ricoeur, Paul, *Freud and Philosophy. An Essay on Interpretation*, New Haven and London: Yale University Press, 1970.
——, *The Conflict of Interpretations – Essays in Hermeneutics*, Evanston: Northwestern University Press, 1976.
——, *Hermeneutics and the Human Sciences*, Cambridge: Cambridge University Press, 1981.
——, *Time and Narrative*, Eng., 3 vols., Chicago: Chicago University Press, 1984–8.
——, *Oneself as Another*, Eng. Chicago: University of Chicago Press, 1992.
Roberts, Richard, *Hope and its Hieroglyph: A Critical Decipherment of Ernst Bloch's Principle of Hope*, Atlanta: Scholars Press, 1990.
Rorty, Richard, *Philosophy and the Mirror of Nature*, Princeton: Princeton University Press, 1979.
——, *Contingency, Irony and Solidarity*, Cambridge: Cambridge University Press, 1989.
——, *Objectivity, Relativism and Truth. Philosophical Papers*, vol. 1, Cambridge: Cambridge University Press, 1991.
——, *Essays on Heidegger and Others: Philosophical Papers*, vol. 2, Cambridge: Cambridge University Press, 1991.
Runzo, Joseph, *Is God Real?* London: Macmillan, 1993.
Rutherford, Jonathan, *Identity: Community, Culture, Difference*, London: Lawrence & Wishart, 1990.
Sallis, John (ed.), *Deconstruction and Philosophy. The Texts of Jacques Derrida*, Chicago: University of Chicago Press, 1987.
Sarot, Marcel, *God, Passibility, and Corporeality*, Kampen: Kok Pharos, 1992.
Schleiermacher, F. D. E., *Hermeneutics. The Handwritten Manuscripts*, ed. H. Kimmerle, Eng. Missoula: Scholars Press, 1977.

Searle, John R., *Speech Acts. An Essay in the Philosophy of Language*, Cambridge: Cambridge University Press, 1969.
——, *Expression and Meaning. Studies in the Theory of Speech Acts*, Cambridge: Cambridge University Press, 1979.
Searle, John R. and D. Vanderveken, *Foundations of Illocutionary Logic*, Cambridge: Cambridge University Press, 1985.
Seidler, Victor J., *Recovering the Self. Morality and Social Theory*, London: Routledge, 1994.
Shaw, Graham, *The Cost of Authority. Manipulation and Freedom in the New Testament*, London: SCM, 1983.
——, *God in Our Hands*, London: SCM, 1987.
Silverman, Hugh J., *Textualities. Between Hermeneutics and Deconstruction*, New York and London: Routledge, 1994.
—— (ed.), *Derrida and Deconstruction*, New York and London: Routledge, 1989.
—— (ed.), *Gadamer and Hermeneutics*, London: Routledge, Chapman & Hall, 1991.
Silverman, Hugh J. and D. White (eds.), *Postmodernism and Continental Philosophy*, Albany: State University of New York Press, 1988.
Speidell, T. H., 'A Trinitarian Ontology of Persons in Society', *Scottish Journal of Theology* 47 (1994).
Stell, Stephen L., 'Hermeneutics in Theology and the Theology of Hermeneutics: Beyond Lindbeck and Tracy', *Journal of the American Academy of Religion* 61 (1993), 679–703.
Sullivan, Robert R., *Political Hermeneutics. The Early Thinking of Hans-Georg Gadamer*, University Park: Pennsylvania State University Press, 1989.
Thiselton, Anthony C., 'Truth, *alētheia*' in Colin Brown (ed.), *The New International Dictionary of New Testament Theology*, 3 vols., vol. 3, Exeter: Paternoster Press, 1978, 874–902.
——, *The Two Horizons. New Testament Hermeneutics and Philosophical Description*, Carlisle and Exeter: Paternoster Press, and Grand Rapids: Eerdmans, 1980 (rp. 1993) [also in Korean].
——, *New Horizons in Hermeneutics. The Theory and Practice of Transforming Biblical Reading*, London: HarperCollins, and Grand Rapids: Zondervan, 1992.
——, 'Christology in Luke, Speech-Act Theory, and the Problem of Dualism in Christology after Kant', in Joel B. Green and M. Turner (eds.), *Jesus of Nazareth. Lord and Christ*, Grand Rapids: Eerdmans and Carlisle: Paternoster Press, 1994, 453–72.
——, 'New Testament Interpretation in Historical Perspective', in Joel B. Green (ed.), *Hearing the New Testament: Strategies for Interpretation*, Grand Rapids: Eerdmans and Carlisle: Paternoster Press, 1995, 11–37.
Tillich, Paul, *Systematic Theology*, 3 vols., London: Nisbet, 1953–64.
Tsohatzidis, S. L. (ed.), *Foundations of Speech–Act Theory*, London and New York: Routledge, 1994.
Tuttle, Howard N., *Wilhelm Dilthey's Philosophy of Historical Understanding. A Critical Analysis*, Leiden: Brill, 1969.

Van den Brink, Gijsbert, *Almighty God. A Study in the Doctrine of Divine Omnipotence*, Kampen: Kok Pharos, 1993.

Vattimo, Gianni, *The End of Modernity. Nihilism and Hermeneutics in Post-modern Culture*, Eng. Cambridge: Polity Press, 1988 and 1991.

Ward, Keith, *Rational Theology and the Creativity of God*, Oxford: Blackwell, 1982.

Warnke, Georgia, *Gadamer. Hermeneutics, Tradition and Reason*, Cambridge: Polity Press, 1987.

Watson, Francis, *Text, Church and World. Biblical Interpretation in Theological Perspective*, Edinburgh: T&T Clark, 1994.

White, Stephen R., *Don Cupitt and the Future of Doctrine*, London: SCM, 1994.

White, Vernon, *The Fall of a Sparrow. A Concept of Special Divine Action*, Exeter: Paternoster Press, 1985.

Wittgenstein, Ludwig, *Philosophical Investigations*, German and Eng. Oxford: Blackwell, 1967.

——, *Zettel*, German and Eng. Oxford: Blackwell, 1967.

Index of Names and Subjects

accountability 63–5, 74, 82–3, 97, 131
address 63–4, 102–3
Anscombe, G. E. M. 70
apocalyptic 145
Apel, K.-O. 70, 114
apostleship 20, 143
Arendt, H. 77
Ast, F. 50
atheism 4, 122–4, see also 'death of God'; idols
Austin, J. L. 63, 99, 130
autonomy 11–12, 77–8, 83–98, 103–5, 107, 121–4, 126, 130
Ayer, A. J. 112

Babel 85–6, 130
Bacon, F. 5
Barrett, C. K. 20, 36
Barth, K. 27, 42, 63, 109, 150, 154, 156
Barthes, R. 13–16, 41–2, 68–9, 85, 88, 112, 131–2
Bartsch, H.-W. 102
Baudrillard, J. 16, 111, 131, 141, 144
Bauman, Z. 48
Baur, F. C. 109
Beauvoir, S. de 162
Beethoven, L. van 42, 65, 138
Benhabib, S. 131
believing 38–9, see also faith
Berger, P. 133
Berman, D. 123
Bernstein, R. J. 11, 12, 34, 112
Bethge, E. 19, 23
Betti, E. 41, 42, 51, 53, 70, 158
Boff, L. 156–7
Boison, A. 54, 75
Bonhoeffer, D. 19, 21–5, 27, 39, 89, 94, 142
Brandt, R. B. 50, 95
Braun, H. 102–4, 112
Brink, G. Van den 75, 116

Brown, D. 158
Brown, J. 92
Brown, R. E. 36
Brown, R. H. 76, 77, 159
Brümmer, V. 13, 30, 84, 112, 116, 155, 156
Brunner, E. 129, 140, 143
Buber, M. 53
Buddhism 84, 86, 92–5, 106–7, 113
Bühler, K. 99
Bultmann, R. 13, 14, 64, 65, 94–102
bureaucracy 12–13, 125, 133–4
Buri, F. 102, 112

Cairns, D. 101–2
Calvin, J. 103
Campbell, C. A. 74, 106
Capps, D. 54
Caputo, J. D. 15
Carlstadt, A. 149
Castelli, E. A. 21, 37, 140–2, 144
cave allegory 90–1
Chan, M. L. Y. 162
Chatman, S. 88
cheap grace 22
Chilton, B. D. 147
Clark, A. D. 142
class interests 12, 15, 138
Clifford, P. R. 74
Collange, J.-F. 37
conflict 12–13, 130–5, 143, see also violence
consumerism 22–3, see also contextual pragmatism
contextual pragmatism 92, 122, 135
Cowdell, S. 87, 112
creation 96–7, 99–100, 130, 140
Croatto, J. Severino 146
cross, the 22–5, 89, 100, 142, 147, 149
Cullmann, O. 128, 148
Cupitt, D. viii, 16, 30, 81–118, 126, 145, 151, 158

Darwin, C. 6, 113
'death of God' 25, 105, 107–10, 113, 115, 117, 123, 125
deception 3–7, 13–14, 19–40, 67–72, 109, 115, 124–44, 160
deconstruction 15–16, 91, see also Derrida
Deleuze, G. 16
Denzin, N. K. 11, 159
Derrida, J. 13–16, 28–9, 39, 41, 69, 85, 86, 105, 107, 111–15, 122, 131–2
Descartes, R. 49, 61, 73, 77, 111, 121, 122, 129, 133
despair 12, 24, 127–35, 143, 148
Dewey, J. 111
dialectic 70–1, 122–3
dialogue 70–1, 134
Dilthey, W. 13, 47–51, 54–7, 59–65, 67, 70, 73, 76–7, 158, 160
docility, mediocrity, servility 11, 19–22, 25, 141, 144, 147, 148, 154–5, see also Foucault and Nietzsche
Dodd, C. H. 147
double-forked rhetoric 111–16, 135, 144
dreams 3, 4, 67–72
Droysen, J. G. 70
Dunn, J. D. G. 7, 143

Ebeling, G. 24, 64–7
Edwards, D. 113
effective-history 62, 150–3
Ellingworth, P. 148
empiricism viii, 47–51, 57, 60, 64, 67, 69, 89, 101, 106
Engels, F. 124
enlargement 28
Enlightenment, the 83, 121, 123
Epicurus 122, 123
Evans, D. D. 99
expecting 38–9

'facts' 34, 99–100
faith, faithfulness 20, 22–5, 114, 121, 148
fast food 117
Feenstra, R. J. 158
feminine, feminism 12, 56, 96, 124, 131, 134, 137–8, 140, 145, 162
Fergusson, D. 102
Feuerbach, L. 7, 23, 77, 81, 83, 95, 105, 107, 109, 122–6
Fichte, J. G. 7, 50, 90
Fish, S. 114
Fitzmyer, J. A. 144
Flacius 57

forked rhetoric, see double-forked rhetoric
Foucault, M. vii, 12–13, 16, 21, 85, 105, 107, 125, 131–4, 140–4, 147
Fox, R. 137
Freeman, A. 30, 31, 82–4, 95, 114–17
Freud, S. 12, 13, 15, 54, 67–70, 73, 83, 93, 95, 108, 113, 127–30, 160
Froelich, K. 66–7
Fuchs, E. 55, 64
Funk, R. 64
future viii, 59–62, 63, 73–8, 121–6, 128–9, 139, 145–64

Gadamer, H.-G. 13, 41, 48–50, 55, 60–2, 67, 69–71, 75, 144, 152, 153
Geach, P. 30
'genetic fallacy' 55–6
Genette, G. 88
Gerkin, C. V. 53–4, 75–8
Gerrish, B. A. 95, 96
Gibson, A. B. 101
Gill, J. H. 95
God as 'dead', see 'death of God'
God as living God 153–63
God as personal
    as self-imparting 23–4, 41–3, 94–5, 100–4, 108, 129–30, 147–8, 150, 152–63
God as projection 3–7, 30–1, 81–117, see also deception; myth
God as Trinity 71, 76, 90, 116, 150, 154–63
Goethe, J. W. 138
Gollwitzer, H. 84, 103, 104, 112
Green, J. 47
Gunton, C. E. 156–8

Habermas, J. 11, 55, 70, 99
Hainz, J. 130
Harries, R. 84, 116, 137
Hart, D. A. 82, 108, 116
Hart, K. 131
Hartmann, N. 70
Harvey, D. 130, 159
Heal, J. 34
Hebblethwaite, B. 109, 112
Hegel, G. W. F. 47, 49, 59, 85, 88–90, 94, 109, 123–4, 151
Heidegger, M. 15, 25, 55, 65, 70, 85, 122, 126, 146
Hempel, C. 70
Heraclitus 88
hermeneutics 15–16, 41–3, 47–79, 90, 91–6, 100, 103–4, 151, 160
Hobbes, T. 3, 4

Hodges, H. A. 61
Holy Spirit 25, 42, 78, 128–30, 148,
    154–63
hope 24, 59, 76, 101, 121–6, 128–9,
    134–5, 145–63
Hume, D. 47, 51, 57, 60, 61, 67, 73–4,
    101, 106, 127
Husserl, E. 15

identity vii, viii, 50–8, 64–6, 67, 73–8,
    106, 113, 130, 132, see also
    reconstituted identity; self
'idol meat' 142–3
idols, idolatry 5–7, 69, 82–3, 117, see
    also atheism
incommensurability 122, 144
infantile regression 22–4, 128, see also
    Freud
integrity 84, 107, 114
internalization 84–97, 105–6
interpretation, see hermeneutics
Irenaeus 39

Jaspers, K. 102
Jauss, H.-R. 66
Jeremias, J. 147
Jesus Christ 7, 20, 22–5, 89, 91, 92,
    100, 107, 142, 147, 152–63
Jewett, R. 14, 142
Jonas, H. 97
Judge, E. A. 20, 37
Jüngel, E. 54

Kant, I. 7, 25, 41, 47–51, 59, 77, 81–4,
    87, 89–91, 93–5, 100–2, 105, 107,
    109, 111–12, 121–6, 130
Käsemann, E. 20
Kasper, W. 156–7
Kaufmann, W. 5
Kelsey, D. 66, 77
Kierkegaard, S. 87, 91, 92, 109, 111,
    122
Kimmerle, H. 48
Kingdom of God 147
Klemm, D. 48, 60
Kristiva, J. 131
Kuhn, T. S. 90
Küng, H. 108, 109, 112, 127, 160

Lacan, J. 16, 67, 105, 106, 114–15, 131
language 3–6, 27–39, 55–7, 61, 67–70,
    84–8, 94–7, 105–6, 117, 132, see
    also especially Wittgenstein;
    Barthes; Derrida; Ramsey; speech-
    acts

language, action and life, see
    Wittgenstein and speech-acts
law, bondage to 7, 128, 154–5
liberal-pluralist credentials 111–16, see
    also double-forked rhetoric
liberal (vs radical) theology 114,
    116
liberation 23, 116, see also autonomy,
    transformation
Liberation theology 157–8, see also
    feminism
life 17, 24–6, 47, 53–62, 65, 125–6
Lindars, B. 36
Lindbeck, G. 116
listening, art of 50–1, 54–5, 69, 75, see
    also pastoral theology
Locke, J. 4, 47, 73
Lonergan, B. 112
love 13, 16, 22, 24, 32, 35, 42–3, 49,
    51, 63, 94, 126, 129, 139, 143–5,
    154–63
Luckmann, T. 133
Lundin, R. 39
Luther, M. 21, 22, 24, 27, 39, 89, 103,
    137, 139, 149, 154, 160
Lyon, D. 131–2, 159
Lyotard, J.-F. 16, 28, 33–4, 41, 88,
    107, 111, 131, 144, 159

McFadyen, A. I. 71, 77
MacIntyre, A. 108, 122, 134
Mackintosh, H. R. 95
Macquarrie, J. 95, 100–2, 109
Malcolm, N. 38
manipulation 4–7, 11–13, 19–27, 30–2,
    36–44, 47–51, 65, 68–70, 77,
    108–9, 113–15, 124–44, 156–7,
    162–3
Mannheim, K. 48
Martin, R. P. 20, 37
Marx, K. 6, 48, 68, 107, 109, 113, 123,
    124, 138–9, 146
mass advertising 12, 68–9
Mauthner, F. 6
medicine 42, 55, 100, 131, 141
metaphor 5, 14–15, 28–32, see also
    Nietzsche; Derrida; language
Mitchell, M. M. 142
modernity 11–13, 16, 121–5, see also
    postmodernity
Moltmann, J. vii, 24–7, 39, 71, 76, 90,
    112, 116, 121, 126, 129–30, 142,
    145–9, 154–8
Moore, S. D. 21, 140–4
Mueller-Vollmer, K. 59
Munck, J. 7

myth, 'mythologies' 14–15, 68–9, 84–6, 96–104, see also Hegel; Bultmann, Barthes; Derrida

narrative, narrative plot 27, 60–1, 73–82, 88, 90, 111, 146, 160, 163, see also Ricoeur; future; identity; time
nations, national interests 32, 137–8
Neufeld, D. 36, 39
Newman, J. H. 28
'New Testament introduction' 55–6
Nicholson, L. J. 131
Nidditch, P. 4
Niebuhr, R. 32, 95, 135, 137–43
Nietzsche, F. vii, 4–8, 12, 15–19, 21–9, 36, 68, 73, 83, 88, 91, 101, 105, 107–9, 113, 123–7, 132, 144, 146–7, 149, 155, 161
Noonan, H. 74, 75, 106
Norris, C. 111
Nygren, A. 129, 155

objectification 83–9, 93–7, 100, 102–4
Ogden, S. 102
omnipotence 29–31, see also God as Trinity
O'Neill, J. 117
O'Neill, J. C. 109
order 139–40, 143–4, 159
other, others 13, 22, 26, 47–51, 53–8, 60, 71, 73, 96, 126, 129–30, see also relationality
Otto, R. 95
overdetermination 67–8, see also Freud

Pannenberg, W. vii, 38, 71, 76, 101, 112, 150–3, 156–8, 160–1
parousia, the 38–9
Parsons, T. 48
Pascal, B. 109
pastoral theology, pastoral counsel 50–1, 53–8, 69, 75, see also listening
Paul, the Apostle 7–8, 20–1, 31, 128–30, 137, 140–2, 146, 148
Pearse, R. 81
perichoresis 26, 157–8, 160
Perrin, N. 147
personhood 11–18, 42–3, 47–79, 94, 129, 145–63, see also self; identity
Philo 143
Plantinga, C. 158
Plato 70, 71, 90

Pogoloff, S. M. 142
politics 4, 12, 70, 76, 114, 123, 131, 133–4, 137–9
Poole, R. 91
Popper, K. 70
postmodernism, postmodernity vii, 9, 11–17, 24, 34, 111–35 and throughout. See especially Foucault; Derrida, Lyotard, Baudrillard; Vattimo
power-interests 3–9, 12–16, 20–2, 25, 27, 30–2, 110, 121–35, 137–40, 154–5, 159 and elsewhere. See also Foucault and Nietzsche
prayer 31, 84
priesthood, religious leaders 5–7, 19, 23, 110
promise 63, 76, 101, 122, 128–9, 139, 145–63
psychoanalysis 67–72, see also Freud
public criteria of meaning 34–6, see also Wittgenstein

Rad, Gerhard von 82
Rahner, K. 12, 128, 160
Ramsey, I. T. 29, 89, 94–5, 146
Reardon, B. M. G. 49
reason, rationality, rationalism 4, 6, 11–17, 26, 34, 41, 49, 61, 70–1, 89–90, 112–13, 122, 132–4, 143
Recanati, F. 99
reception theory 66
reconstructed identity, renewed self 75–7, 130, 146, 160–1
relationality 41–5, 49, 50, 71, 77, 92, 96, 129, 144, 155–8, 162–3
resurrection 43, 78, 100, 101, 146, 161
Reventlow, Henning Graf 4
Ricoeur, P. vii, viii, 13, 41, 48–9, 54, 57, 60, 67–9, 70, 73–7, 82, 88, 106, 108, 117, 127, 129, 151, 158, 160
Ridding, G. 60
Robinson, J. A. T. 14, 87, 94, 95
Robinson, J. M. 97
roles, role-performance vii, 11–17, 76, 121–2, 124, 144, 151, 160
Rorty, R. 33, 34, 41, 92, 111, 112, 114
Runzo, J. 171
Ryle, G. 39

Sanders, E. P. 7, 107
Sarot, M. 30
Satterthwaite, P. 149
Saussure, F. de 15, 56, 132
Schelling, F. W. J. 50, 88, 94

Schleiermacher, F. D. E. 13, 41–2,
  48–60, 73, 75, 95, 96
Schmithals, W. 102
Schnackenburg, R. 36
Schopenhauer, A. 123
Schütz, A. 48
Schweitzer, A. 147
science, scientific method 13, 42, 47–51,
  54–6, 60, 61, 90, 95, 101–2, 105,
  108–9, 116, 117, 121, 125, 127
scripture and the self 63–6
Sea of Faith Network viii, 81–6,
  107–10, 114–17
Searle, J. R. 63, 99
self, selfhood vii, viii, 11–17, 47–78, 96,
  104–7, 110–13, 121–6, 151, 154–6,
  160–1, see also identity; person;
  reconstituted self
Shaw, G. 21, 30–2, 141, 144
signs, semiotics 14–15, 28–9, 56–7, 61,
  67–70, 84–6, 88, 105–10, 117, 132
Silverman, H. J. 71
situatedness 11–17, 76, 122, 128, 133,
  143, 145, 150, 154–5
Snyder, J. R. 16
social construction 12, 34, 90, 122,
  124, 132–3, 140, 159
social sciences 42, 47–51, 76–7, 105,
  121, see also science
society 11, 32, 107, 121–63
speech-acts 36–9, 63, 149–50
Stendahl, K. 7
Strauss, D. F. 109
Sullivan, R. R. 70
Suskind, H. 50
suspicion 12–13, 42–3, 67–71, 127,
  133, 160
Swartley, W. 65

Taylor, C. 70
Temple, W. 49
temporal imagery 146–7
time, temporality, plot 59–60, 73–8, 82,
  106, 146–7, 150–1, 160, see also
  future; narrative
Thatcher, A. 158
Thielicke, H. 49

Thiselton, A. C. 34, 36, 37, 99, 109,
  149
Tillich, P. 29, 89, 91, 94, 95
transformation 66, 71, 75–7, 103,
  128–9, 139, 145–63
Travis, S. H. 20, 37
Trinity, see God as Trinity
trust 16, 74, 104, 130–1, 134, 160–1
truth 3–5, 7–8, 11–12, 14–16, 25, 27–8,
  33–9, 89, 92, 95–6, 99, 107–9, 111,
  116, 124, 128–9, 132, 134, 135,
  145, 160 and throughout
Tuttle, H. N. 62
two kingdoms 139
Tyndale, W. 149

vandalism 135
Van den Brink, G. 30, 32
Vattimo, G. 16, 131
Vawter, B. 85
violence 134–5, 141, 143–4
virtual reality 111, 117, 131–2
vocation 22, 151

Ward, K. 116
Warnke, G. 34, 114
Watson, F. viii, 39, 71
Weber, M. 48, 70
Weil, S. 27
Weiss, J. 147
West, C. 114
White, S. R. 112
Whybray, N. 82
Wiles, G. P. 37
Willis, W. L. 142
Wittgenstein, L. 6, 28–39, 56, 60, 70,
  108, 109
Wolf, F. 50
Wolterstorff, N. 112
Wright, N. T. 7, 99, 112

Young, F. 66, 77

Zagzebski, L. T. 75
Zen Buddhism 106, see also
  Buddhism
Zizioulas, J. 158

Index of Biblical References

Genesis
1:26   163
42:16   38

Psalms
57:3   38
130:1   149

Isaiah
44   83
44:14–17   82

Jeremiah
17:9   129

Joel
2:28, 29   130

Zechariah
8:8, 16, 17   38

3 Macc.
6:2   30

Wis. Sol.
14:25–26   143

Matthew
6:10   147
10:39   139
12:28   147
23:5, 6   19
23:7, 11, 27, 33   20

Mark
1:15   31, 147

Luke
11:20   147
15:11–32   64

John
1:1–14   36
3:21   36
5:44   19
10:30   156
14:9, 10   156
14:16   36
17:10–24   156

Acts
2:17   130
7   148
7:2–53   147
7:3, 5, 46–48   148

Romans
1:18–39   143
1:21   14
1:25   36
2:16, 29   141
3:24   155
4:18   148
5:5   129, 130
6–8   128, 129
8:23, 24   148
8:29   153
9:1   36
12:18   144
13:1–7   143, 144
13:11–12   14
15:7   161

1 Corinthians
1:18–2:5   20
1:30   155
2:3, 4   20
3:18   128
4:5   129, 141
4:16   141
5:1–5   141
5:8   37
6:20   155

7:10–11	141	**Colossians**	
8:1	130, 161	1:14	155
9:27	141	1:15	153
11:1	140		
11:3, 27–32	141	**1 Thessalonians**	
13:8, 10, 12	129	1:6	140
15:35–49, 50–57	78	5:4–8	14
15:43–44	154	5:24	148
15:49	128, 153, 154		
		2 Thessalonians	
		2:10	37
2 Corinthians			
1:22	148	**Titus**	
3:18	128, 153	1:12, 13	37
4:2	36		
6:4–10	36	**Hebrews**	
7:14	36	1:1–3	153
11:3, 4, 13, 15, 20	20	1:3	163
11:21–12:10	20–1, 36	2:8b–17	163
12:10	20	3:13	128
12:15	21	4:16	163
13:8	37	5:17	163
13:13	130	6:13–18, 19, 20	163
		9:15–22	163
Galatians		9:15	155
3:13	155	11:1, 7, 29–31	148
3:28, 29	162	11:26	25
4:12	141	12:2, 3	163
5:20–22	162	13:13, 14	25
6:12	14		
		1 John	
Ephesians		1:8	128
2:14	162	1:6	36
4:13–15, 17	14	3:2	153
4:15, 24, 25	37	4:8, 16	156
5:8–14	14		
		Revelation	
Philippians		16:14	30
3:17	141		